BLAKE'S COMPOSITE ART

BLAKE'S COMPOSITE ART

A Study of the Illuminated Poetry

W. J. T. Mitchell

PRINCETON UNIVERSITY PRESS
PRINCETON, NEW JERSEY

Published by Princeton University Press, Princeton, New Jersey
In the United Kingdom: Princeton University Press,
Guildford, Surrey

Library of Congress Cataloging in Publication Data will
be found on the last printed page of this book

Printed in the United States of America
by Princeton University Press,
Princeton, New Jersey

TO

THE MEMORY OF

EARL R. WASSERMAN

Contents

List of Illustrations

ALL illustrations are by Blake unless otherwise designated. Copies of illuminated books are identified by the letter assigned to them in the Keynes-Wolf *Census*. Plate numbers follow Erdman, *TIB*.

TEXT FIGURES

Preface

T. S. ELIOT defined the proper aims of criticism as the elucidation of the text and the correction of taste. These goals may seem quaint or narrow in a time when literary criticism is haunted by the structuralist goal of a unified theory of knowledge, and by the widely shared notion that taste is purely subjective and not subject to any standard of correction. When applied to the work of William Blake, however, these aims seem less modest. Modern criticism has only begun the task of defining, much less elucidating Blake's text, especially the visual-verbal text of his unique illuminated books. And the taste for Blake's work in our time is grounded in such widely diverse and often contradictory values that it must be subject to some degree of correction or we are faced with a hopeless muddle.

This book is an attempt to fulfill Eliot's first aim directly (and perhaps the second indirectly) by defining and elucidating those unique texts in which the poetic and pictorial aspects of Blake's genius were wedded, the series of illuminated poems which form the central achievement of his life. The first two chapters are primarily concerned with defining the nature of Blake's composite art as an expression of his own aesthetics, and with examining the way in which Blake transforms traditional theories about the relationships of the "sister arts" into the principles of his own visionary art form. The next three chapters attempt to balance this theoretical introduction with practical application, consisting of detailed formal analyses of three illuminated books (*The Book of Thel*, *The Book of Urizen*, and *Jerusalem*) which provide a survey of a wide diversity of thematic and stylistic expression and which represent, in a rough way, major phases in Blake's development.

This is not, of course, the first time this subject has been broached, but it is, I think, the first extended, systematic attempt to define the nature of Blake's composite art from the inside out, as an expression of his own theories of art rather than as a late example of the long tradition of pictorial and poetic marriages which includes the emblem book and the illuminated manuscript. This is not to say that Blake abandons tradition or creates his forms *ex nihilo*: quite the contrary, my argument is that Blake's originality is a result of his ability to assimilate and transform a wide variety of traditional techniques to his own purposes. My subject is the manner and method of transformation, the way in which Blake reshapes the venerable doctrines of pictorialism, *ut pictura poesis*, and the sister arts into the principles of a new form. I am heavily indebted, therefore, to critics such as Jean Hagstrum who have provided a comprehensive picture of the traditions on which Blake drew. My argumentative treatment of these traditions is not an attempt to deny the relevance of tradition, but an effort to clarify the uses Blake made of it.

The second chapter is an essay in the definition of Blake's pictorial style. As in the first chapter, the emphasis is primarily intrinsic, attempting to analyze Blake's style in terms of his own theory of vision and to treat his adoption of traditional stylistic elements such as mannerist elongation, medieval space and iconography, and Renaissance concepts of the human figure in terms of their transformation into a coherent whole. We know that Blake's style has affinities with all these historical periods; the question is *why*, to what purpose does he place a Michelangelesque nude in a Romanesque or Gothic space? My debts in this chapter are to art historians such as Anthony Blunt and Robert Rosenblum, who have clarified the historical parameters of Blake's style. I have also drawn heavily on the work of theorists and historians such as E. H. Gombrich, Rudolf Arnheim, Meyer Schapiro, Henri Focillon, and Erwin Panofsky, especially insofar as they treat style as the objective correlative of epistemology, ways of showing as metaphors for ways of knowing.

The three chapters of practical criticism draw upon such a wide variety of Blake scholarship that it would be impossible to itemize my debts here. The attempt in these chapters is to analyze each illuminated book as a distinct, unique interaction of pictorial and poetic elements. The principle of organic wholeness is nothing new in literary criticism, but it has never been applied systematically and simultaneously to both the visual and verbal aspects of Blake's illuminated books. I have examined each book with the hypothesis that it contains its own "interinanimating principles"—that is, a distinctive poetic form or structure of images and values, and a distinctive pictorial style and iconography that interacts with this poetic form. Blake's composite art attains its "wholeness," I argue, at three levels: as poetic form, as pictorial gallery, and as dialogue or dialectic of poetic and pictorial forms. The most useful, indeed an indispensable reference work for anyone interested in this sort of investigation is David Erdman's *The Illuminated Blake*. I am very grateful to Professor Erdman for letting me consult his work in progress while preparing this book.

One aspect of the organization of the analytical chapters may need some explanation. In spite of my argument that Blake's illuminated books must be read as unified formal entities, I have divided the essays into sections which deal primarily with text or design respectively, rather than writing a "contrapuntal" commentary in imitation of Blake's own form. One reason for this division is simply the matter of ease and clarity. Talking about complex poems and pictures at the same time is like trying to carry on two conversations at once; it will have to await someone more ambidextrous than myself.

But a more fundamental reason for the divided presentation has to do with my understanding of the nature of Blake's art. I will argue in what follows that the "unity" of the illuminated book is a dynamic one, built upon the interaction of text and design as independent or contrary elements, and that an important part of understanding Blake's form is to allow each element "its own proper sphere of invention and visionary conception" (*DC*, E 532). In practice, this usually means compensating for our natural tendency to reduce pictures to visual translations of verbal text, and trying instead to see the pictures on their own terms, as distinct kinds of meaning systems, containing nonverbal forms, allusions, and stylistic implications. I have tended, therefore, to treat the illustrations to each book as an independent picture gallery which may be investigated for its own significance quite apart from the text. Needless to say, this is an artificial act of overcompensation, and the intimate relationship of picture and poem continually reasserts itself in the process of interpretation. My hope is that the relationship of text and design, given this kind of trial separation, will then be understood as the marriage of equals Blake surely intended.

I began by suggesting that the mere elucidation of Blake's "text" (understood as an interaction of verbal and graphic elements) is a more ambitious project than it might seem at first glance. His illuminated books may be unique as artifacts, but the theoretical problems raised as we try to interpret them are not unique; they bear upon fundamental aesthetic questions about the unity of the arts and the basic epistemological problem of relating distinct kinds of symbolic systems. The practical interpretation of Blake's illuminated books is fascinating, in other words, not just because his work is interesting in itself, but because it demands continuous cross-fertilization and discrimination between the hermeneutic strategies of literary criticism and art history. Blake's work provides us with a unique experimental laboratory in which to explore the nature of transactions between the poetic and the pictorial, the linguistic and the visual, the temporal and the spatial. In a time when humanistic discourse is searching for a unified poetics of culture, Blake provides a medium and a catalyst for bringing different intellectual disciplines into significant contact. I would hope, then, that this book will interest not just Blake specialists, but aestheticians, semiologists, iconographers, art historians, and literary theorists—anyone, in short, who is fascinated with the problem of unifying human knowledge.

The first chapter of this book grew out of a shorter, more polemical piece, "Blake's Composite Art," in *Blake's Visionary Forms Dramatic*, ed. David Erdman and John Grant (Princeton, 1970), pp. 57-81. The fourth chapter is a substantially revised, rewritten, and rethought version of "Poetic and Pictorial Imagination in Blake's *The Book of Urizen*," *Eighteenth-Century Studies* III (Fall 1969), 83-107, which was reprinted in a slightly revised form in *The Visionary Hand: Essays on William Blake's Art and Aesthetics*, ed. Robert Essick (Los Angeles, 1973). Portions of the second chapter dealing with synaesthesia and linear schemata in Blake's pictorial style are developed more fully in "Style as Epistemology: Blake and the Movement toward Abstraction in Romantic Art," *Studies in Romanticism*, 16:2 (Spring, 1977), 145-164.

My acknowledgments for help in this work could go on indefinitely. First priority must certainly go to Earl Wasserman, who supervised my first work on Blake and who taught me to believe in the possibility (at least in *his* classroom) of total intelligibility as the goal of criticism. To him this book is dedicated. My thanks also to Hazard Adams for introducing me to Blake; to Martin Butlin, David Erdman, John Grant, Jean Hagstrum, and Ronald Paulson for encouragement and criticism; to Lessing Rosenwald, Geoffrey Keynes, and George Goyder for helping me with access to materials. Special thanks must go to Thomas Minnick, Linda Peterson, and Walter Scheps, who read and criticized the manuscript in its final stages; Judith Ott, who helped with matters iconographic; and Morris Chafetz, who advised on matters graphic. For initial financial assistance I am indebted to the American Philosophical Society, and for long-term, continuous, and renewed support, I wish to thank the College of Humanities at the Ohio State University. For keeping me firmly grounded in physical reality while writing this book I must thank Carmen and Gabriel, and for being an acute listener, critic, and skeptical muse I am grateful to my wife, Janice.

Abbreviations

1. ILLUMINATED BOOKS AND OTHER WORKS BY BLAKE

A	*America*
Ah	*The Book of Ahania*
BL	*The Book of Los*
DC	*Descriptive Catalogue*
E	*Europe*
Exp	*Songs of Experience*
FZ	*The Four Zoas*
GP	*The Gates of Paradise*
Inn	*Songs of Innocence*
J	*Jerusalem*
M	*Milton*
MHH	*The Marriage of Heaven and Hell*
PA	*Public Address*
SL	*Song of Los*
U	*The Book of Urizen*
VDA	*Visions of the Daughters of Albion*
VLJ	*A Vision of the Last Judgment*

2. SECONDARY WORKS AND EDITIONS

BSA	*Blake's Sublime Allegory*, ed. Stuart Curran and Joseph Wittreich, Jr. (Madison, 1973)
Census	*William Blake's Illuminated Books: A Census*, compiled by Geoffrey Keynes and Edwin Wolf (New York, 1953)
E	*The Poetry and Prose of William Blake*, ed. David Erdman, commentary by Harold Bloom (New York, 1965)
K	*The Complete Writings of William Blake*, ed. Geoffrey Keynes (London, 1969)
TIB	*The Illuminated Blake*, annotated by David Erdman (New York, 1974)
VFD	*Blake's Visionary Forms Dramatic*, ed. David Erdman and John Grant (Princeton, 1970)

Unless otherwise indicated, all quotations from Blake's works in the text are from the Erdman edition.

BLAKE'S
COMPOSITE ART

Chapter One

BLAKE'S COMPOSITE ART

It has become superfluous to argue that Blake's poems need to be read with their accompanying illustrations. Almost everyone would now agree with Northrop Frye's remark that Blake perfected a "radical form of mixed art," a "composite art" which must be read as a unity.[1] It is not superfluous, however, to ask in what precise sense Blake's poems "need" their illustrations, and vice versa. Neither element of Blake's illuminated books is unintelligible or uninteresting without the support of the other. Indeed, a notable feature of the history of Blake's reputation has been the extraordinary success which his paintings and poems have enjoyed without the mutual support of one another. For over a century Blake's admirers had a truncated view of his art, some admiring the bust, others the torso, all finding a sufficient aesthetic unity in the fragment they beheld. This suggests that Blake's poems do not need their illustrations in the same sense that Wagner's libretti need their musical settings to be aesthetically successful. It suggests that his composite art is, to some extent, *not* an indissoluble unity, but an interaction between two vigorously independent modes of expression. "When a Work has Unity," Blake reminds us, "it is as much in a Part as in the Whole. the Torso is as much a Unity as the Laocoon" ("On Homer's Poetry," E 267).

Suzanne Langer has argued that this sort of composite art is impossible, that "there are no happy marriages in art—only successful rape."[2] Her argument must be borne in mind by anyone who would ravish one of Blake's art forms for the sake of elucidating the other. Langer suggests that the juxtaposition of two art forms always re-

[1] Frye, "Poetry and Design in William Blake," in *Discussions of William Blake*, ed. John Grant (Boston, 1961), p. 46; reprinted from *Journal of Aesthetics and Art Criticism*, X (Sept. 1951), 35-42. Jean Hagstrum, *William Blake: Poet and Painter* (Chicago, 1964), was, I believe, the first to refer to Blake's illuminated books as a "composite art."

[2] *Problems of Art: Ten Philosophical Lectures* (New York, 1957), p. 86. Langer goes on to say that "every work has its being in only one order of art; compositions of different orders are not simply conjoined, but all except one will cease to appear as what they are."

sults in the absorption of one form into the other, poetry being subordinated to musical values in song, musical values subordinated to visual considerations in ballet. A picture hanging on the wall in a set for *Man and Superman* is not seen as an aesthetic object in its own right, but is absorbed into the dramatic illusion. Similarly, an illustrated book tends to become either a portable picture gallery with running captions or a literary text with attendant illustrations. The historical fact that Blake's illuminated books have been read in *both* of these ways strongly suggests that his composite art is an exception to Langer's rule, a successful marriage of two aesthetically independent art forms.

This is not to say that the partnership is equal or harmonious on every plate of Blake's illuminated books. There are many individual instances of the subordination of one mode to the demands of the other. Many of Blake's visual images move toward the realm of language, operating as arbitrary signs, emblems, or hieroglyphics which denote the unseeable, rather than as "natural" representations: an eagle is "a portion of Genius" and a serpent may symbolize nature as a whole.[3] Similarly, the text sometimes derives its coherence not primarily from its verbal order, but from the series of pictures for which it provides titles, as in *The Gates of Paradise* series. In general, however, neither the graphic nor the poetic aspect of Blake's composite art assumes consistent predominance: their relationship is more like an energetic rivalry, a dialogue or dialectic between vigorously independent modes of expression.

I. VISUAL-VERBAL DIALECTICS

The most obvious manifestation of the independence of design from text is the presence of illustrations which do not illustrate. The figure of a young man carrying a winged child on his head in the frontispiece to *Songs of Experience* [1], for instance, is mentioned

[3] I am employing here the conventional distinction between language as a system of arbitrary signs and pictorial representation as a system of more or less "natural" signs, containing intrinsic resemblances to that which is signified. Emblems and hieroglyphics thus occupy something of a middle ground between linguistic and pictorial representation. The key phrase in the distinction is "more or less," some kinds of pictorial representation being more explicitly verbal (and thus less "natural") than others. Further elaboration of this concept may be found in E. H. Gomrich, *Symbolic Images: Studies in the Art of the Renaissance* (London, 1972), p. 212, and Ronald Paulson, *Emblem and Expression* (Cambridge, Mass., 1975), p. 8.

nowhere in the *Songs*, nor for that matter anywhere else in Blake's writings. In the absence of explicit textual associations we are forced, I would suggest, to concentrate on the picture *as a picture in the world of pictures*, rather than seeing it as a visual translation of matters already dealt with in words. We have to look at the picture's expressive content, "reading" facial expressions, bodily gestures, and details for their innate significance, and we tend to see it not in relation to words but in the context of other, similar compositions both in and out of Blake's *œuvre*. It is inevitable, of course, that this concentration on the picture as picture will move over into the world of verbal language at some point—the moment, in fact, that we begin to articulate an interpretation, or the moment that we encounter a related composition that *does* have an explicit verbal equivalent.[4] The mysterious figure carrying the cherub has an obvious pictorial relative, the figure looking up at a child on a cloud in the frontispiece to *Songs of Innocence* [2]. And this latter composition *does* have an explicit verbal equivalent: it serves as an illustration to the song of the Piper "piping down the valleys wild" and seeing a child on a cloud, the introductory poem to *Songs of Innocence.* We cannot, however, make a direct verbal translation of the frontispiece to *Experience* from the Piper's song by way of the intermediate association of the picture of the Piper. It is clear that the two frontispieces function not just as companion pieces with similar compositions but as "contraries" whose differences are as important as their similarities. Any words we find to describe the frontispiece to *Experience* will have to involve transformations and reversals of the language discovered in the poem and illustration which introduce *Songs of Innocence.*

This process of transformation goes on quite unobtrusively and

[4] Roland Barthes argues for the tendency of all symbolic forms to aspire to the condition of language: "it appears increasingly difficult to conceive a system of images and objects whose *signifieds* can exist independently of language: to perceive what a substance signifies is to fall back on the individuation of language: there is no meaning which is not designated, and the world of signifieds is none other than that of language" (*Elements of Semiology*, tr. Annette Lavers and Colin Smith [Boston, 1968], p. 10). Barthes' difficulty in conceiving of a system independent of language may, however, say as much about the linguistic bias of structuralism as it does about the actual nature of things. If Blake teaches us anything about symbolic systems, it is that there is an equally strong tendency for language to fall back into that which cannot be designated, the wordless realm of pure image and sound, and that this realm may have systematic features independent of language.

perhaps unconsciously whenever we interpret a problematic illustration in Blake's illuminated books. It is generally assumed without question that since the frontispiece to *Innocence* clearly depicts the Piper, the frontispiece to *Experience* must depict the analogous figure in the latter group of poems, the Bard whose voice is heard in the opening poems to *Songs of Experience*. This assumption seems wholly justified, but it is important for us to remember that it is not directly "given" by the text or its illustrations, but must be arrived at by a series of associations, transformations, and creative inferences. And once this initial inference has been made, the problem of interpretation has only begun. We must then account for other transformations suggested by a comparison of the two frontispieces: in one the child floats without the aid of wings on a cloud above the Piper; in the other the child has wings and yet must be carried by the Bard. The Piper looks up at the child, his setting an enclosed grove of trees; the Bard looks straight ahead, backed by a vista of open fields. The significance of these contrasts may not strike us as terribly complex, but the process by which we arrive at that significance is rather involved and it entails a good deal more than simple matching or translating of visual signs into verbal.

The creative inferences involved in reading this sort of picture are multiplied when we make associations in pictorial realms outside of Blake's own art. The Bard carrying the child is rather similar, for instance, to representations of St. Christopher carrying the Christ-child across the river, a theme which Blake and his readers could have seen in many English churches and in the works of European masters such as Dürer [3].[5] The implication that the child on the Bard's head is Christ is certainly consistent with the symbolism of *Songs of Innocence and Experience*, and it introduces a whole new set of verbal associations to be found in the legends of St.

[5] The widespread familiarity of the St. Christopher image is suggested by H. C. Whaite in *Saint Christopher in English Medieval Wallpainting* (London, 1929). Whaite notes that despite the tendency to casually obliterate medieval paintings with whitewash in the eighteenth and nineteenth centuries, "it is surprising how much material has survived. Of the hundreds of paintings of St. Christopher which at one time adorned the walls of English churches, there are still over sixty known to exist in fair condition. In Keyser's list of 1883 one hundred and eighty representations of the subject are mentioned" (p. 13). The best general work on this theme is Ernst K. Stahl, *Die Legende vom Heil Riesen Christophorus in der Graphik des 15 und 16 Jahrhunderts* (Munich, 1920). Stahl cites Dürer, Cranach, Altdorfer, Schongauer, Bosch, and van Veen (whose work Blake definitely knew) among the artists who made prints of St. Christopher carrying the Christ-child.

Christopher, the saint who, according to Jacobus de Voragine, is not only the "Christ-bearer," but "hast . . . borne all the world" upon his shoulders.[6] For some readers the allusion might evoke the popular image of the patron of travelers (English folk belief had it that anyone who saw St. Christopher's image in a church could not die that day),[7] giving the Bard a kind of protective significance, as guide and guardian in the approaching journey through the dangerous world of Experience. The allusion would thus reinforce the contrast with the carefree, wandering figure of the Piper, who is blissfully unaware of the road ahead and need not carry his Christ-child muse as a burden.

For readers more deeply versed in the lore of St. Christopher more complex intersections with Blake's imagery would emerge. St. Christopher was called "reprobus" (reprobate or outcast) before his conversion, a striking analogue to Blake's later description of the prophetic Bard as an angry "Reprobate" crying in the wilderness.[8] Disparities between Blake's frontispiece and the saint's iconography also invite transformational inferences: Blake's Bard carries his child on his head rather than in the traditional place, on the shoulders, perhaps a way of stressing the suggestion in *The Golden Legend* that the burden of Christ's weight is mental rather than physical.[9] The presence of wings on the child (something that never occurs in traditional representations of the Christ-child), and the ironic contrast between this weighty cherub and the weightless but unwinged child of the Piper may suggest sinister overtones: Geoffrey Keynes sees the winged child as a "Covering Cherub," an image of what Blake called the Selfhood, that burden of alienated consciousness which emerges in the state of Experience.[10] In this reading, our

[6] *The Golden Legend*, tr. William Caxton, ed. Frederick S. Ellis (Hammersmith, 1892), pp. 645-48. Blake was probably familiar with Caxton's translation of this classic collection of saints' lives, perhaps learning of it during his apprenticeship among the antiquarians.

[7] Whaite, *Saint Christopher*, p. 9.

[8] Blake did not arrive at the term "Reprobate" for his wrathful prophet until writing *Milton*, but he certainly presents a clear image of the "just man raging in the wilds" in the Argument to the earlier *Marriage of Heaven and Hell*. I would not argue that he *meant* his readers to see the Bard of Experience as a "Reprobate" in 1794; but his later use of that term to describe the prophetic stance may have been an outgrowth of the St. Christopher legend.

[9] Voragine, *The Golden Legend*, p. 645.

[10] Commentary in Keynes' facsimile edition of *Songs of Innocence and of Experience* (London, 1967). Keynes' interpretation, like my association of the

Bard/St. Christopher may begin to resemble Christian of *Pilgrim's Progress*, whose burden is his own sense of guilt, depicted in Blake's illustrations to Bunyan as a childlike form swaddled in a fleshy bundle that grows from Christian's back and shoulders [4]. This darker reading of the winged child is not really incompatible with our earlier association of the child with Christ; it serves rather as a way of complicating the image, and rendering what Blake saw as the ambiguity of the poet's relation to his own inspiration in the state of Experience. Unlike the Piper, the Bard must carry the weight of his inspiration (or perhaps hold it down to prevent it from flying away), and he has to watch where he is going. The burden of Christian prophecy is, for Blake, inseparable from the burden of the Selfhood, and its weight, as he was to suggest in a later sketch in the pages of *The Four Zoas* [5], is equivalent to the weight of the world, the burden of Atlas.

The absence of direct illustrative function in the frontispiece to *Experience* allows the picture to be experienced as the focus for an invisible text compounded from a wide range of verbal and visual associations. While these associations involve creative inferences and transformations, they are anything but "free" in the sense of random, arbitrary, or capricious: the test of their validity is their coherence and adequacy in returning us to our point of departure, the picture itself, with a more precise and comprehensive sense of its significance. A more discriminating and lengthy analysis would differentiate between historically probable "meanings" and the more open realm of "significance" (Blake could not have "meant" in 1794 to link his Bard figure with his later drawing of Atlas in *The Four Zoas*, but the figure could have assumed that significance for him at a later date).[11] The crucial element in either kind of reading is the demand for creative participation. It is almost as if there were a missing poem that Blake could have written to go with this picture. By refusing to supply this poem, he challenges us to fill the void, and places us in a position analogous to that of his Bard/St. Christopher,

Bard with the Reprobate, involves an anachronism: we go forward in Blake's writing to find words adequate to pictures he conceived much earlier. I think this procedure is justified as long it is done consciously. It seems highly probable that Blake often developed graphic images long before he found the words adequate to describe them, and the act of anachronistic interpretation may have real value in tracing the process of Blake's imagination as it moves from vision to verbalization.

[11] The distinction between "meaning" and "significance" here is drawn from E. D. Hirsch's *Validity in Interpretation* (New Haven, 1967), p. 8.

making us work for our meanings rather than passively receive them as we do in the frontispiece to *Innocence*. The Bard is thus an emblem not only of the poet but of the reader in the state of Experience, and a full encounter with the picture is not just a glimpse through the window into Blake's world, but a look at ourselves in the mirror he provides.

The wealth of independent, nonillustrative pictorial significance which Blake can deposit in a given design is, of course, most obvious in "illustrations which do not illustrate," and the frontispiece to *Experience* is a kind of limiting example of how far this process can go. But other, subtler kinds of visual-verbal independence and interplay occur—as, for instance, when Blake plays text and design off against one another, an effect rather like counterpoint in music, or, more precisely, like the interaction of image and sound in cinema. In plate 8 of *America* [6], for example, the text begins with the words "The terror answerd: I am Orc, wreath'd round the accursed tree" (8:1, E 52), printed on a cloud bank which hangs over the sea. Seated on this cloud bank, however, we find not the youthful Orc but the aged Urizen, or his political equivalent, Albion's Angel. For a moment Orc's voice seems to emerge from the figure of his aged antagonist. This effect lasts only a moment, however, for Orc's voice goes on to describe how "Urizen perverted to ten commands" the "fiery joy" of human energy (8:3), and we begin to see the design at the top of the page as an image not of the speaker but of the speaker's *vision*. We are invited, in other words, to see Urizen through Orc's eyes by his presence as an invisible narrator-commentator on the image before us.

Two plates later in *America* [7] a similar effect occurs: the text, printed among flames which wash up the page, begins, "Thus wept the Angel voice & as he wept the terrible blasts/ Of trumpets, blew a loud alarm across the Atlantic deep"—lines which evoke the seascape of *America* 8 with its "angelic" aged Urizen on the bank of clouds. But the picture now shows Orc, not Urizen or Albion's Angel, and the accompanying voice belongs not to one of the characters but to the omniscient narrator of the poem, Blake himself, describing the "perturbation" of Albion's Thirteen Angels as they sit in their Atlantic kingdom. Why does Blake couple his vision of Orc with a verbal description of Orc's apparent opposites, Albion's Angels? The answer comes at the top of the very next plate: "Fiery the Angels rose, & as they rose deep thunder roll'd/ Around their shores: indignant burning with the fires of Orc" (*A* 11:1-2). What we have witnessed in the orchestration of this series of texts and designs is a kind of cinematic transformation or conversion. The angel has become a devil (a conversion that Blake presents in a narrative fashion in plate 24 of *The Marriage of Heaven and Hell*). The cold, oppressive, aged figure of plate 8 has become the flaming youth of plate 10, a transformation which can be seen even more dramatically if one superimposes mentally (or with film transparencies) the "lineaments" of one figure over the other. The aged figure can then be made to "dissolve" into his youthful counterpart, and vice versa. The effect is a kind of counterpoint in which each medium proceeds with its own independent formal integrity, while interacting with the other to form a complex, unified whole.

In Blake's longer books he employs a technique of maintaining the independence of design from text which Northrop Frye has called "syncopation"—the placement of a design at a considerable distance from its best textual reference point.[12] In general, however, this sort of syncopation is achieved not by physical distance but by the introduction of iconographic disparities which complicate and attenuate our equations of text and design. Blake invites us, for instance, to see the title page of *The Marriage of Heaven and Hell* [8] as an "illustration" of the textual episode on plate 24 near the end of the book, the conversion of the angel into a devil. And yet he complicates this equation with a number of disparities: (1) the textual devil and angel seem to be males, while the pictured figures look female, or (in some copies) sexually ambiguous; (2) the text describes a single conversation followed by a self-immolation, while the design depicts a sexual encounter followed by a flight (if we can infer that the couple in the foreground will soon join the others floating up the center of the page); (3) none of the other details in the design refers directly to the scene of conversion related in plate 24, particularly the figures arranged along the "ground line" at the top of the page. These disparities produce a metaphorical richness which multiplies the independent complexities of text and design: conversation becomes copulation, immolation becomes flight, single conversion becomes catalyst for mass resurrection.[13]

[12] "Poetry and Design," p. 48. Frye's example of "syncopation" is the female figure harnessed to the moon at the bottom of plate 8 of *Jerusalem*, a figure which is not mentioned in the text until plate 63. Even more important than the physical distance, however, is the fact that the textual reference ("the Fairies lead the Moon along the Valley of Cherubim"; *J* 63:14) does not really explain the picture, but simply gives us a clue for further investigation.

[13] Note, too, that all these metaphors can and perhaps should be reversed,

The most interesting feature of the title page to the *Marriage* is that Blake manages to play upon all these metaphoric lines while keeping the design a simple and direct evocation of the book's central theme, the interaction of contraries. Every aspect of the composition—the strong contrasts of color and shape of flames and clouds, the thrust and recoil of the opposed trees at the top of the page, the aggressive inward thrust of the devil versus the receptive outward pose of the angel—is designed to embody the encounter of active and passive contraries. These contraries are seen not as they are perceived by the religious, as categories of good and evil (Blake employs none of the conventional imagery of horns, tails, wings, or halos to distinguish devil from angel), but as mutually "necessary to Human existence" (*MHH* 3). This does not mean that they are presented in an absolutely symmetrical balance, however. Blake clearly sides with the devils in the text because he sees the history of his culture as the deification of the angelic virtues of rational passivity and self-restraint. Thus, despite the theoretical and representational equality of devils and angels, the thrust of the design cuts diagonally across the page rather than vertically down the middle, tipping the balance of the composition in favor of the devil's party. And in one detail at least, this implicit preference verges on overt satire: on the ground line, the left (devil's) side shows a harmonious vision of the sexes, a couple walking beneath the trees, while the right side displays an inharmonious "di-vision" in the figure of a young man playing a musical instrument, apparently unable to stir a reclining female out of her bored passivity.[14]

The independence of Blake's text and designs, then, allows him to introduce independent symbolic statements, to suggest ironic

---

since the scene of mass sexual resurrection comes before the more personalized encounter of devil and angel. This analysis, by the way, is the product of an exchange with John Grant in the footnotes of *Blake's Visionary Forms Dramatic*, ed. David Erdman and John Grant (Princeton, 1970), pp. 63-64 (hereafter cited as *VFD*).

[14] The reclining figure is clearly a woman in copies C and D. The instrument held by the kneeling figure is only suggestively etched—perhaps a flute, shepherd's pipe, or lyre. The absence of conventional imagery to distinguish devil from angel (noted above) must be qualified in copies A and I, where, as Erdman notes (*TIB*, p. 98), the devil and angel *share* a halo. This humorous little touch may suggest that the conversion is, from another point of view, the transformation of the devil into an angel; similarly, the androgynous ambiguity of the devil's and angel's sexes stresses the major point of conversion, transformation, marriage of equals, rather than the superiority and victory of one point of view.

contrasts and transformations, and to multiply metaphorical complexities. The most important kind of independence to watch for, however, is found not where the picture clearly departs from or contradicts the text, but in cases where the design seems nothing more than a literal illustration. The second illustration to "The Little Black Boy" in *Songs of Innocence*, for instance, seems to be a merely literal rendering of the concluding stanzas:

> When I from black and he from white cloud free,
> And round the tent of God like lambs we joy:
>
> Ill shade him from the heat till he can bear,
> To lean in joy upon our fathers knee.
> And then I'll stand and stroke his silver hair,
> And be like him and he will then love me.

The design shows a white boy leaning on the knee of a shepherd Christ, the black boy standing behind him to "stroke his silver hair" [9]. The details not mentioned in the text, such as the flock of sheep in the background or the willow tree (emblem of paradise), do not introduce complications, but are predictable features of the heavenly state which the black boy envisions. And yet this design is not simply an imitation of the text, but introduces its own symbolic dimensions. Blake seems to be making a pictorial allusion to the theme of a guardian angel presenting a human soul to God, as treated in the seventeenth-century emblem book *Amoris Divini Emblemata* by Otto von Veen (Vaenius) [10].[15]

This allusion completes the transformation in consciousness which is only implicit in the text: the black boy's emerging sense that despite his lessons in racial self-hatred ("I am black, but O! my soul is white"), he is equal and even superior to the English boy because he has had to suffer (ironically referred to as "bearing the beams of love"). Whereas the poem begins with the English boy "white as an angel" and the black boy in a fallen, damned condition ("bereav'd of light"), the design presents a near—but not total—

[15] Hagstrum suggests that van Veen, among other well-known emblematists, "surely caught Blake's young eye in the engraver's shop where he worked and in the print shops he frequented as a boy" (*Poet and Painter*, pp. 50-51). The *Amoris Divini Emblemata* would probably have been more congenial to Blake's temperament than van Veen's emblems after Horace, or those on secular love. Mario Praz notes three editions of this work, two published in Antwerp (1615 and 1660) and one in Amsterdam (1711). See his *Studies in Seventeenth-Century Imagery*, rev. ed. (Rome, 1964), p. 526.

reversal of roles. The black boy is now the angel who has absorbed and been refined by God's light and heat, and the white boy has, in a sense, been "bereav'd of light" in that he has not yet learned to bear the beams of love. Thus the design puts him in the position of the lost soul who has been rescued by his black "guardian angel." Even without the added dimension provided by its design, "The Little Black Boy" is a great poem, but it is a great fragment whose unity is part of a larger whole produced by its interaction with a design that has its own independent symbolic integrity.

The most pervasive kind of rivalry between text and design in Blake's illuminated books is simply the matter of conflicting aesthetic appeals. To open one of Blake's books is to be confronted with two equally compelling art forms, each clamoring for primary attention. Frye suggests that in some books this contest is clearly won by one art (text in *The Marriage of Heaven and Hell*, design in *Urizen*), but that in general Blake moves toward a balance of pictorial and poetic elements.[16] I suspect, however, that there are many readers like myself who find it difficult to read Blake's text in his illuminated books with any extended concentration. This difficulty must have been felt by contemporaries of Blake such as Dawson Turner, who despite what Blake considered "the Loss of some of the best things" asked for separate prints from the Lambeth books without their texts.[17] The difficulty arises in part from occasional illegibility and frequent smallness of print, from the distraction continually offered by rather striking designs, and from a tendency of readers to take the line of least interpretive resistance. Blake's pictures may contain "mythological and recondite meaning, where more is meant than meets the eye" (*DC*, E 522), but they are also clear and distinct pictures *of* something. His text makes fewer concessions to the "corporeal eye" and is thus most readily grasped, as a text, in a form

16 "Poetry and Design," p. 46.

17 Blake later complained, "Those I printed for Mr Humphry are a selection from the different Books of such as could be Printed without the Writing, tho' to the Loss of some of the best things. For they when Printed perfect accompany Poetical Personifications & Acts, without which Poems they never could have been Executed" (Blake to Dawson Turner, 9 June 1818 [K 867]). It is interesting to note further that when Blake supplied these separate plates, the captions he inscribed on them were in no case quoted from the poems they were supposed to "illustrate," but were apparently written as Blake's latest responses to the independent symbolic meaning of the designs. Thus the title page of *Urizen* is inscribed not with a line about Urizen or the "primeval priest" but with a playful question evoked by the symmetrical quality of the design: "Which is the way, the right or the left?"

where it can be underlined, annotated, and easily read. The total effect is rather like that of one of those medieval illuminated bibles, a *biblia pauperum* which provides us visionary paupers and illiterates with something to feed our imaginations.

Northrop Frye has remarked that the independence of Blake's designs from his words is rather surprising in view of the prevailing conventions within which he worked. The tradition of historical painting, Frye argues, tended to dictate a slavish fidelity to the text, and the naïve allegories of the emblem books were generally "an attempt to simplify the verbal meaning."[18] Blake's departures from these traditions have too often been explained, however, by recourse to value judgments and odious comparisons.[19] Not all the allegories were naïve, and history painting had its masterpieces. Blake's departures from traditional ways of connecting poetry and painting cannot, I would suggest, be understood simply as an improvement in the quality of his use of the two modes of expression. In the eighteenth century the ideal of relating the "sister arts" of painting and poetry had become grafted to aesthetic concepts which were in many ways alien to Blake's philosophy of art. In order to understand his stylistic departures from these conventions we need to compare the assumptions that lay behind them with Blake's own understanding of the purposes of art, and of the nature of composite art in particular.

II. BLAKE AND THE TRADITION OF THE SISTER ARTS

It is probably an exaggeration of Blake's originality and uniqueness to say that his composite art has "scarcely a parallel in modern culture."[20] Blake seems so original because—to invoke Eliot's paradox in "Tradition and the Individual Talent"—he is so deeply traditional. His art is not reducible to the conventions of manuscript illumination, the emblem, the *impresa*, the book of icons, or other forms of book illustration, because he is capable of using any and all of these forms when it suits his purpose. But he does not seem particularly eclectic in the loose sense: there are important aspects of the tradition of the sister arts that he conspicuously avoids, both in relations

[18] Frye, "Poetry and Design," p. 45.

[19] Rosemary Freeman, for instance, compares Wither's marigold emblem with Blake's sunflower, but she can only point to the superiority of Blake's poem, not the underlying difference in purpose. See her *English Emblem Books* (New York, 1970), pp. 24-29; reprinted from original edition (London, 1948).

[20] Frye, "Poetry and Design," p. 46.

between text and design and in the formal qualities of his poems and pictures taken separately. Jean Hagstrum is certainly right to see in Blake "a theoretical commitment to the values of pictorialism, broadly conceived,"[21] but this could be said with equal force of Keats or Hogarth. The question is, what unique modification did Blake give to the tradition of the sister arts, and at what point was he likely to depart from it?

As illustrated books, of course, nothing like Blake's illuminated poems had been seen since the Middle Ages.[22] Although book illustration had become a minor industry in the eighteenth century, it was essentially a business of assembling work by different hands (printer, engraver, painter, and writer) into a final product which reflected the division of labor that went into it. The free interpenetration of pictorial and typographic form so characteristic of Blake's books is technically impossible in a medium which separates the work of the printer from that of the engraver. Blake's books unite the labors of the craftsman and the artist: he invents both the text and its illustrations (often at the same time), cuts both into the copper plate as parts of one total design, and prints them on his own press, retouching and adding final color by hand. In one sense, then, there is almost something perverse about discussing the "relations" between the constituent parts of an art form which is so obviously unified in both conception and execution.

Blake could hardly have been unaware, however, that his age was obsessed with the idea of unity in general, and with the goal of uniting the arts of painting and poetry in particular. The eighteenth century was, after all, the age that discovered that art could be spelled with a capital "A," and Abbé Batteux could entitle his 1746 treatise *Les beaux arts réduits à un même principe.*[23] As he set about uniting

[21] Much of the following section is the product of an exchange between Hagstrum and myself in *Blake's Visionary Forms Dramatic.* Professor Hagstrum's brief essay there, "Blake and the Sister Arts Tradition," was written partly in response to my claim in "Blake's Composite Art" that Blake was more critical than appreciative of the sister arts tradition. I have tried in the following pages to meet his objections and have altered my own views where appropriate. I should stress, however, that my debts to Professor Hagstrum's splendid scholarship far outweigh any disputes with his conclusions.

[22] For an informative survey of the history of style and technique in this field, see David Bland, *The Illustration of Books* (London, 1951).

[23] For a general study of the rise of aesthetics as a distinct discipline in the eighteenth century, see Paul O. Kristeller, "The Modern System of the Arts: A Study in the History of Aesthetics," *Journal of the History of Ideas* III

his two art forms in a single composite form, then, Blake must have meditated on the kinds of "unity" he did and did not want to achieve. It seems evident, for instance, that he had an instinctive antipathy to abstract notions of unity, systems based on the assumption that "One Law" governs the multiplicity of phenomena. If "One Law for the Lion & Ox is oppression," it seems reasonable to suppose that one law for painting and poetry is oppression too.

The problem is only aggravated when that one law or "même principe" is called "nature," and is defined as a reality external to and independent of human consciousness. Blake's rejection of an art based in the imitation of nature transcends the usual boundaries which divide artistic movements of the eighteenth and nineteenth centuries. Wordsworth and Pope get equally bad marks for "following nature," despite the fact that they mean radically different things by the word. In Blake's view the reliance on nature encouraged a tendency to evaluate art not in terms of its imaginative or visionary coherence, but in terms of its correspondence to the general idea of what is "out there." It did not matter to him whether the "there" was defined as the Lockean "ratio of five senses" or a Platonic realm of abstract forms to be apprehended through memory and reason. The problem with both concepts was that they split the perceiver from an "objective" world outside himself, and they encouraged, not just technical verisimilitude in art ("fac-simile representations of merely mortal and perishing substance"; *DC*, K 576), but conventionality and a tame correctness.

The doctrine of nature as the source, end, and test of art also had important consequences for the understanding of the relationship between the arts. If painting and poetry were imitations of the same thing, they ought to be reducible to their common origin. *Ut pictura poesis* ("as a painting, so also a poem") became, in eighteenth-century aesthetics, not a casual comparison but a commandment for poets and painters.[24] The dominance of this principle had, I would

(1951), 496-527. Useful recent studies include Lawrence Lipking, *The Ordering of the Arts in Eighteenth-Century England* (Princeton, 1970), and James S. Malek, *The Arts Compared* (Detroit, 1974). Malek notes that "comparative discussions of the arts, along with aesthetic speculation in general, gradually increased in popularity during the eighteenth century in Britain. In terms of total numbers of works produced, this branch of aesthetics achieved its most rapid growth between 1760 and 1790" (p. 154), precisely the period in which Blake was growing up.

[24] Of the enormous body of literature on this subject, the most useful studies

suggest, three major consequences for the practice of poetry and painting: (1) It encouraged a sense of *translatability*, a conviction that differences in mediums, like those of language, are superficial distinctions. It can hardly be an accident that an age believing so firmly in the possibility of translation turned book illustration and literary painting into a light industry. (2) It encouraged a belief in the *transferability* of techniques from one medium to the other; painting was not merely similar to poetry, it was supposed to borrow techniques from its sister art. (3) Where differences between the two arts were acknowledged, the issue of unity was resurrected in the notion of *complementarity*, the idea that the coupling of the two arts would provide a fuller imitation of the total reality. Blake had, I would suggest, a highly critical attitude toward these notions of the sister arts, and thus a basic foundation for the understanding of his style is an analysis of the way he confronts the prevailing conventions in his own stylistic choices, sometimes rejecting, sometimes assimilating and transforming traditional notions for his own purposes.

1. *Illustration: Visual Translation and Visionary Transformation*

The belief in the translatability of literature into painting is everywhere evident in the eighteenth century's liking not only for individual designs illustrating literary texts but for entire galleries de-

are Mario Praz, *Studies in Seventeenth-Century Imagery*; Robert J. Clements, *Picta Poesis: Literary and Humanistic Theory in Renaissance Emblem Books* (Rome, 1960); Jean Hagstrum, *The Sister Arts* (Chicago, 1958); Rensselaer Lee, *Ut Pictura Poesis: The Humanistic Theory of Painting* (New York, 1967), reprinted from *Art Bulletin* XXII (1940), 197-269; and Ralph Cohen, *The Art of Discrimination: Thomson's "The Seasons" and the Language of Criticism* (London, 1964). One obvious gap in our history of critical theory is the transformation of the idea of *ut pictura poesis* in the nineteenth and twentieth centuries. One of the few treatments of this subject is Roy Park's "*Ut Pictura Poesis*: The Nineteenth Century Aftermath," *Journal of Aesthetics and Art Criticism* XXVIII (1969), 155-64, which suggests that the critical, antipictorialist, and antivisual attitudes which I ascribe here to Blake are characteristic of Romantic criticism in general. Blake would surely have been aware of his friend Fuseli's sentiments in the matter: "From long bigotted deference to the old maxim that poetry is painting in speech, and painting dumb poetry, the two sisters, marked with features so different by nature, and the great masters of composition, her oracles, have been constantly confounded with each other by the herds of mediocrity and thoughtless imitation" (From the *Analytical Review* of 1794, quoted in *Encounters*, ed. John Dixon Hunt [London, 1971], p. 7).

voted to the pictorial translation of poets. Macklin's "Poets' Gallery" and Boydell's "Shakespeare Gallery" were symptomatic of the belief that painting would be enhanced by an alliance with literature, and that, despite some technical problems, translation from one medium to the other was possible and even inevitable. The pleasures of imagination were, as Addison had pointed out, the pleasures of "the most perfect and delightful of all our senses," our *sight*.[25]

Blake is entirely within the mainstream of eighteenth-century literary painting in the sense that all of his pictures are in some way related to texts. But his usual approach to those texts, in contrast to the general practice of eighteenth-century illustrators, is to provide not a plausible visualization of a scene described in the text but rather a symbolic recreation of the ideas embodied in that scene. The symbolic independence of his designs for Job and Dante has been well-documented,[26] but the peculiar quality of Blake's illustrations is probably best exemplified in his treatment of Milton, the poet who more than any other was illustrated in the eighteenth century. As Marcia Pointon puts it in *Milton and English Art*: "unlike any other illustrator of Milton, Blake incorporated into his designs his own interpretations of the poem. Various artists ranging from Medina to John Martin embroidered on the text in order to portray more convincingly the scene described, but Blake actually contributes to the symbolic content of the poem through his own very personal interpretation . . . his illustrative method is symbolic rather than representational. He is concerned with the idea rather than the narrative."[27]

Blake's vigorous independence as a literary illustrator has often been traced to his intellectual disputes with the texts he illustrated. The Bible must be seen as well as read, presumably, in its "infernal

[25] "The Pleasures of the Imagination," *The Spectator*, No. 411, 21 June, 1712, reprinted in *Eighteenth-Century Critical Essays*, ed. Scott Elledge (Ithaca, N.Y., 1961), I, 42. Elledge also quotes John Dennis: "The eye is a sense that the poet ought chiefly to entertain, because it contributes more than any other to the exciting of strong passion" (I, 501). Malek's survey of theoretical statements on this issue indicates the prevalence of visual norms: "painting was to strive for more or less accurate representation of visual particulars; *no one* argued that the province of painting (or sculpture) might include anything other than natural concretes" (*The Arts Compared*, p. 155, italics mine).

[26] The classic study of the *Job* series is Joseph Wicksteed's *Blake's Vision of the Book of Job* (London and New York, 1910). For the Dante series the basic work is Albert S. Roe, *Blake's Illustrations to the Divine Comedy* (Princeton, 1953).

[27] (Toronto, 1970), pp. 137-38.

sense," and Dante's Caesarism, like Milton's Puritanism, must be corrected, not merely reflected by the conscientious illustrator. But these pictorial "wars of intellect" which Blake conducted with the texts of the past continue, in a sense, even into his designs for his own poems. This suggests that his illustrative independence, his refusal to provide visual translations of texts, is not merely a sign of doctrinal differences with his subject, but is a basic principle in his theory of illustration.

The difference between "symbolic" and "representational" illustration can be seen when we compare Blake's treatment of the theme of the expulsion from paradise with that of a contemporary, E. F. Burney [11, 12]. Burney's version is designed as a plausible visualization, with great attention to details of vegetation and drapery. The only clue that this is a supernatural, Biblical scene is the presence of Michael's wings; otherwise, we would simply be seeing a large warrior dragging a half-nude couple through a dense woodland. Blake, on the other hand, makes no attempt to place his scene in a realistic setting. Natural details are schematized, and the human figures, while classically rendered, are placed in a frontally composed row across the surface of the picture plane, rather than (as in Burney) twisting back into the interior space of the design. This symmetrical frontality permeates Blake's entire composition: the lighting does not streak across a distant sky, but forms a jagged border around each figure. The "Flaming Brand" which waves over paradise is not in the distance, but forms a stylized whirlpool of color which seems, like the horsemen of the apocalypse around it, to hover directly over the heads of Adam, Michael, and Eve. In short, Blake's version is the more primitive, stylized, and emblematic of the two, and it is dominated not by the concerns of visual illusionism or verisimilitude but by pictorial ideas, or what Blake would call "Intellectual Vision." This does not mean the picture is a diagrammatic system of abstract symbols, nor is this style completely unique to Blake. Contemporaries such as Fuseli, Barry, Mortimer, and Flaxman were moving in the same direction. But Burney's treatment, with its emphasis on visual translation, is the more typical product of the sister arts tradition as the eighteenth century understood it, because it locates Milton's episode in visualized nature, the realm in which poetry and painting were supposed to converge. The difference between Blake and Burney is the difference between a visionary and a visualizer, a transformer and a translator.[28]

28 Morse Peckham makes a strong case that Blake's treatment of the expulsion

2. *Pictorialist Poetry and Visionary Prophecy*

The belief in a homogeneous visualizable nature ("Single vision & Newtons sleep") was also the basis for mutual transference of techniques and standards of taste between the visual and verbal arts. Superficial symptoms of this transference were the taste for attaching long quotations to paintings as captions and the construction of elaborate systems of analogies between the two arts by eighteenth-century critics. The test of a poem became its ability to evoke pictures in the reader's mind, pictures like the ones he would see "in nature," or in those faithful imitations of nature, postmedieval paintings—not, Lord Shaftesbury would assure his readers, in those "magical, mystical, monkish, and Gothic" pictures of the "emblem kind" which had dominated the vision of a less reasonable age.[29] Nature, reason, and visual (i.e., homogeneous, single-perspective, three-dimensional) space made it possible for the pleasures of imagination (i.e., visualization) to mean the same thing in poetry and painting.

The most obvious consequence of the vogue for "painterly poetry" was, of course, the descriptive poem, a form which, like the nature it described, cut across the boundaries between classicism and romanticism. From Thomson to Wordsworth to Keats we find a continuing fascination with verbal paintings of real or ideal places and things.[30] Blake seems especially alien to this tradition. The main thrust of his poetry is dramatic, from the dramatized states of mind in *The Songs of Innocence and of Experience* to the thunderous dialogues of the "Visionary Forms Dramatic" in his prophetic poems. More important, the scenes in which these poetic dramas are set tend to be consistently and increasingly nonvisual. The landscapes

---

theme was based on Burney, a fact which would bring into clearer focus Blake's consciousness of stylistic transformation. See Peckham's "Blake, Milton, and Edward Burney," *Princeton University Library Chronicle* XL (Spring 1950), 109. For a survey of other treatments of the expulsion, see Merritt Hughes, "Some Illustrators of Milton: The Expulsion from Paradise," *Journal of English and Germanic Philology* LX (1961), 670-79, but note that Hughes mistakenly attributes the first "gentle" treatment of the expulsion (the angel holding Adam and Eve by the hands rather than driving them out with a sword) to Blake. Actually, as Thomas Minnick has shown, such a treatment was conceived earlier by Frances Hayman ("On Blake and Milton," Ph.D. diss., Ohio State University, 1973, p. 17).

[29] Shaftesbury, *Second Characters, or The Language of Forms*, ed. Benjamin Rand (Cambridge, Mass., 1914), p. 92.

[30] On this subject see Cohen, *The Art of Discrimination*, Chap. III.

of the early lyrics are simply identified as "valleys wild" or "eccho-ing greens": there is none of the dwelling on the patterns of light and shade or the effects of distance which we find in the "pic-turesque" poetry of the eighteenth century. Blake seems to have heeded Johnson's remark that "scenery is fine—but human nature is finer," for his settings never become the subject of the poem, and are never treated as if they were independent of the human theme Blake is dramatizing. This obliteration of the visual and objective aspects of the poetic landscape reaches its radical extreme in the phantasmagoric "fluxile" spaces of the prophetic books, in which the "look" of Blake's scenery changes with every change in the mind of the perceiver. Thus we find Blake, like the blind Milton, avoiding painterly or picturesque descriptions in favor of visual paradoxes such as "darkness visible" and "the hapless Soldiers sigh" which "Runs in blood down palace walls." And we also find him going beyond Milton, using the vast, cosmic abysses of *Paradise Lost* as an interior distance whose shape is not fixed or picturable, as it is in Milton, but rather is seen as the raw material of psychological transformation:

> First I fought with the fire; consum'd
> Inwards, into a deep world within:
> A void immense, wild dark & deep,
> Where nothing was; Natures wide womb.
> And self balanc'd stretch'd o'er the void
> I alone, even I! the winds merciless
> Bound; but condensing, in torrents
> They fall & fall; strong I repell'd
> The vast waves, & arose on the waters
> A wide world of solid obstruction
> (*U* 4: 14-23, E 70-71)

The "scene" around this narrator is indistinguishable from his con-sciousness of it: he *is* the "wide world of solid obstruction" which arises on the waters within himself. The visual world Blake creates here is not the objective, homogeneous "natural" perspective of postmedieval painting; it is more like the kaleidoscopic world of the modern cinematographer.

It is possible, of course, for poetry to be pictorial without con-taining descriptions of natural scenes. Jean Hagstrum has argued that despite Blake's disregard for the picturesque he was a pictorialist in his use of "verbal icons" (imagery that "suggests or is organized into pictures or other works of graphic art"), "picture gallery form" (in which "the reader moves like a spectator from tableau to tableau"), and the "visualizable personification."[31] It is true that all these elements may be found in Blake's poetry, but they are not used in a visual or pictorialist manner, as the eighteenth century understood it. Blake frequently alludes to icons or artifacts: shields, buildings, sculpture, tools, ornamented fabrics, books, and whole cities are mentioned or described—but not in a way that invites us to visualize them, or to think of their visual appearance as especially significant. Despite his fondness for the artifact, Blake never makes one of them the controlling image of a poem, in the manner of Keats's Grecian urn. When a single image such as, for instance, a tree does become the focus of a poem, its visual, natural properties as an object of description are minimized:

> The Gods of the earth and sea,
> Sought thro' Nature to find this Tree
> But their search was all in vain:
> There grows one in the Human Brain
> ("The Human Abstract," *Exp*; E 27)

When Blake does pause to describe a fixed object, such as the city of Golgonooza, the result is anything but a visualizable set of images:

> The great City of Golgonooza: fourfold toward the north
> And toward the south fourfold, & fourfold toward the east
> & west
> Each within other toward the four points. . . .
> (*J* 12:46-48, E 154)

There is a similar problem with the idea of "picture gallery form." Blake does not move, as Spenser or Thomson does, from one picture or visualizable scene to another, but rather from vision to vision—and these visions tend to be not visual but synaesthetic, tactile, and phantasmagoric. Their relationship, moreover, is not like that of items in a sequential gallery of distinct visual structures. They tend rather to be linked in a dramatic fashion, as the oratory or stream of consciousness of characters who have conflicting visions to express. The effect is more like watching a furious debate, in which the contestants are capable of projecting vast multimedia displays to demonstrate their arguments.

31 "Blake and the Sister Arts Tradition," *VFD*, p. 85.

Blake's deepest connection with the pictorialist tradition is in his use of personification, but not, I think, the "visualizable" personification. Blake rarely describes his personae in visual terms, perhaps because he knew his own illustrations were worth the proverbial thousand words, but also because they are, in the corporeal, three-dimensional sense, invisible. Keats's "Ode to Psyche" treats a visualized personification in the typical pictorialist fashion (as his Grecian urn treats the icon). Keats has never really seen his goddess outside of pictures and statuary,[32] but he adopts the fiction that he *has* seen her in a dream or with "awakened eyes," placing her and Cupid in a lavishly detailed natural landscape. Such a treatment of personification is alien to Blake's whole sense of where his characters exist, the human mind. Keats recognizes the mental nature of Psyche in a theoretical way, but when he tries to give her a home in his mind, he visualizes that home as a picturesque landscape, where thoughts become pines "murmuring in the wind," receding into the distances of a Claude Lorrain or Salvator Rosa landscape: "Far, far around shall those dark-clustered trees/ Fledge the wild-ridged mountains steep by steep." Blake would probably have sympathized with the humanistic theme of "Ode to Psyche," but he would have seen Keats's treatment of it as that of a fanciful voyeur, too obsessed with his externalized visualization of Psyche.[33]

Perhaps the simplest test of Blake's antipictorialism, however, is the fact that his poems do not refer us visually even to his own illustrations. His characters are rarely described in terms that would allow us to "see" them if we did not have actual pictures of them. Urizen is "this Demon of smoke,/ . . . this abstract non-entity/ This cloudy God seated on waters/ Now seen, now obscured" (*Ah* 2:10-13, E 83). Los is too busy hammering and building and dividing to hold still for a verbal portrait. This lack of verbal visualization makes the task of identifying characters in the illustrations rather problematic. We conventionally assume, for instance, that Urizen looks like the old man with the white beard we find in the illustrations. But in the poems Urizen frequently acts not like a patriarchal deity but like the Satanic rebel against a heavenly order (he is characterized as the "prince of light" in *The Four Zoas* 25:5). Similarly, Los

[32] Ian Jack suggests some of the specific pictorial sources Keats may have used in *Keats and the Mirror of Art* (Oxford, 1967), Chap. XII.

[33] Walter Jackson Bate points out that Keats himself was "aware of the limitations of the genre" of descriptive poetry, and worked to free himself from its influence. See Bate's *John Keats* (Cambridge, Mass., 1963), p. 124.

is not invariably depicted as the heroic artist-liberator: he sometimes adopts the role of jealous patriarch and oppressor, forming "nets & gins" like his adversary Urizen. While Blake's illustrations provide a stable visual element that is absent in his poetry, then, even they do not provide us with unambiguous portraits of his personae or their settings. They are more likely to be what David Erdman has called "multi-purpose emblems,"[34] designs in which a few simple forms can be "seen" in several different ways.

It is, of course, impossible to write poetry for very long without introducing some visual imagery. Blake acknowledges that "it is impossible to *think* without images of somewhat on earth" (Annotations to Lavater, E 590; italics mine). But he does his best to place his visual imagery in a nonpictorial, nonobjective context, treating it as the malleable content of a consciousness that sees much more than meets the eye in three-dimensional spatial perspective. One suspects that Keats was on a parallel track: his interests in dramatic poetry and in synaesthesia were both motivated, in part, by a desire to free himself from the luring sirens of description ("I am getting a great dislike of the picturesque"; "descriptions are bad at all times").[35] Blake seems not to have been so tempted by the pleasures of the eighteenth century's version of pictorialism, deriving his imagery from the older and more radical pictorialism of sacred literature, in which language becomes vision and the word is made flesh:

> Hear the voice of the Bard!
> Who Present, Past, & Future sees
> Whose ears have heard,
> The Holy Word,
> That walk'd among the ancient trees.
> (Introduction to *Experience*)

> I saw no God, nor heard any, in a finite organical perception; but my senses discover'd the infinite in every thing. . . .
> (*MHH* 12, E 38)

3. *The Picture as Text: Narrative, Allegory, and Vision*

The other half of the pictorialist program for the sister arts was to make painting more "poetical." If this goal is seen in the sense of the Leonardesque *paragone*, as the attempt to make painting as intellec-

[34] Erdman, *TIB*, p. 209.

[35] Quoted in Bate, *John Keats*, p. 124.

tually respectable as poetry, then Blake is certainly a poetical painter. But the tradition as Blake received it had become more particular and demanding. It had come to mean not only the literal, visual fidelity to historical and literary texts epitomized by Burney, but also a tendency to see pictures as literary texts in themselves, containing narrative episodes, "depth" characterization, and allegorical details to be "read" like words, as signs of a reality not presented in the picture.[36]

Hogarth (who like many eighteenth-century painters referred to himself as the "author" of his compositions) exemplifies the attempt to give a narrative, temporal dimension to the visual arts. The simplest way of doing this was to fill the picture with details that would evoke various stages in the "story" behind the scene depicted. The first plate of *A Harlot's Progress* [13] for instance, shows the York stagecoach which brought the girl to town at the left, her initial encounter with the procuress in the center, and the would-be seducer waiting in the doorway at the right. The other details (toppling baskets, dead goose, the haggard woman on the balcony in the background) are all omens of the more distant future. So pervasive was the taste for pictures that could be "read" in this fashion that some critics even found narratives where none were intended. Le Brun, for instance, insisted on reading the different reactions of the Israelites in Poussin's *Fall of the Manna* as a narrative sequence, showing the state of the Jews before, during, and after the descent of the manna.[37]

Although Blake considers himself in some sense to be a "history painter,"[38] it is clear that he has little interest in attempting to construct his compositions as narrative texts.[39] His designs concentrate on a few foreground images, usually arranged symmetrically, with a minimum of subordinate detail, encouraging an instantaneous grasp of the whole design rather than an impression of sequence. Occa-

[36] See Lee, *Ut Pictura Poesis*, Chap. IX, "The Unity of Action."

[37] For a fuller analysis of *A Harlot's Progress* and the traditions of literary, historical painting that lie behind it, see Ronald Paulson, *Hogarth: His Life, Art, and Times* (New Haven and London, 1971), I, 259-76.

[38] Blake's exhibition of 1809 contained "Poetical and Historical Inventions," according to his *Descriptive Catalogue*, and he regularly identified himself as a painter of history, meaning heroic, sublime, epic subjects.

[39] This generalization applies mainly to the illuminated books. It is also generally true in Blake's other works, but there are notable exceptions, such as the *Arlington Court Picture*, which has several centers of interest and seems designed to be read.

sionally, to be sure, he does present metamorphic sequences across the foreground plane,[40] usually in marginal designs where (for obvious reasons) radial and bilateral symmetry must give way to some sort of sequential presentation. But these marginal murals embody the passage of time not as a progression from the near to the distant, or from the clear to the obscure, as in Hogarth, but as a movement from the near to the near. All moments in the sequence are immediate and immanent, just as in the poetry the prophetic narrator sees "Present, Past, & Future" as an eternal *now*.[41]

The other desideratum of poetical painting, the representation of the interior life of its human subjects, not just their outward features, likewise seems difficult to apply to Blake's practice. His human figures have a kind of allegorical typicality, and are clearly not designed as subtly differentiated portraits of real persons. We see very little subjectivity or individuality in the faces of Blake's figures for the same reason we do not find complex motivation or intricate personalities in his poetical personifications. Urizen cannot have his own interior life like the character of a novel; he is only an aspect of the interior life of the single human mind that constitutes the world of his poem. Blake certainly expresses passions and states of mind in his pictures, but he does not present them as residing *within* human figures, subtly disclosed (as in Rembrandt) by the way a shadow descends from an eyebrow. He presents the parts of the psyche *as* human figures. His portraits are thus not of men with minds, but of the mind itself, seen as human form. One consequence of this strategy is that the expressiveness of the human figure tends, for Blake, to be diffused throughout the body rather than focused primarily in the face: "I intreat then that the Spectator will attend to the Hands & Feet to the Lineaments of the Countenances they are all descriptive of Character" (*VLJ*, E 550).

The branch of literary painting which seems closest to Blake is, of course, the allegorical world of Dürer, the emblematists, and the Neoplatonists whose *icones symbolicae* point toward an invisible reality. We should beware, however, of assuming that Blake simply rejects in a circular fashion the eighteenth century's rejection of "magical, mystical, monkish" painting of "the emblem kind," and returns to the sacramental pictorialism of the Middle Ages and

[40] See, for example, plates 1, 4, and 15 of *America*.

[41] Sometimes these sequences can be read in both directions, which further undercuts the temporal, sequential impression. See Erdman, *TIB*, p. 139, for a reading of *America* 1 in this manner.

Renaissance. While his pictures do have a more emblematic, allegorical quality than the naturalistic world of eighteenth-century painting, he nevertheless seems, as Hagstrum argues, to have avoided the "Oriental, mystical, diagrammatic grotesques," and the arbitrary, intentionally obscure imagery of the arcane mystery cults.[42] Blake's pictures do contain some grotesques (swan-maidens, human dragons, griffins, etc.) and numerous emblematic attributes (compasses, globes, hammers, veils, books), but never in the profusion that we find in Dürer or the emblematists. Blake is reported to have kept a print of Dürer's *Melencolia I* [108] hanging above his workbench for most of his life.[43] But when he adapted this theme for use in one of his own illuminations, he drastically simplified and condensed the iconography. In *Jerusalem* 78 [105] he depicts a figure in the traditional melancholic pose, seated like Rodin's *Thinker* with his head resting on his left hand. The bird's head on this figure (probably an eagle, reflecting the traditional association of Saturn with melancholy, an association Dürer makes with the eaglelike wings on his figure; for Blake the eagle is primarily a symbol of genius) is the only "emblematic" departure from a rather spare naturalism.[44] Otherwise, Blake has stripped his character naked in both the literal and figurative sense: the elaborately rendered draperies and the labyrinth of allegorical detail which fill Dürer's composition are completely absent in Blake. But this divesting of detail does not reduce the iconographical complexity of the composition. It tends rather to open up the range of allusive contexts that Blake may be evoking, linking his "bird-man" not only with *Melencolia* but with treatments of St. John (author of Revelation) as a man with an eagle's head [106], and further with Blake's own verbal descriptions of "Los's Melancholy," especially the one that appears in the text just below this picture: "Los laments at his dire labours . . ./ Sitting before his Furnaces clothed in sackcloth of hair" (*J* 78:10-11, E 231). What we are seeing in Blake's picture, then, is a portrait of Los as a melancholy

[42] "Blake and the Sister Arts Tradition," *VFD*, pp. 88-89.

[43] Arthur Symons, *William Blake* (New York, 1907), p. 122.

[44] Dürer's figure and the paraphernalia around it have many other intersections with Blake's symbolism. The best discussion of *Melencolia I* is found in Erwin Panofsky's *The Life and Art of Albrecht Dürer* (Princeton, 1955), pp. 156-71. For the association of the eagle with Saturn, see Raymond Klibansky, Erwin Panofsky, and Fritz Saxl, *Saturn and Melancholy* (London, 1964). The link between Dürer's print and Blake's use of it in *Jerusalem* was pointed out to me by Judith L. Ott and is developed in her note "The Bird-Man of *Jerusalem*," *Blake Newsletter* X: 2, no. 38 (Fall 1976), 49-51.

prophet of apocalypse, rendered in a fusion of Christian iconography, Renaissance humor theory, and classical mythology. Dürer's composition is the more "literary" piece in the sense commended by the doctrines of *ut pictura poesis*: it is a kind of text full of symbolic details to be "read" by the knowing reader. Blake's design is as iconographically complex as Dürer's, but that complexity has been focused in imagery that can be grasped (although not explicated) almost instantaneously. The ideal of a visionary *biblia pauperum* could not have been better served.

Blake's stripped-down and condensed treatment of the *Melencolia* theme is obviously *not* what Shaftesbury had in mind when he called for eighteenth-century painters to create "True, natural, and simple" compositions to replace the "False, barbarous and mixed" hieroglyphics of the seventeenth century.[45] Blake's style resides somewhere between these two extremes, in a middle ground which may be defined by bracketing one of his designs between examples of what Shaftesbury meant by true and false art. Rosemary Freeman provides these brackets: a seventeenth-century emblematic rendition of *The Choice of Hercules* and an eighteenth-century version of the same theme by an Italian artist commissioned by Shaftesbury to carry out his idea of naturalness [14, 15].[46] Between these let us place a similar composition by Blake, which in the absence of a title we may call *The Choice of Jerusalem between Classical and Gothic Form* [16]. Shaftesbury's version is clearly designed as a plausible visualization of a dramatic moment in time. In Wither's version, on the other hand, "none of the three characters has any particular interest in the others: it is a tableau in which each is posed in an attitude appropriate to his own nature."[47] Shaftesbury subordinates the mythical, symbolic nature of his characters to the demand that the picture be "natural, credible, and winning of our assent: that she may thus acquit herself of what is her chief province, the specious appearance of the object she represents."[48] For Wither, "all objects have an allegorical significance. Both in their patterned arrangement and in the fact of their being present at all, the claims of verisimilitude are ignored. . . . Shaftesbury's criterion of the natural and credible is irrelevant here since in such pictures objects are introduced not for their 'specious appearance' but for their significance."[49]

How does Blake's composition relate to these two? It is clearly

45 Shaftesbury, *Second Characters*, p. 92.

46 *English Emblem Books*, p. 9.

47 *Ibid.*, p. 11.

48 *Ibid.*, p. 55.

49 *Ibid.*, pp. 13-14.

more unified visually and dramatically than Wither's composition. The characters interact even more intimately and intensely than Shaftesbury's, and Blake, like Shaftesbury, seems to have chosen the moment of decision: if Hercules is depicted in "the moment when Pleasure has ceased to plead and Virtue is still speaking," Blake chooses the moment when Vala is about to throw her veil over Jerusalem, and her attendants are still urging her to flee. On the other hand, there are emblematic elements in Blake's design (the icons of classical and Gothic architecture), and the whole composition has a supernatural, unreal quality (produced by the flight of the figure at the right, the clouds around the central group, and the schematic nature of the setting) which draws it closer to Wither's way of seeing things. "Specious appearance," the plausible visual illusion, is not negligible in the picture, but it does not govern the composition as it does for Shaftesbury.

If we meditate a little further on the dramatic unity of Blake's design we notice that this is not the unity of a realistic theatrical scene, but more like the visual presentation of melodrama, mime, or dance, forms which depend upon exaggerated bodily and facial gestures to make up for their lack of verbalization. Shaftesbury's dramatic unity is based, by contrast, on a verbal unity: Virtue speaks and Hercules listens—for a long time, evidently, judging by the boredom conveyed by his face and posture. This sort of verbal unity, the sense that the characters are speaking or about to speak, is perhaps the most literal kind of *ut pictura poesis*, and the kind which is most conspicuously absent in Blake. His characters do not say anything: they are too busy acting out a visionary dumb show in a realm of sensuous (not primarily visual) immediacy, somewhere between the hieroglyphical world of Wither and the visual, verbal world of Shaftesbury. Blake's style of presentation does not reside exclusively in either world, but unites elements of the classical, naturalistic mode of vision with the "Gothic" supernatural. Is it only an accident that his Jerusalem has not yet made her choice either, but stands poised, like her creator, between the illusory veils of Nature, "specious representation" and classicism, and the naked glory of Gothic form?

We will pursue this question further when we come to a more detailed consideration of Blake's pictorial style. What should be clear at this point is the distinctness of Blake's visual art from the "literary" traditions of allegorical and narrative painting. Blake would undoubtedly have accepted the fundamental idea of *ut pictura poesis*, in that it insists on the intellectual respectability of painting.

As he proclaims in the *Descriptive Catalogue*: "Painting, as well as poetry and music, exists and exults in immortal thoughts" (E 532). All the arts are unified in the imagination. They are the "Powers of conversing with Paradise which the flood did not Sweep away" (*VLJ*, E 548). But for Blake, painting does not attain visionary, intellectual status merely by imitating the story-telling or signifying procedures of language and literature. It must be "elevated into *its own proper sphere* of invention and visionary conception" (*DC*, E 532; italics mine)—"The apple tree never asks the beech how he shall grow, nor the lion. the horse, how he shall take his prey" (*MHH* 9, E 36). The "proper sphere" of painting may include some of the techniques of literary painting, but it does not define its essential character in literary, verbal ways.

4. *Painting Plus Poetry or Painting Times Poetry*

One of the more obvious contradictions in the tradition of *ut pictura poesis* was the idea that despite the desirability of making poetry and painting more similar, each had a distinct role to play in the imitation of nature. The personification of painting and poetry as sisters was no accident. It expressed concisely the conviction that the two arts were daughters of the same nature, and that they provided complementary representations of the basic modalities in which reality was apprehended—space and time, body and soul, sense and intellect, and, in the realm of aesthetics, *dulce et utile*.[50] Painting was linked with the spatial, bodily, sensuous world, and poetry with the temporal, mental realm, a division which reflected the traditional feeling that poetry was the "higher" art. The emblem book enjoyed a particularly privileged role in this scheme because it seemed to provide the most comprehensive possible imitation of a bifurcated reality. As the anonymous essayist of *The Plain Dealer* put it in 1724: "*Two Sister Arts*, uniting their different *Powers*, the one transmitting *Souls*, the other *Bodies* (or the outward Form of Bodies), their combining Influence would be of Force to frustrate

[50] The space-time distinction was invoked by Lessing in his *Laocoön* (1766) to refute the pictorialist tendency to blur the differences between the arts. A typical example of the "complementary" use of the distinction appears in an unsigned essay in *The Free Thinker*, no. 63 (22 October 1718; reprinted London, 1722), II, 34-36, which argues that poetry is chiefly effective in time because mass publication permits it to endure. Painting, on the other hand, is ineffective in time because it is perishable, but conquers space because it leaps the language barrier. Poetry and painting as an aesthetic *dulce et utile* is documented in Praz, *Studies in Seventeenth-Century Imagery*, p. 168.

Death Itself: And all the Ages of the world would seem to be *Cotemporaries*."[51]

Blake's critique of this notion of the sister arts can be understood most clearly in terms of his reception of the idea of nature that lies behind it. For Blake, the dualistic world of mind and body, time and space, is an illusion which must not be imitated, but is to be dispelled by the processes of his art: "the notion that man has a body distinct from his soul, is to be expunged; this I shall do, by printing in the infernal method, by corrosives, which in Hell are salutary and medicinal, melting apparent surfaces away, and displaying the infinite which was hid" (*MHH* 14, E 38). Relief etching with acid or "corrosives" was the process by which Blake cut his copper plates, melting away the apparent surface of the copper to reveal an art form in which soul and body, rendered in the modalities of poetic time and pictorial space, are united. Blake would agree with the program of the emblematists to unite the two arts, not, however, as a means of imitating or transmitting the full range of reality, but to expose as a fiction the bifurcated organization of that reality. Blake sees the separation of body and soul, space and time, as various manifestations of the fall of man, "His fall into Division" (*FZ* 4:4). The function of his composite art is therefore twofold: it must "melt apparent surfaces away" by satirizing and exposing the illusion of a dualistic nature (thus "All Bibles or sacred codes" have caused the erroneous notion "That Man has two real existing principles Viz: a Body & a Soul"; *MHH* 4, E 34); and it must "display the infinite which was hid," by overcoming the fall into a divided Nature with a "Resurrection to Unity" (*FZ* 4:4). For the emblematists, painting was to be *added to* poetry in order to imitate the larger sum of spatial and temporal reality; for Blake, poetry and painting were to be *multiplied by* one another to give a product larger than the sum of the parts, a reality which might include, but not be limited by, the world of space and time.

Blake never refers to his painting and poetry as "sister arts," a curious omission for a man who lived in the age which systematized this metaphor so extensively. The reason may lie in his conception of the dualities that his art was designed to overcome. Blake's most pervasive metaphor for the fall into "division" is the separation of the sexes. The temporal and spatial modalities in which poetry and painting are created are consistently defined in sexual terms: "Time & Space are Real Beings a Male & a Female Time is a Man Space is a

[51] *The Plain Dealer*, II, no. 60 (London, 1730).

Woman" (*VLJ*, E 553). Even more significant is Blake's attribution of spatial and temporal *forms* to masculine and feminine creative forces: "The Female . . . Creates at her will a little moony night & silence/ With Spaces of sweet gardens & a tent of elegant beauty:/ . . . And the Male gives a Time & Revolution to her Space" (*J* 69:19-23, E 221). In Blake's myth the sexes are, like the time and space, soul and body which they personify, illusions that have arisen with the fall of consciousness from primal unity (the fact that he refers to them as "Real Beings" is a way, I would suggest, of affirming the vitality of this illusion, perhaps even its inevitability). Blake generally describes this fall into division as the paradoxical consequence of the attempt to impose an abstract unity of "One Law" on the multiplicity of phenomena. Urizen's attempt to rationalize experience into a homogeneous continuum always begets its own opposite, a chaotic multiplicity which will not obey his iron laws for a moment, and, in particular, a world of polarized forces such as time and space, mind and body, man and woman. Blake describes this process in *Jerusalem*: "When the Individual appropriates Universality [i.e., imposes one law]/He divides into Male & Female" (*J* 90:52-53, E 248). The danger then arises that these divisions will become permanent, that masculinity and femininity will no longer be seen as contraries within a larger consciousness but will "appropriate Individuality," becoming definitive categories of individual human beings or basic modes of human nature in the way time and space are basic modalities of physical nature: "when the Male & Female,/ Appropriate Individuality, they become an Eternal Death" (*J* 90:53-54, E 248).

The analogy may be extrapolated in physical nature as follows: when Nature appropriates Universality, it divides into Space and Time. When Space and Time appropriate Individuality, they come to be seen as irreducible realities, the "nature of things." Space then becomes indefinite extension, the vast, homogeneous abyss of "Bacon, Newton, & Locke," and time becomes indefinite duration, an endless Heraclitean flux or the "dull round" of cyclical determinism. For the painter, spatial form becomes increasingly visual: the tyranny of sight and the "Druidical Mathematical Proportions of Length Bredth & Highth" (three-dimensional perspective) replace the synaesthetic field of visionary perception in which the senses "discover the infinite in every thing." For the poet, temporal form becomes an art of memory, the endless refinement of classical models, or the raking up of the poet's own past, an indefinitely extended realm for the egotistical sublime.

The eighteenth-century version of *ut pictura poesis* sought to overcome the separation of time and space, body and soul, by making poetry and painting more similar, adding them together as complementary representations, or reducing them to their common denominator, nature. Blake's strategy, I would suggest, was to transform the dualism into a dialectic, to create unity out of contrariety rather than similitude or complementarity. Blake wanted to combine spatial and temporal form in his illuminated books not to produce a fuller imitation of the total objective world, but to dramatize the interaction of the apparent dualities in our experience of the world and to embody the strivings of those dualities for unification. The aesthetic and iconographic independence of Blake's designs from their texts can thus be seen as having two functions. First, it serves a mimetic purpose, in that it reflects Blake's vision of the fallen world as a place of apparent separation between temporal and spatial, mental and physical phenomena. Second, it has a rhetorical or hermeneutic function, in that the contrariety of poem and picture entices the reader to supply the missing connections. In this light, the problematics of relating text and design serve as an "allegory address'd to the Intellectual powers" which is "fittest for Instruction, because it rouzes the faculties to act."[52] David Erdman suggests that we regard the illuminated poem as a "prompt book" which leads us to make "an imaginative leap in the dark, a leap *beyond* the dark" to "Visions, Expanses, New Songs, and Thunderous Dramatic Forms."[53]

[52] Blake to Thomas Butts, 6 July 1803; and Blake to Dr. Trusler, 23 August 1799 (K 825, 793). The idea of throwing difficulties in the path of the interpreter is, of course, as old as allegory itself, and was a favorite technique of the emblematists in making witty, obscure connections between the visual and verbal aspects of their emblems. As Paulson notes (*Emblem and Expression*, p. 14), "the emblem is not merely illustrating a device (motto), a known adage, or an apothegm; it may use one or more of these topoi as its raw material, both visual and verbal, in order to produce a total image that is more than the sum of its parts, that is independent, problematical, to be deciphered." The difference in Blake's art appears to be one of degree, not of kind; his visual and verbal art forms attain more aesthetic independence, each in their own sphere, than we find in the emblem books, and his metaphysic of contrariety demands a multiplicative rather than an additive relationship between visual and verbal form.

[53] "America: New Expanses," *VFD*, p. 93.

The total presentation of Blake's illuminated books, then, is a kind of living embodiment of his theory that "without Contraries is no Progression." The unity of his composite art depends upon the vigorous independence of its component parts. Only in this light can we resolve the apparently contradictory facts that (1) Blake's illuminated books are, technically speaking, the most integrated forms of visual-verbal art since the medieval illuminated manuscript; and (2) the constituent elements of these books, the poems and their illustrations, have a vigorous aesthetic independence which makes them satisfactory, if fragmentary, works of art in and of themselves.

III. THE UNITY OF BLAKE'S COMPOSITE ART

The tradition of the sister arts as modified in the eighteenth century is useful for showing the kinds of things Blake was reacting against as he set about uniting the verbal and graphic arts. But it also sets the stage for an understanding of the positive principles which animate his stylistic choices. Blake would probably not have been impressed by Lessing's attack on the excesses of *ut pictura poesis*, because it only tried to reaffirm the obvious differences between the sister arts rather than to discover a new basis for their unification, and it did not question the basic doctrine of nature as the source, end, and test of art. In Blake's view the attempt to make poetry visual and to make pictures "speak" and tell a story was inherently flawed, not just because it ignored fundamental differences between the two art forms, but because it presumed the independent reality of space and time and treated them as the irreducible foundations of existence. As we have seen, Blake considers space and time, like the sexes, to be contraries whose reconciliation occurs not when one becomes like the other, but when they approach a condition in which these categories cease to function. In the simplest terms, his poetry is designed to invalidate the idea of objective time, his painting to invalidate the idea of objective space. To state this positively, his poetry affirms the power of the human imagination to create and organize time in its own image, and his painting affirms the centrality of the human body as the structural principle of space. The essential unity of his arts, then, is to be seen in the parallel engagements of imagination and body with their respective mediums, and in their convergence in the more comprehensive idea of the "Human Form Divine." For Blake, in the final analysis the body and the imagination are separable principles only in a fallen world of limited perception, and the business of art is to dramatize their unification: "The Eternal Body of Man is The IMAGINATION. . . . It manifests itself in his Works of Art" (*Laocoön*, E 271).

Blake's specific techniques for constructing his art forms as critiques of their own mediums are becoming increasingly clear. In the poetry he creates a world of process and metamorphosis in which the only stable, fixed term is the imagining and perceiving mind. Cause and effect, linear temporality, and other "objective" temporal structures for narrative are replaced, in the prophetic books, by an imaginative conflation of all time in the pregnant moment. The prophetic narrator-actor perceives "Present, Past & Future" simultaneously, and is able to see in any given moment the structure of all history: "Every Time less than a pulsation of the artery/ Is equal in its period & value to Six Thousand Years" (*M* 28:62-63). Consequently, the narrative order of the poem need not refer to any incontingent, nonhuman temporal continuum. Most narrative structures employ what Blake would call "twofold vision": that is, the imaginative arrangement of episodes is constructed with reference to an implicitly objective time scheme. The narrative selects its moments and their order in terms of some imaginative rearrangement of the objective sequence: *in medias res*, *ab ovum*, or *recherche du temps perdu*. All of these selective principles assume, however, that there is an order of nonhuman, "natural," or "real" time which flows onward independent of any human, "subjective," or "imaginary" reorganization of its sequence. For Blake, this objective temporal understructure is an illusion which is to be dispelled by the form of his poetry, or adumbrated in the single mythic episode. The beginning, middle, and end of any action are all contained in the present, so the order of presentation is completely subject to the imagination of the narrator. Hostile critics have always recognized this quality in Blake's major prophecies when they indicted them for being "impossible to follow." That is precisely the point. Blake's prophecies go nowhere in time because time, as a linear, sequential phenomenon, has no place in their structure. *Jerusalem* is essentially a nonconsecutive series of epiphanies or visionary confrontations with the total structure of history (six thousand years) encapsulated in the poet's experience of the personal and historic moments in his own life. That is why Blake has Los, his alter ego, personify Time, Poetry, Prophecy, and the Imagination simultaneously. In this way Blake could dramatize the poet's management of fictive time and the prophet's quarrel with history as versions of the struggle of the individual with himself. It is also why Blake continues Milton's task of consolidating the forms of epic and prophecy in the embracing form of revelation.[54] The epic form provides the forward pressure, the sense of a journey through time and space (the "passage through/ Eternal Death"). The prophetic strain emphasizes the visionary moment, continually asserting that the time is at hand, the journey really a dream ("the Sleep of Ulro") from which we can awake at any moment. The apocalyptic form provides windows into that awakened state which is found at the center (moment) and circumference (beginning and end) of time, the "awaking to Eternal Life." Blake's prophetic works stress these forms in different ways (*The Four Zoas* is more like a narrative epic, *Milton* a dramatic epic like *Paradise Regained*) which all tend to the final consummation in *Jerusalem*, an encyclopedic song "Of the Sleep of Ulro! and of the passage through/ Eternal Death! and of the awaking to Eternal Life."

A similar consolidation of epic and prophetic styles can be observed in Blake's illuminated prints, in which the human figures of classical, Renaissance history (i.e., epic) painting, are placed in a Gothic (i.e., prophetic or apocalyptic) spatial setting.[55] Art historians have begun to recognize that this sort of hybrid style, far from making Blake a historical maverick, places him in the mainstream of experimental movements in late eighteenth-century art.[56] In historical terms, Blake's style must be defined (along with that of many of his contemporaries) as a kind of "Romantic classicism," an oxymoron which helps us to see that his art has affinities with Michelangelo, Raphael, and the mannerists in his treatment of the human figure, with Gothic illumination in his primitivism and anti-illusionism, and with contemporaries such as Flaxman in his stress on pure outline, Fuseli in his use of the terrific and exotic, Barry and Mortimer in their treatment of the mythic and heroic.

Historical terminology cannot explain, however, how and why

[54] The best recent work on this subject is that of Joseph A. Wittreich, Jr. See, for instance, his "Opening the Seals: Blake's Epics and the Milton Tradition," in *Blake's Sublime Allegory*, ed. Stuart Curran and Joseph A. Wittreich, Jr. (Madison, 1973), pp. 23-58 (hereafter cited as *BSA*).

[55] In the sister arts tradition, history painting was considered the analogue of epic poetry, a comparison which Blake echoes when he writes in the margin of Reynolds' *Discourses*, "A History Painter Paints The Hero, & not Man in General" (E 641).

[56] Robert Rosenblum's essay "Toward the *Tabula Rasa*," in his *Transformations in Late Eighteenth-Century Art* (Princeton, 1967), does a great deal to demonstrate Blake's centrality.

these elements are transmuted into something unified and unique in Blake's pictorial style. His art is a curious compound of the representational and the abstract, the picture that imitates natural forms and the design that seems to delight in pure form for its own sake. The "flame-flowers" which are so characteristic of his early work, and which later inspired the arabesques of art nouveau, exemplify the interplay between representation and abstraction that informs all his work. Abstract linear forms such as the vortex or the circle provide the structural skeletons for a seemingly infinite range of representational appearances, and the postures of his human figures are repeated so systematically that they suggest a kind of pantomimic body-language, a repertoire of leitmotifs that can be repeated in widely differing contexts.[57] Blake provides a kind of emblem of the "life of forms" in his art in his picture of a serpent metamorphosing into a flame, then a leaf, and finally into the tendrils of a vine [17].

The effect of this sort of pictorial strategy is to undercut the representational appearance of particular forms and to endow them with an abstract, stylized existence independent of the natural images with which they are identified: serpent, flame, and vegetative form participate in one sinuous formal life. Blake frees his style, in this way, from the task of accurately representing nature ("fac-simile representations of merely mortal and perishing substances"; *DC*, E 532), and develops a style which demonstrates that the appearances of nature are to some extent (but never completely) arbitrary, and subject to transformation by the imagination of the artist.

All art, of course, even that which claims only to provide a mirror image of external reality, transforms its subject matter in some way, through the imposition of some style or convention. But the very subject of Blake's art is this power to transform and reshape visual imagery, and, by implication, the ability of man to create his vision in general. This is what he means when he says that his art "copies Imagination" ("Men think they can Copy Nature as Correctly as I copy Imagination this they will find Impossible"; *PA*, E 563). The word "imagination" does not mean, I would suggest, a transcendent body of archetypal, quasiplatonic forms; it is rather the name of a process ("The Imagination is not a State: it is the Human Existence itself"; *M* 32:32, E 131). And this process is the activity by which

[57] Northrop Frye ("Poetry and Design," p. 48), was the first to suggest an analogy with Wagner's use of the leitmotif. Janet Warner's important essay "Blake's Use of Gesture," *VFD*, pp. 174-95, attempts to categorize the basic body positions.

symbolic form comes into being, not just the state of its finished existence. Blake's pictorial style embodies the interaction between imagination and spatial reality, then, just as his poetic form enacts the encounter between imagination and time.

The concrete symbol or icon of the imagination in Blake's pictures is, of course, the human body. The nonillusionistic, stylized character of the settings which surround the body is Blake's iconographic way of restating his central stylistic premise, that the shape and significance of spatial reality is not objective or given, but derives its form and meaning from the human consciousness that inhabits it. The environments of Blake's paintings thus serve as a kind of malleable setting for human form: there are no mathematically consistent perspectives, and very few landscapes or architectural backgrounds which would make any sense without the human figures they contain.[58] Pictorial space does not exist as a uniform, visually perceived container of forms, but rather as a kind of extension of the consciousness of the human figures it contains.

The essential unity of Blake's composite art, then, lies in the convergence of each art form upon the goal of affirming the centrality of the human form (as consciousness or imagination in the poetry, as body in the paintings) in the structure of reality. The coupling of Blake's two art forms is thus an enactment of his central metaphor, "The Eternal Body of Man is The IMAGINATION. . . . It manifests itself in his Works of Art" (*Laocoön*, E 271). Blake's art is neither representational, imitating a world of objective "nature," nor allegorical, rendering an invisible, abstract, transcendent reality. It is, rather, an art of "Living Form," built upon the stylistic interplay between linear abstraction and concrete representation, the iconographic drama of the human body in pictorial space, and the poetic drama of the imagination in time, working to find the form and meaning of the moment, the individual life, and the total expanse of human history, "Six Thousand Years."

The consequences of this definition of Blake's art are perhaps more apparent in his poetry than his painting. Since Frye's *Fearful Symmetry* the nonallegorical nature of Blake's poetry has been regularly acknowledged,[59] and recent criticism has begun to explore

[58] On Blake's adventurous distortions of perspective, see Rosenblum, *Transformations*, pp. 189-91.

[59] Allegory, that is, in the "corporeal" sense, as a kind of code whose "real meaning" lies behind the symbols rather than dwelling in their sensuous par-

the question of form in the major prophecies. *Jerusalem* is no longer treated simply as a quarry for Blakean "philosophy," but is being investigated as a poetic structure whose generic elements are just now coming into focus. The recognition of traditional structural topoi such as the epic quest, the descent into the underworld, the dream vision, the prophecy and apocalypse has become much more eclectic and pluralistic. We are now in a position to assimilate these structures into Blake's theory of poetry as a critique of time, a project which may reveal that the major prophecies have formal and thematic intersections with works like *Tristram Shandy* as well as with the Bible and *Paradise Lost* (more on this in Chapter V).

It is generally acknowledged that the understanding of Blake's pictures has progressed more slowly, partly because art historians are not usually equipped to deal with the formidable complexities of Blake's verbal "system"; consequently the commentary on Blake's pictures has been mostly literary, i.e., concerned with the identification of imagery whose meaning is felt to reside primarily in the text, not in the formal treatment provided by the picture.[60] Our problem, then, is to go beyond the identification of Blake's symbolic figures to a grasp of his symbolic *style*, not just in a historical sense, but as a repertoire of specific formal devices, as a personal expression of the artist's ideology, and as a strategy for manipulating the visual field of the reader/spectator—a kind of visual rhetoric. To this problem let us now turn our attention.

---

ticulars. Blake obviously approves, on the other hand, of sublime allegory which "rouzes the faculties to act," stirring up the imagination of its readers.

60 Erdman (*VFD*, p. vii) notes that "in the reading of Blake's illuminations the advance has been slower and less steady," and Hazard Adams (*Blake Newsletter* VII: 3, no. 27 [Winter 1973-74], 69) traces this problem to excessive literariness of commentary on the pictures. A good primer on the thicket of methodological interference between literary criticism and art history is provided in *New Literary History* III (Spring 1972), an issue devoted to this subject; see especially Svetlana and Paul Alpers, "*Ut Pictura Noesis*? Criticism in Literary Studies and Art History," 437-58.

Chapter Two

BLAKE'S PICTORIAL STYLE

I. TECHNICAL DISCRIMINATIONS AND THE LIFE OF FORMS

FIRST, a general inventory of Blake's graphic productions. Any examination of his style must begin with a sharp distinction between his reproductive engravings, which are technically indistinguishable from the work of many other journeyman engravers, and Blake's original compositions, whether executed in etching, engraving, woodcut, line drawing, watercolor, tempera, or some combination of techniques. A second distinction may be drawn, much less sharply, between his original illustrations of subjects from other writers (Dante, Milton, the Bible, Blair, Young) and his illustrations for his own poetry, the works in illuminated printing. These illuminated books, the main subject of our present inquiry, are distinguished by a technique known as relief etching, a process which seems to have died with Blake.[1] Small wonder: in an age that believed in progress, this technique looked like a regression from the "science of engraving" back to earlier forms of printing such as the medieval block book or its ancestor, the sculptured relief.[2] The lines of relief

[1] *Ahania* and *The Book of Los* are the only illuminated books which were not relief etched. The best study of this process is still Ruthven Todd's "The Techniques of William Blake's Illuminated Printing," in *The Visionary Hand*, ed. Robert N. Essick (Los Angeles, 1973), pp. 19-44; revised and reprinted from *The Print Collector's Quarterly* XXIX (Nov. 1948), 25-37. See Essick's postscript, p. 44, for further studies of Blake's techniques. One obvious need in Blake scholarship is further exploration of his technical resources, beyond relief etching and color printing. Many of his plates seem to be in the "mixed method" (main outlines etched, subordinate lines engraved). We need some reliable way of discriminating between these graphic techniques, not to mention the wide range of coloristic effects in the illuminated books. The complexities of the relief etching process are described in minute detail by John Wright, "Blake's Relief-Etching Method," *Blake Newsletter* IX: 4, no. 4 (Spring 1976), 94-114.

[2] Blake sometimes signed his plates "W Blake sculpsit" rather than "Engraver," a signature which, while not unique to Blake, reflects his feeling that the copper plate is a surface or wall to be hollowed out like a bas-relief, not

etching are generally thicker and coarser (and hence unfashionable in a refined England which preferred the delicate tonalities of Woollett, Strange, and Bartolozzi to the hard "dry" style of Renaissance engraving) than lines bitten directly into copper with acid or burin.[3] The presence of both kinds of lines in Blake's designs for his own poetry indicates that he used a mixed method, with the emphasis on relief etching as a kind of sculptured relief in copper which could be further refined, finished, and colored, both on the plate and its impressions.

Blake's original compositions for subjects other than his own poems are often quite similar, as compositions, to his illuminated prints. Many of his stylistic and iconographical motifs can be found in both groups: the manneristic elongation of human proportions, the symmetrical, frontally arranged forms, and the primitive, schematic quality of natural images. The main difference between the two groups is that Blake's designs outside the illuminated books are frequently directed toward a final condition as line engravings (Job,

---

just a plane for the inscription of lines. Blake expresses his sense of having recovered a primitive technique in his illuminated books in the prefatory remarks to *Jerusalem*, where he links his printing process to the mythic origins of writing:

> Reader! [*lover*] of books! [*lover*] of heaven,
> And of that God from whom [*all books are given,*]
> Who in mysterious Sinais awful cave
> To Man the wond'rous art of writing gave,
> Again he speaks in thunder and in fire!
> (*J* 3: 1-4, E 144)

Etching words and pictures in metal with fiery acid is, for Blake, a way of recovering the primeval inspiration that expressed itself by cutting words in stone with fire.

3 The eighteenth-century preference for "tonal" engraving styles over the more primitive linearism of Raimondi and Aldegrever is documented by Arthur M. Hind in his *History of Engraving and Etching*, rev. ed. (London, 1963), pp. 204-206, 209. Blake's resentment of this fashionable style is recorded most fully in his *Public Address* (E 560-71). Blake was not, however, isolated in his preference for linearity. Winckelmann's ideal of archaic purity based on ancient sculpture was having a wide effect both in England and on the Continent. Diderot's hope for a reincarnation of Poussin was being fulfilled, as Jean Seznec has shown, by David's meticulous historicism and sculptural purity ("Diderot and Historical Painting," in *Aspects of the Eighteenth Century*, ed. E. R. Wasserman [Baltimore, 1965], p. 139). Even more radical experiments with pure linearism were being conducted by Blake's own circle, notably Flaxman and Cumberland. The preference for linearity has, moreover, a long tradition in idealist aesthetics (see Dora and Erwin Panofsky, *Pandora's Box* [New York, 1956], for an account of this tradition).

Dante, Young's *Night Thoughts*, Blair's *Grave*), or they are executed as finished paintings in nonreproducible forms, drawn or painted directly on the surface rather than cut in a copper plate. There is a general sense, then, of higher technical finish and of greater technical orthodoxy in Blake's compositions for other authors. The technical complexity of the Job engravings, for instance, is never remotely approached in Blake's illuminated prints. The Job series has been recognized as the only rival to Dürer's masterpieces in line engraving, while the illuminated prints have been regarded by print connoisseurs as "rough productions . . . more interesting from the printer's than the engraver's point of view, being meant only as foundations for the final colouring by hand."[4] If we subtract the overtones of a value judgment from this statement, it becomes a fairly accurate observation. Blake's illuminated prints *do* often seem rougher and sketchier than his designs for others, although they sometimes exhibit great technical subtlety, especially in the full-page designs which might be ordered separately. More precisely, then, we might say that they are less uniform and orthodox, showing a wider variation in technical finish than any other group of Blake's works and exemplifying his disregard for the fashionable "dots & Lozenges" and "Clean Strokes" which dominated reproductive engraving: "I defy any Man to Cut Cleaner Strokes than I do or rougher when I please" (*PA*, E 571).

Blake probably began etching rather than engraving his own poems because it was cheaper ("less than one fourth of the expense" of letterpress and engraving; Prospectus, E 670) and easier (at least in the etching of the text; the completed copper plate, however, was often the result of numerous etching stages and laborious refinements of the original design). Blake's "New Method of Printing" allowed him to avoid the setting of type and the expensive labor of engraving letters in reverse, and it eliminated division of labor and aesthetic effect, producing both typographic and pictorial form with the same process. The greater finesse and higher finish of line engraving could be reserved for separate plates and commissioned works, or employed in combination with relief etching as a way of achieving special effects. Blake clearly had high hopes that "Illuminated printing" would make his fortune and open English eyes to a whole new

[4] Laurence Binyon, "The Engravings of William Blake and Edward Calvert," in *The Visionary Hand*, ed. Essick, p. 54; reprinted from *Print Collector's Quarterly* VII (1917), 305-32.

realm of expression.[5] Perhaps he also saw its potential as an instrument of an underground radical press, a way of producing a revolutionary *biblia pauperum*, a "Bible of Hell" by, as well as for, the politically conscious working classes of London.[6]

The main chance and the revolution turned out in different degrees to be illusions. Blake was never able to mass-produce his books as he hoped, partly because the new method was not so easy as he supposed, and partly because "republican art" was in the 1790s a dangerous commodity.[7] But art was not neglected. Blake's method of illuminated printing became the vehicle for a remarkably flexible and various pictorial style which ranges from the barest, sketchiest suggestions of form to plates of relatively high finish. The opening sequence of plates in *Milton* exemplifies this flexibility. The title page [18], which shows Milton returning to earth from the "Heavens of Albion," is rendered in white-line engraving, with extremely fine lines used to model Milton's body. Plate 2 [19], Milton descending as a star (really the same subject seen from a different point of view), is executed in much rougher, thicker lines, a style reminiscent of Blake's first experiments in illuminated printing. Finally, plate 3 [20] presents the human form as half-finished, struggling into formal life (or perhaps resisting it) like Michelangelo's *Captives*, rendered in the roughest graphic style Blake could muster.

It is a mistake, I would suggest, to view these prints in terms of the pictorial values of the engraving connoisseur. Taken separately, plates 2 and 3 of *Milton* would not do very well as exhibits of Blake's graphic genius. As a series, however, they present a living visual continuum which shows not just the final, finished product of visionary experience, but some sense of its process. (It is interesting, in this regard, to look at Blake's pencil drawings, which rarely start from a firm, assured, linear basis, but seem rather to grope through numerous erasures and trial alternatives before focusing themselves clearly.)[8] In these plates from *Milton* Blake is "copying Imagination"

[5] Erdman describes Blake's pursuit of "the main chance" in *Prophet Against Empire*, rev. ed. (New York, 1969), p. 101.

[6] If this was part of his intention, Blake's fears of political reprisal kept him from speaking very plainly in his illuminated books, and they seem ultimately to have silenced him, at least from 1795 until around 1804 when he first issued *Milton*. See Erdman, *Prophet*, pp. 152-53.

[7] *Ibid.*, p. 152.

[8] This assertion would seem to contradict Blake's well-known liking for strong, linear facility in drawing. Note, for instance, Samuel Palmer's remark

—that is, copying the process by which form is discovered and created, searching for what Henri Focillon has called "the life of forms in art."[9]

II. THE INTERPLAY OF COLOR AND LINE: A CRITIQUE OF THE *DESCRIPTIVE CATALOGUE*

The stylistic and technical differences among Blake's illuminated books, his original designs for other authors, and his commercial reproductive engravings must be kept in mind when we try to relate his artistic practice to his aesthetic theories. The main source for Blake's thoughts on style is the *Descriptive Catalogue* of 1809, a polemic against all forms of painterly style in painting and engraving.[10] In this manifesto Blake divides the world of art into sheep and goats, aligning himself with the great "linear" artists Michelangelo, Raphael, and Dürer, and against the "demons" of the Venetian and Flemish schools, Rembrandt, Rubens, and Titian. Blake's theoretical preference for outline and form over color and light ("Colouring does not depend on where the Colours are put, but on where the lights and darks are put, and all depends on Form or Outline"; *DC*, E 520), carries over into a related preference for naked as opposed

on one of Blake's drawings, that it contained "the first Lines on the preservation of which Mr. Blake used so often to insist" (quoted in Keynes, *Pencil Drawings* [Toronto, 1970], p. v). Blake undoubtedly had a facility for original composition, arranging the relation and proportion of figures and space with sureness and rapidity, but his "first lines," on the evidence of the drawings themselves, are rarely preserved as the last lines of the finished engraving, but are tentative, sketchy explorations of a pictorial idea. See [5], for instance, in which the four smaller figures are only suggestively sketched. On the main figure there is evidence of erasure along the left side, and there are two "trial" lines above the left shoulder which would have preceded the final bounding line. This use of drawing as pictorial exploration is quite frequent in Blake, as a quick survey of Keynes's *Pencil Drawings* will show.

[9] For a more detailed analysis of these three plates and the problem of engraving styles in *Milton*, see my "Style and Iconography in the Illustrations to *Milton*," *Blake Studies* VI (Fall 1973), 47-71. The concept of a "life of forms" is drawn from Henri Focillon, *The Life of Forms in Art*, tr. C. B. Hogan and G. Kubler, (New York, 1957).

[10] Also important are the Annotations to Reynolds's *Discourses*, the *Public Address*, and the *Vision of the Last Judgment*. The best commentary on the theory presented in these writings is Edward J. Rose's "'A Most Outrageous Demon': Blake's Case Against Rubens," in *The Visionary Hand*, ed. Essick, pp. 311-36; reprinted from *Bucknell Review* XVII (March 1969), 35-54. Rose does not, however, test Blake's theory against his practice.

to draped figures: "Art can never exist without Naked Beauty displayed" (*Laocoön*, E 272), and "the Drapery is formed alone by the Shape of the Naked" (Annotations to Reynolds, E 639).

The value judgments of Blake's *Descriptive Catalogue* cannot be taken seriously or literally as a basis for the appreciation of his pictures. We do not have to despise Rembrandt in order to like Blake—although an understanding of Blake may cause us to see Rembrandt differently, just as it may lead us to read Milton differently. But the *descriptive* categories (linear vs. painterly) which form the basis of Blake's argument do have some validity, especially in the remarkable precision with which they anticipate the fundamental stylistic distinctions of modern histories of art.[11] The question is, how accurate are these categories as a description of Blake's own style? Did he in fact create a purely linear style of naked figures, and completely avoid the painterly concern with drapery, chiaroscuro, the picturesque, and the "blotting and blurring" devices which produce tonality? Did he consistently subordinate color to line, and light to form?

The answer is clearly no—or at least, not completely. Blake frequently drapes his human figures in garments which do not take their form from the "Shape of the Naked" figure beneath them; he frequently employs coloristic effects which are not only independent of form, outline, and the demands of light and shade, but which also tend to obscure or completely obliterate outline.[12] And an en-

[11] These are the famous distinctions between classical and baroque first systematized by Heinrich Wölfflin in *Kunstgeschichtliche Grundbegriffe; das Problem der Stilentwicklung in der neueren Kunst* (Munich, 1915). The seventh edition of this work, translated by M. D. Hottinger as *Principles of Art History* (New York, 1932), is probably the single most influential book in modern art historical studies, despite the skepticism of later scholars about the limitations of its binary system of categories.

[12] The obscuring of outline is especially notable in the mid-1790s, the period when Blake turned from the technique of translucent watercoloring to opaque color printing. As Martin Butlin notes, "he seems to have realized that, if the designs were to be heavily color-printed, there was no point in etching even the outlines on the plate." See Butlin, "The Evolution of Blake's Large Color Prints of 1795," in *William Blake: Essays for S. Foster Damon*, ed. Alvin S. Rosenfeld (Providence, 1969), p. 115. Further confirmation of the inadequacy of the *Descriptive Catalogue* as a basis for generalizations about Blake's style has come from Morton Paley in "The Truchsessian Gallery Revisited," *Studies in Romanticism*, 16:2 (Spring, 1977), 165-177. Paley notes that prior to 1804 Blake's pictorial style was much more eclectic than the *Catalogue* would suggest, and that the remark in the letter to Hayley (23 October 1804) about

graving such as the one based on Hogarth's illustrations of *The Beggar's Opera* [21] demonstrates that he was capable of working in a painterly, tonal style, capable of concentrating his light in the middle like the hated Rembrandt.[13] Blake concedes, in fact, in his *Descriptive Catalogue* that he has not always been faithful to his own aesthetic goals, but has been "tempted" by the painterly demons:

> These Pictures, among numerous others painted for experiment, were the result of temptations and perturbations, labouring to destroy Imaginative power, by means of that infernal machine, called Chiaro Oscuro, in the hands of Venetian and Flemish Demons; whose enmity to the Painter himself, and to all Artists who study in the Florentine and Roman [i.e., linear] Schools, may be removed by an exhibition and exposure of their vile tricks. (E 537)

Whenever Blake defines his position in opposition to a set of demonic adversaries, as he does here, we must beware of taking him too literally, and watch for the possibility that he is merely "resolved to be a contrary fellow" and is trying to desecrate the ruling pieties of the artistic establishment—in this case, the Royal Academy and the British Institution, both of which had "regularly refused" to exhibit paintings like those described in Blake's catalogue (E 518). More fundamentally, we need to remember that devils and angels change places very rapidly in Blake's writings, not only in *The Marriage of Heaven and Hell* but throughout Blake's works, and that it is very dangerous to rely on them as absolute categories of good and evil. Just when we are ready to write off Satan as the personification of unredeemable error and evil in *Milton*, our hero announces that his mission is to release Satan from hell (14:31), and when Milton finally confronts his adversary, he refuses to destroy him, preferring the paradoxical strategy of "giving thy life to thy enemies" (40:8). Similarly, in *Jerusalem* Blake's lifelong intellectual enemies "Bacon, Newton, & Locke" are lined up with "Milton &

---

being "enlightened with the light which I enjoyed in my youth, and which has for exactly twenty years been closed from me" may refer to this long period of experimental eclecticism. I would argue further that even after the "enlightening" experience of the Truchsessian Gallery visit, Blake does not adhere to a *purely* linear style, especially in his illuminated books, and continues to enrich his work with complex effects of light and color.

[13] Blake states in his letter to Butts, 22 Nov. 1802: "There is nothing in the Art which our Painters do that I can confess myself ignorant of" (K 814).

Shakespeare & Chaucer" in the apocalyptic vision of a redeemed humanity. Blake's intellectual and stylistic enmities are rarely expressed by avoidance or destruction or casting out of the enemy: his strategy is rather to make the adversary part of his own system, that the "enmity . . . may be removed by an exhibition and exposure."

Some "devils" are worse than others, of course. Blake's feeling that "Shakspeare & Milton were both curbd by the general malady & infection from the silly Greek & Latin slaves of the Sword" (*M* 1, E 94) does not prevent him from stealing from both poets, and further, from making Milton the hero of his own epic poem.[14] Blake's condemnations of Milton are obviously different from his diatribes against the Flemish and Venetian demons, and in the case of the latter he never reverses the judgment explicitly by making Rubens or Rembrandt into heroes in his poetry. The closest he ever comes to forgiving or tolerating the painterly school is his remark to Thomas Butts: "My Pictures are unlike any of these Painters, & I would have them to be so. I think the manner I adopt More Perfect than any other; no doubt They thought the same of theirs" (K 815).

What all this suggests is that the *Descriptive Catalogue* is more polemical than descriptive, that it is not to be trusted as an account of Blake's stylistic practice, and that Blake's actual use of the relation of color and outline is more complex and balanced than his theory. Thus, we should not be surprised to find a tree rendered in a sketchy, picturesque style in the pages of *Jerusalem* [92]; we should not be surprised to find many plates in which color seems to take on a life of its own, or in which drapery obscures the human body. This is *not* to say that Blake imitates the whole style of Rembrandt, Rubens, or Titian (as he does with Milton): rather he assimilates antilinear and painterly elements, motifs, and techniques into the context of his own basically linear style.

This process of assimilating contrary styles seems to be more pervasive in the illuminated books than in any other part of his work, occurring most obviously in the color printed books of the mid-1790s, but also in delicately washed illuminations such as those in *The Book of Thel*. As we shall see in Chapter III, below, even a translucent, nonopaque use of washes can produce effects which are independent of the linear structure of the print, and which interact with that structure to produce a complex whole. It seems very wide

14 Blake's withdrawal, in later editions, of the Preface to *Milton* with its condemnation of Milton and Shakespeare may imply a wish to retract these remarks.

of the mark, then, to regard color as an "afterthought" in the illuminated books, or even to see it as consistently governed by the principles of light and shade. One suspects that Blake's commitment to these principles ("Colouring does not depend on where the Colours are put, but on where the lights and darks are put, and all depends on Form or Outline. On where that is put"; *DC*, E 520) is expressed more as a reaction to the "cold light and hot shade" of Rubens than as a dispassionate description of his own work.[15] The idea that color depends upon light and shade assumes the opacity of bodies in space: shadows are the result of the obstruction of light traveling in a line. But Blake does not consistently present bodies as opaque forms. His general practice is to treat form and light in terms of illumination—light passing through or emanating from bodies, rather than falling on them. Thus the linear foundation of a print such as the title page of *Jerusalem* [93] is not elaborated in terms of the principles of light and shade, but is washed by independent bands of color. As Ruskin was to remark, "the distinctive difference between illumination and painting proper" is "that illumination admits of *no* shadows, but only gradations of pure colour."[16] Blake does not completely banish shadows, but he certainly does not lay on his colors in strict accordance with the principles of light and shade. His practice is simply much more "Gothic" than the theory expressed in the *Descriptive Catalogue*.

The remark that Blake is supposed to have made to Benjamin Haydon—"Ah, that is what I have been trying to do all my life—to paint round and never could!"[17]—may be apocryphal, but it points up an essential feature of Blake's style. His figures are rarely "round" in the sense of freestanding sculpture in three-dimensional space. They are closer to the medieval bas-relief (or Wedgewood frieze) which entangles the figure in a relatively two-dimensional background. Blake could and did "paint round" in the more limited sense of presenting his bodies as if revealed by external light, but the

[15] Cf. Annotations to Reynolds, E 644: "Rubens's Colouring is most Contemptible His Shadows are of a Filthy Brown somewhat of the Colour of Excrement these are filld with tints & messes of yellow & red His lights are all the Colours of the Rainbow laid on Indiscriminately & broken one into another. Altogether his Colouring is Contrary to The Colouring. of Real Art & Science." See also E 625 and 651.

[16] *Modern Painters*, 5 vols. (New York, 1923), I, 96.

[17] Quoted in Keynes, *Blake Studies*, 2nd ed. (London, 1971), p. 86.

placement of these shadows does not control his arrangement of color.[18]

Blake sometimes uses light and color not only as the internal property or emanative energy of a body, but also as a focus of pictorial interest which is completely independent of any etched outlines or forms. One is reminded, for instance, of the magnificent color print of Sir Isaac Newton as a seated nude, bending over to inscribe with compasses a half-open scroll at his feet [22]. The figure of Newton is a perfect example of what Blake means by linear form: the body is a clear, distinct, almost enamel-like entity, frontally composed (that is, placed parallel to the picture plane, not at an angle), and cleanly demarcated from its surroundings. And yet there is a secondary focus of interest in the picture, the ambiguous setting which surrounds Newton. Is this a night scene, a subterranean realm, or an undersea world? And what are those vaguely vegetative, gently flowing forms which seem to encrust the stony shelf on which Newton sits? Whatever the answers, it is clear that the effect of this picture is not definable in exclusively linear terms. Color enters into it as a positive force with a life, significance, and even "form" all its own.

Blake's prophetic writings provide a more balanced and complex notion of his pictorial style, I would suggest, than his *Descriptive Catalogue*. In *The Four Zoas* he suggests that the two elements of composition are like a man and a woman:

> Los . . . planting his right foot firm
> Upon the Iron crag of Urizen then springing up aloft
> Into the heavens of Enitharmon in a mighty circle
> And first he drew a line upon the walls of shining heaven
> And Enitharmon tincturd it with beams of blushing love
> It remaind permanent a lovely form inspird divinely human
> (*FZ* 90:32-37, E 356)

Note that Enitharmon is linked not only with color, but with the *space* ("heavens of Enitharmon") in which form is inscribed. Like

[18] Rudolf Arnheim distinguishes two kinds of shadows, those "attached" to figures, and those "cast" by figures. Blake frequently employs the former to give a sense of contour to bodies, but rarely the latter. The "cast" shadow is the property of freestanding sculpture in three-dimensional space, while the "attached" is more characteristic of bas-relief. See Arnheim, *Art and Visual Perception* (Berkeley, 1954), p. 305.

Blake's other female characters, she is associated consistently with bodily coverings—drapery, garments, embroidery, and the weaving process itself—which suggests that the naked figure beneath these "integuments" will be conceived of as masculine. This turns out to be exactly the case. Blake is clearly an artist who prefers the male to the female nude, and even more significant, his female nudes, like those of his master Michelangelo, tend to have masculine traits, often looking like men with breasts or very athletic women. The frequent difficulty commentators have had in determining the sex of Blake's figures suggests further that his ideal nude is more like an androgynous athlete than a purely masculine figure.

Los and Enitharmon are also associated, as we saw in the discussion of relation of text and design, with Time and Space, a notion which bears upon Blake's understanding of line and color. Blake talks of his outlines as the compositional elements which persist through time: "Reengravd Time after Time/ Ever in their youthful prime/ My Designs unchangd remain" (E 472). His colors, on the other hand, change drastically through time. Each version of an illuminated print is unique, an expression of the mood in which Blake colored it. Outline is thus linked with permanence and recurrence in time, and the linear element of Blake's art is accordingly a repertoire of schematic figures, gestures, and positions which are repeated in widely different contexts. Coloring, drapery, and the space of the design, the "feminine" elements, are thus linked with impermanence and evanescence, the fleeting mutable world in which linear archetypes may be incarnated, the "Moment" or "pulsation of the artery" which "Is equal in its period & value to Six Thousand Years" (*M* 28, 29).

Ideally, Blake envisions a harmonious unification of outline and color, form and light, the body and its drapery:

> In Great Eternity, every particular Form gives forth or
> Emanates
> Its own peculiar Light, & the Form is the Divine Vision
> And the Light is his Garment. This is Jerusalem in
> every Man
> A Tent & Tabernacle of Mutual Forgiveness Male & Female
> Clothings.
>
> (*J* 54:1-4, E 201)

But the drama of Blake's poetry is built upon the "fall into Division" of the human psyche. The Individual ("every particular Form") is split from its Emanation in the fallen world, and so the elements of composition, like the sexes, are at war with one another. Sometimes the female "outer surface" may dominate:

> As a beautiful Veil so these Females shall fold & unfold
> According to their will the outside surface of the Earth
> An outside shadowy Surface superadded to the real Surface;
> Which is unchangeable. . . .
>
> (J 83:45-48, E 239)

Thus Blake's compositions are often designed as a kind of dialogue between clothing and nakedness: Jerusalem must choose between Vala's veils of classical form and the nakedness of Gothic form [16]; Los enters the fallen world in the frontispiece to *Jerusalem* clothed in his printer's smock [86] and emerges from that world with "Naked Beauty displayd" ninety-six plates later [87]; the old man enters "Death's Door" in the illustrations to Blair's *Grave* wearing heavy clothes, but is resurrected as a youthful nude [88]. It would be a mistake, however, to conclude that the garment is simply a negative symbol in these designs. It is more accurately seen as ambiguous, having a protective or mediating function as well as suggesting a descent into the fallen world.[19]

A similar dialectic may be seen in Blake's designs between the elements of outline and color. One of Blake's favorite devices is the use of "coloristic chaos," the application of heavy, mottled pigments whose shapelessness contrasts sharply with the etched outlines of the plate. The frontispiece to *The Song of Los* [23], for instance, shows Urizen kneeling before a sun which contains a riot of disorganized pigments—a literal emblem of the disorder that arises, paradoxically, from Urizen's worship of absolute order (see a similar technique in *Urizen* 5, copy D; the Leviathan of *MHH* 20, copy I; and the ground of *Albion rose*). But the non- or anti-linear use of color is not an invariably negative symbol, any more than is the garment. In the *Newton* color print [22], in fact, the welter of color seems to present a positive alternative: if Newton's concentration on his abstract, mathematical universe has contracted his body into a circle like the one he is drawing with his compasses, the space around him provides a contrary vision of flowing organic life. The vegetative world of "Generation," presented as a kind of improvisation in free,

[19] The ambiguity of the garment is demonstrated by Morton Paley in "The Figure of the Garment in *The Four Zoas*, *Milton*, and *Jerusalem*," *BSA*, pp. 119-39.

random coloristic shapes,[20] may be an image of "Regeneration"—an alternative to the sterile world of "Single vision & Newtons sleep."

The sarcastic address "To Venetian Artists" in Blake's notebook,

> That God is Colouring Newton does show
> And the devil is a Black outline all of us know
> (E 507)

somehow loses its sting (or becomes, by a double irony, Blake's literal meaning) in the presence of his *Newton* print. Our problem in reading Blake is to avoid settling for single-level ironies, translating the devilish outline as "good" and Newton's godly coloring as "evil." Blake's point is that God and the devil are ultimately present in both elements, and are revealed according to the context:

> God Appears & God is Light
> To those poor Souls who dwell in Night
> But does a Human Form Display
> To those who Dwell in Realms of day
> ("Auguries of Innocence," E 487)

Despite Blake's engagement in the historical struggle to preserve linear style he does not reduce the elements of the opposition—the "feminine" qualities of light, shade, color, and drapery—to a merely subordinate or negative role in his pictorial hierarchy.[21] The "painterly" elements in Blake's style are more accurately seen as the contraries of outline, form, and figure, capable of assuming positive significance in their own right. Blake's total presentation is thus, at one level, a drama of color and line which reenacts or embodies the drama of a divided, polarized consciousness seeking reunification—the subject of his prophetic books. This compositional dialectic includes a wide variety of relationships, ranging from antagonism

[20] Blake seems to have printed his colors with millboard, the mottled, random appearance resulting from the tacky "pulling apart" of the printing surface and the board. While the colors were still wet, he would touch up the chaotic impression with a brush, creating the vegetative and crystalline forms of the final state. See Butlin, 45n above.

[21] Robert Essick has suggested that Blake integrates the tonal engraving styles which he had to master as a journeyman into his prophetic style. There is a tendency in Essick's argument, however, to attach a negative connotation to these "commercial" reproductive engraving techniques. It would seem a more promising hypothesis to regard them, along with other coloristic, tonal, or antilinear devices, as "contraries" in Blake's style. See Essick, "Blake and the Traditions of Reproductive Engraving," *Blake Studies* V (1972), 59-103.

(when, for instance, color or drapery becomes "an outside shadowy Surface" obscuring outline, or when outline becomes a constricting boundary that crushes its contents) to unity (when light serves as a translucent ambience, freely interpenetrating the form and its surrounding space). Blake's total vision incorporates a multiplicity of relationships between color and line, light and form, and the purely linear composition is only one aspect of this larger totality.

III. COMPOSITIONAL DYNAMICS AND THE LIFE OF THE BODY

Blake's tendency to construct his compositions in terms of stylistic oppositions gives a peculiarly dynamic appearance to his designs, not only in the individual plate, but also in the graphic series. The illuminated prints have sometimes been referred to as a "visionary cinema,"[22] a metaphor which suggests that the single design can be seen as a "frame" or moment in a larger visual continuum. Blake provides us with a vocabulary for describing these dynamics in his mythic account of the relation of form and light to the vicissitudes of consciousness. When man falls from his state of visionary perfection, according to Blake's myth, a finite universe or space must be created to set limits to the fall: "The Divine Hand found the two Limits: first of Opacity, then of Contraction" (*M* 13:20, E 106). These two limits are personified as Satan and Adam, and represent the lower boundaries of man's fall into spiritual darkness and the shrinking of his soul into an egocentric, self-enclosed organism. "But there is no Limit of Expansion! there is no Limit of Translucence" (*J* 42:35, E 187) except in the limitations of the artists' ability to create glowing images of bodily freedom. The dynamics of Blake's pictorial style seem to be organized as a kind of systole and diastole of expanding and contracting forms, darkening and brightening spaces, created "In periods of Pulsative furor" (*FZ* 113:6, E 362). The polar limits of this style are defined on the one hand by the numerous crouching figures in opaque, contracted spaces, and on the other by the ubiquitous leaping, flying figures in fiery, expansive spaces. It is obvious, however, that there is an infinite range of intermediate possibility: contracted figures in expansive spaces, and vice

[22] Harold Bloom, "The Visionary Cinema of Romantic Poetry," in *Essays for Damon*, ed. Rosenfeld, pp. 18-35. Bloom does not consider the application of the metaphor to Blake's pictorial style in any detail.

versa, and figures or spaces which suggest a combination of expansion and contraction such as, for instance, the leaping figure whose head and shoulders are contracted (see [31]). Any given design, then, is a "frame" or "Moment" in the visionary cinema of the "Universal Man" who contains all of Blake's characters within his body. When we "stop the action" to contemplate one of Blake's designs, what we are seeing is the "pulsation of the artery" in the body of a much larger form:

> . . . for tho we sit down within
> The plowed furrow. listning to the weeping clods till we
> Contract or Expand Space at will: or if we raise ourselves
> Upon the chariots of the morning. Contracting or Expanding
> Time!
> Every one knows, we are One Family: One Man blessed for
> ever
>
> (*J* 55:43-46, E 203)

Two of Blake's most famous designs, the frontispiece to *Europe* [24] and *Albion rose* [25], exemplify the polarities between which Blake's pictorial style oscillates. The figure captioned (in the black and white engraved version) "Albion rose from where he labour'd at the Mill with Slaves:/ Giving himself for the Nations he danc'd the dance of Eternal Death" (K 160) expands in a sunburst of radiant colors. Albion serves as both the hub and spokes of a color wheel whose rim (since there is no limit to expansion) is not depicted, except perhaps in the area just below his knees, where the darkness seems to retreat and melt at the approach of the expanding light (the melting effect appears in the colored versions; a kind of rainy effect appears in the line engraving). The ground on which Albion stands presents the contrary vision of color, as a riot of disorganized, opaque pigments that symbolizes the spiritual blindness from which Albion/ Samson has arisen (in the line engraving the blindness is rendered emblematically with the figures of a bat and a worm).[23] In the vi-

[23] This reading of the *Albion rose* engraving as an image of liberation has been challenged recently by Joseph Wittreich, Jr. in *Angel of Apocalypse: Blake's Idea of Milton* (Madison, 1975). Wittreich contends that the line engraving conveys a completely different meaning from the color print, the former showing "Albion in the posture of error" and the latter presenting "Albion transfigured" (p. 65). I cannot do justice to the full complexity of Wittreich's argument here. Although I am impressed by its subtlety and the breadth of knowledge in both Blake and Milton studies implicit in it, I remain unconvinced by a reading that depends upon seeing Samson (Albion's proto-

sionary cinema of the Universal Man, this may be seen as the moment of birth and liberation, or as the moment of death, Albion sacrificing himself like Samson by destroying himself along with the oppressive structures he opposes.

Albion rose has long been recognized as an adaptation of the traditional diagrams of ideal human proportions found in treatises on painting such as Scamozzi's *Idea dell'architettura universale.*[24] Blake has of course eliminated the diagrammatic circle or grid which allows the novice to grasp the quantitative, rational proportions of the figure. But then no artist would include these textbook scaffoldings in a finished picture: on the contrary, the idea was to make the figure look as natural as possible, and to make the spectator forget its mechanical basis. But Blake, by isolating his figure in a composition of simple frontality, and by suggesting a wheel with the radiant bands of light and the rim at Albion's knees, *reminds* us of the diagrammatic wheel, and thus implies that Albion/Samson's liberation from the mill is also a pictorial triumph over the tyranny of "mathematic form." This liberation involves not a suppression or avoidance of the mathematical model, but its transformation and inclusion in a new context, just as Blake's liberation from "painterly" conventions is accomplished by incorporating them into a new set of pictorial values.[25]

The contrasts with the frontispiece to *Europe* need hardly be elaborated. Urizen, his body bent and contracted into itself, is shown enclosed in a circle, his one expansive gesture a thrust downward into the abyss to inscribe yet another circle with his compasses. Unlike Albion, who is the center and source of all the dynamism in his design, Urizen is subject to the elements: the wind blows his hair, and the clouds seem to be closing in to obscure his radiance. If Albion breaks the oppressive mill of mathematical proportion, Urizen creates that circle, and Blake's treatment of him must remind us of one of his most audacious epigrams:

---

type) as "a destroyer and perverter" (p. 52), and which views the activities of Orc (whom Wittreich also links with Albion in this design) through the eyes of Edmund Burke (see p. 57) as nothing more than "the death-like dance of . . . revolution," without redemptive potential.

24 Anthony Blunt was the first to note this connection in "Blake's Glad Day," *Journal of the Warburg and Courtauld Institutes* VI (1943), 225-27.

25 Note also that the center of Blake's figure is the loins rather than, as in the Renaissance figure, the navel. This is Blake's way of stressing the use of the erotic image "Naked Beauty displayed" as a central means of "Improving sensual enjoyment" and disclosing "the infinite which was hid".

To God
If you have formed a Circle to go into
Go into it yourself & see how you would do
(E 508)

But Urizen is not being treated simply as the butt of Blake's irony. In the scenario of the visionary cinema, this is the contracted, embryonic phase in the "pulsations" of figure and space. If Albion presents the creative act as the destruction of boundaries, Urizen is the creator of boundaries, an equally necessary phase in the life of forms, not to mention the life of human beings.

The pictorial or metaphoric forms of expansion and translucence, contraction and opacity cannot be placed, then, in a simple equation with good and evil, any more than outline and color can be assigned value in themselves. Blake always has a "contrary vision" in mind, in which any given symbolic organization can reverse its meaning. The act of creation, for instance, is a demonic act in that it encloses man in the "Mundane Shell," but from another point of view it is an act of mercy in that it prevents man from falling endlessly into the "indefinite." Thus the contracted figures of Newton and Urizen, the archetypal creators of boundaries, are not simply being satirized, and they are certainly not being ridiculed or depicted as evil. When Blake wanted a figure to look ridiculous he knew how to go about it, having good examples before him in the political cartoonists of his day—see, for instance, his treatment of the Popish George III in plate 11 of *Europe* [26]. Urizen and Newton are more accurately seen as examples of heroic or sublime error: they may be mistaken, but they cannot be ignored or dispensed with, and the clarifying power of their mistakes can serve as a catalyst for the progress of vision.

As we might expect, then, expansion and translucence are not always associated with positive subjects. Blake often presents the figures of "corporeal warfare" and vengeance as bright, expansive nudes (see, for instance, the Satan of the Job engravings, the figure of Hand in *Jerusalem* 26 [97], or "Pestilence" in the Bible illustrations [50]. As Janet Warner suggests, even the Christlike cruciform posture cannot be read automatically as a sign of good or evil: it must be seen rather as an image of "man at his spiritual extremes."[26] This does not preclude the possibility of moral judgments on figures

[26] "Blake's Use of Gesture," *VFD*, p. 178. This is true of any of Blake's recurrent postures, as she points out.

in specific contexts. Satan is clearly doing a bad thing to Job, even if (*especially* if) he does it in the pose of the Messiah. But the fact that Blake uses this posture for characters in radically different moral states has a number of interesting effects. First, it prevents us from establishing an imagistic code which will tell us what to think about a given design before we have attended to the particulars of iconography and style. Second, it tends to subvert any attempt to see a moral state as fixed or final. Satan's cruciform posture is not only a parody or travesty, but an emblem of contrary possibilities. In plate 6 of *Urizen* [54] we will be invited to see the image of Satan falling into hell as an upside-down resurrection [cf. 55].[27]

Blake's iconography, his repertoire of visual personifications and attributes, invites, even tempts us to make a whole series of value judgments: Urizen, Satan, Vala are the villains. Compasses or circles or caves symbolize "rationalistic repression." But Blake's style subverts these judgments by placing the images which evoke them in figural equations with images that have opposite meanings: the compass becomes a blacksmith's tongs (or perhaps we just learn to look at compasses differently after meditating on *Newton* for the tenth time); the circle is the sun created by Los, as well as the imprisoning boundary we associate with Urizen; the cave is the "mossy cell" in which Milton reaches his prophetic strain, not just an emblem of psychological enclosure. Blake discourages us, in other words, from *evaluating* his figures in terms of some Blakean moral code in which imagination equals goodness and reason equals evil. The point is rather to *identify* the figures, and to "Enter into these Images in . . . Imagination approaching them on the Fiery Chariot of . . . Contemplative Thought" (*VLJ*, E 550). "Goodness or Badness has nothing to do with Character. an Apple tree a Pear tree a Horse a Lion are Characters but a Good Apple tree or a Bad, is an Apple tree still" ("On Homer's Poetry," E 267). The questions to be answered, then, are *who* is this? how is he seen? what may he become? where does he belong in the larger body of which he is an organic part: "when distant they appear as One Man but as you approach they appear Multitudes of Nations" (*VLJ*, E 546). The meaning of the particular design thus resides in the interplay between the linear skeleton, which will generally allude to a whole gallery of related figures, and the specific appearances which "incarnate" that figure in a particular

27 See my "Poetic and Pictorial Imagination in *The Book of Urizen*," *Eighteenth-Century Studies* III (Fall 1969), 99-101, for a detailed analysis of these themes; and Chap. IV, below.

print. The recurrent figural motif does not in itself have any denotative meaning. It is like the "is" in a metaphor, a way of identifying (i.e., equating and differentiating) two or more different visual phenomena.

IV. LINEAR SCHEMATA: THE STRUCTURES OF THE ELEMENTS AND OF THE SENSES

Within the dialectical parameters of outline and color and the dynamics of pulsative composition, it is possible to discern an even more specific set of conventions which give the sense of a "style," a coherent, unified vision, to Blake's illuminated prints. This is something more pervasive than the recurrent gestures and positions which Janet Warner has catalogued or the "leitmotifs" which Northrop Frye mentions,[28] something which seems to govern not only the position of bodies but the structure of the spaces in which they appear. Ernst Gombrich has suggested that every artistic style is built upon a "developed system of schemata" or pictorial "idiom" that governs the manner of representation rather than upon direct imitation of external appearance.[29] We learn in elementary art classes to draw a cat not just by looking at cats but by assembling a series of circles and triangles until the identity of the figure begins to emerge: the "making" of elementary forms precedes the "matching" of them to external reality. The question is, what are the schemata that structure Blake's visual world? It seems clear that his idea of the human figure and its positions is derived from classical and Renaissance models, with some manneristic distortions, but it also seems clear that this is only the starting point for something quite different, something which is hinted at but not adequately defined as the "Gothic" element in Blake's art.

The human figures in Blake's prints are frequently surrounded, we have noted, by a space which seems relatively primitive and "elemental." Landscapes are schematized and perspective is flattened, or rendered in the medieval manner, as a series of horizontal strips ascending the picture like a ladder, the highest rung being the most distant. Architectural backgrounds do not provide a spacious three-dimensional container for a scene; generally they present a blank, impervious wall which lies parallel to the picture plane (see, for instance, [65] and [81]), rarely at an oblique angle as in post-Renais-

[28] Frye, "Poetry and Design," *Discussions of Blake*, ed. Grant, p. 47.

[29] *Art and Illusion*, 2nd ed. rev. (Princeton, 1961), p. 87.

sance painting. More often no architectural background is provided, and the figure is placed in an "elemental" setting of some basic natural image such as fire, water, clouds, vegetation, or stone.

Blake's preference for the two-dimensional and his tendency to condense and simplify iconographical references we discussed earlier as symptoms of his reaction against "literary" (i.e., narrative and allegorical) painting. But the positive purpose of these stylistic choices is to create a sense that the space "external" to the human form is nonobjective, a created entity or projection of the consciousness it contains. This is most obvious, of course, when Blake is most medieval, when his figures are surrounded by aureoles, mandorlas, halos, fibers, or garments that flow out from the linear surface of their bodies. The flames around Orc, we know, are to be seen as *inside* him, as an externalization or projection of his consciousness. The "wide world of solid obstruction" that crushes Urizen is really himself. Terms such as "outer" and "inner" may mislead us, however, into seeing Blake's style as governed by a kind of subjectivism or solipsism, when his real point is to convey the continuity and interplay between body and space, as a symbol of the dialectic between consciousness and its objects. For Blake as a visual artist everything must in a sense be considered an "outside." Subjective and objective realms, inside and outside must be dealt with as a single formal entity whose constituent elements are divided more or less sharply into figure and background by boundary lines: "There is an Outside spread Without, & an Outside spread Within/ Beyond the Outline of Identity both ways, which meet in One" (*J* 18:2-3, E 161).[30]

Blake avoids the objective, homogeneous, visual rendering of pictorial space, then, not to produce a sense of other-worldly subjectivism, but to restore a tactile, synaesthetic quality to pictorial

[30] I am using this quotation slightly out of context. Blake's immediate point in this passage is to treat "outsideness" as a sense of alienation, both from the self and the world. The "Outsides" which we perceive within and without thus "meet in One: / An orbed Void of doubt, despair, hunger, & thirst & sorrow" (*J* 18:3-4, E 161). The more basic point, however, is that "within" and "without" are for Blake arbitrary or conventional distinctions, both in psychology and in the elements of composition. He anticipates the discovery by modern artists and theorists (perhaps a rediscovery) that "form" in painting is always double. Paul Klee refers to this as "exogenic" and "endogenic" form, the shape which is perceived as body, and the shape seen as surrounding space. Blake does not, like some modern painters, make the distinction between inside and outside totally ambiguous, but he does try to stress the continuity between inner and outer form, and he treats them as equally significant formal elements: space or background is rarely a neutral, homogeneous container for bodies.

form.[31] The continuity of figure and background is a literal emblem of multisensory contact between consciousness and the world. The pervasiveness of elemental forms is a stylistic strategy for providing this sort of contact for the viewer, emphasizing the nonvisual sensations of heat, cold, wetness, dryness, hardness, and softness rather than the sensory alienation of visual distance. The schematization of these elemental forms further reduces the visual sense of their existence, producing a kind of synaesthetic ambiguity. Hair may cascade down a figure's shoulders, becoming a waterfall or a network of veins nourishing an embryo (see [73]). Fire becomes vegetation becomes a wave, a series of transformations which we cannot see in nature, but which can be felt in the underlying dynamics of wave motion.

There are, of course, many ways of stylizing or schematizing elemental forms, ranging from the geometrical ornaments of Islamic art to the translucent latticework of medieval painting to the flowing arabesques of art nouveau. Blake seems closest to the spirit of medieval stylization in its understanding of linear form as a surface for light to be seen *through* rather than on (which accounts for the effectiveness of his work in slide presentations), but his linear foundation is, as Hagstrum points out, "more fluid and eccentric, and bolder in its movement, than that of the medieval artist."[32] For Blake, the lattice or linear pattern of composition is not nearly so fixed or stable as it was for the medieval artist: the linear structure is itself a fluid entity which dissolves in radiance, darkens, or expands and contracts.

In a comparative study of medieval art and philosophy, Erwin Panofsky (quoting Aquinas) suggests that the translucent lattice of medieval illumination was not only an image of objective reality as a medium through which God's light is transmitted, but an analogue to the structure of the senses: "The senses delight in things duly proportioned as in something akin to them; for the sense, too is a kind of reason as is every cognitive power."[33] The "doors of per-

[31] This point is suggested in a much more general context by Marshall McLuhan in *The Gutenberg Galaxy* (Toronto, 1962), pp. 265-66.

[32] *Poet and Painter*, p. 32.

[33] *Gothic Architecture and Scholasticism* (New York, 1964), pp. 37-38. Panofsky also links the medieval understanding of the senses to Gestalt psychology, in that it " 'refuses to reserve the capacity of synthesis to the higher faculties of the human mind' and stresses 'the formative powers of the sensory processes.' Perception itself is now credited . . . with a kind of 'intelligence' that organizes the sensory material under the pattern of simple, 'good Gestalten' in

ception" are not merely neutral passageways: they have distinct structures and proportions analogous to the forms they perceive. As Ernst Curtius explains it, "the visual power of the physical eye is transferred to the perceptive faculty of the intellect. Inner senses are co-ordinated with the outer. The mind has ears as well as eyes."[34]

Blake adapts the medieval notion of illuminated form to his own purposes in a remarkably simple and inevitable way, by comparing *both* works of arts and sensory openings to windows. "Five windows light the cavern'd man," his five senses. But these windows are not simply "there" by nature: they can be ornamented, cleansed, multiplied, and improved. "Eno, a daughter of Beulah," one of Blake's muses, "with much care & affliction/ . . . made windows into Eden/ She also took an atom of space & opend its center/ Into Infinitude & ornamented it with wondrous art" (*FZ* 9:10-13, E 300). But if both the senses and works of art are windows, the implication is that Blake sees his illuminated prints as sensory openings in the walls of our dark skull or body-cave. The Palace of Art is the human body, and the illuminated windows and pictures which glow on its walls are the portals of perception. The systole-diastole effect in Blake's designs is thus also an image of the dilation and contraction of sensory openings:

> If Perceptive organs vary: Objects of Perception seem to vary:
> If the Perceptive Organs close: their Objects seem to close also. . . .
>
> (*J* 30:55-56, E 175)

As the Eye—Such the Object
(Annotations to Reynolds, E 634)

But suppose that not only the "pulsative" dynamics of outline and color but the very *structure* of the linear lattice were an image of the senses. The formal structure of the illuminated print would be permeated with schematic correspondences to Blake's structural con-

---

an 'effort of the organism to assimilate stimuli to its own organization.'" Panofsky is quoting Rudolf Arnheim, "Gestalt and Art," *Journal of Aesthetics and Art Criticism* II (1943), 71-75, and "Perceptual Abstraction and Art," *Psychological Review* LIV (1947), 66-82.

[34] *European Literature and the Latin Middle Ages*, tr. Willard R. Trask (New York, 1963), p. 136.

cepts of the senses. Let us test this supposition by examining the imagery he associates with the senses.

For Blake the senses are windows, inlets, doors, gates, portals, or chinks in a body which is a wall, cave, shell, or building. They are capable of being cleansed, enlarged, opened, multiplied, decorated, even passed through—or conversely, of being locked and barred, bricked up, narrowed, or dirtied. Ideally, the senses are "all fluxile," capable of being expanded and contracted at will, in accord with the object of perception; but in actuality, Blake suggests, man has "shut himself up" in a very reduced form of his total sensory capability. The painterly, picturesque technique of giving pictures a single light source ("Rubens . . . blocks up all its gates of light, except one, and that one he closes with iron bars"; *DC*, E 538) is thus analogous to the reduction of perception to the primacy of sight, "Single vision & Newtons Sleep." Blake's enumeration of the senses varies. He usually associates the conventional five senses with empiricism and rationalism, but sees them nevertheless as potential avenues of vision; "portions of the eternal world" may be seen through them in *Europe* iii:4, for instance. More frequently he talks of four senses corresponding to the four gateways in the skull—eye, ear, nose, and tongue—and associated with the four-gated city of "spiritual" London and the four "humours," faculties, elements, and Zoas (see *J* 98:12-22 for a summary of the four senses).

Blake consistently associates particular images with these sensory openings. The ear is generally seen as a spiral or vortex, sometimes like a conch shell with "intricate volutions," sometimes as "a whirlpool fierce to draw creations in" (*Thel* 6:17). The eye is generally depicted as an orb or globe "concentrating all things" (*E* 10:12) in circles around itself. The tongue is usually linked with fire and vegetative, serpentine forms, sometimes several of these at the same time: "the False Tongue Vegetated beneath your land of Shadows" (*M* 2:10) is also the serpent who creeps in "narrow form" through the garden. The nostrils are sometimes seen as gates, "barr'd and petrify'd against the infinite" (*E* 10:15), but more often they are simply described as "bended . . . down to the earth" (*J* 34:47). In *Urizen* and *The Four Zoas* Blake describes "two nostrils bent down to the deep" (*U* 13:1; *FZ* 54:29, E 330), and in *Jerusalem* Albion threatens Luvah as follows:

> I will turn the volutions of your ears outward, and bend your nostrils

Downward, and your fluxile eyes englob'd roll round in fear:
Your withring lips and tongue shrink up into a narrow circle,
Till into narrow forms you creep. . . .

(*J* 43:67-70, E 190)

Anyone who is familiar with Blake's pictures will immediately recognize that these four clusters of images correspond to some of the most characteristic linear schemata in his pictorial style. The spiral image appears in an astonishing variety of contexts, sometimes as a major structural device, as in the "whirlwind" compositions in the Dante and Job series (see [37] and [34]), sometimes as a secondary decorative motif, as in the numerous designs where vines coil around tree trunks, or yet again as a tiny but potentially significant detail such as the coil at the end of Newton's scroll [22]. When the spiral is stretched out in two dimensions it becomes a serpentine S-curve, like the flowing arabesques of flame, vegetation, or drapery which serve as both structure and ornament in Blake's designs. If the S-curve tends to become a spiral in three dimensions, it tends to rectilinearity at the one-dimensional extreme, modulating into the vertical or horizontal rigidity we find in Blake's "archaic" figures (see [27] and [81]). When the curved line is "bended down to earth" it becomes still another important structural device, the vaulted arch or inverted U-shape which appears not only in "gates barr'd against the infinite" but in the outlines of gravestones, tablets of law, tree branches, opened books, caves, and most important, in the crouching human figure, especially Urizen. The human figures in the S-curve compositions tend, on the other hand, to be climbing, leaping, dancing, running, or flying. When the arch form is allowed to enclose itself at the bottom we have the circular or "globular" composition which can appear as heavenly bodies, the Mundane Shell, wheels, halos and other circular radiances, "bubbles" of consciousness (as in illustrations to *L'Allegro* and *Il Penseroso*), and human forms contracted into a full circle, head and feet coming together like a fetus in the womb [61].

It is important to recognize that the spiral, S-curve, circle, and inverted U are *not* symbolic forms in the iconographical sense, but rather the schematic constituents of a pervasive symbolic style. The spiral form does not represent or symbolize the ear in the way the old man with the white beard symbolizes Urizen. There is little to be learned, then, by trying to equate these four forms to all the other fourfold correspondences of seasons, metals, compass points, and

Zoas. The pervasiveness of these four forms can best be grasped, though, by seeing them all at once, with some of their typical "incarnations," as shown in figure 1.

But if these schematic forms do not represent or symbolize anything in themselves, then what *do* they do?

First, let us note a few characteristics of their behavior. They seem capable of infinite transformation and variation, even in a single design. The title page of *Urizen* [46], for instance, restates the inverted U or rounded arch form in at least seven different ways: as the limbs of the dead, overarching tree whose extremities are "bended down to earth"; as stone tablets; as the knees, shoulders, head, and entire profile of Urizen; and as the flat, horizontal curves of the book he squats on. The design is a kind of study in entropy, the systematic loss of energy portrayed as a series of arches flattening or collapsing under a crushing gravity. The design is so full of exaggerated gravity, in fact, that we are tempted (rightly) to laugh at this scholarly solipsist, crushed under the burden of his infinite knowledge. The end point of this process is flat horizontality, the tablets in which Urizen writes his secrets, or a horizontal, supine figure, dead or asleep, like the one who lies outstretched beneath the final words of *The Book of Urizen* [47]. The fact that Blake considers the horizontal a modulation of the rounded arch is suggested strongly by a rather literal emblem composed of concentric arches flattening into a supine figure in *America* 9 [28].

We can find all these forms, taken separately, in the work of other painters. Van Gogh and the Vorticists, for instance, frequently build their compositions on the schemata of spirals and S-curves, and the frontally composed vertical and horizontal structure was very popular among the archaic neoclassicists of Blake's own period. But only in Blake, to my knowledge, do we find all these forms linked in a series of dynamic modulations. The vision of the condensed and intensified series of variations on the inverted U-form, for instance, is etched on our visual memories (Blake would say on our imaginations), and is evoked in the curves of bat wings, clouds, the moon and rainbow of Beulah, the downturned hands of a figure delivering a curse. The pointed Gothic arch becomes, in this visual context, not an arbitrary emblem of a preferred style but an embodiment of it, an actual breaking open of the entropic circular arch which is felt so oppressively in other designs. The peak of the Gothic arch is, for Blake, the center of the vortex, the critical point of breaking out or through the vaulted ceiling, whether it be the ceiling of a human

SENSORY ORGAN	EYE	EAR	TONGUE	NOSE
SCHEMATIC FORM	circle, orb	spiral, vortex	arabesque, S-curve	arch, inverted U
LINEAR VARIATIONS	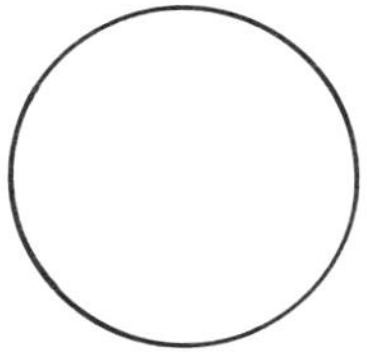			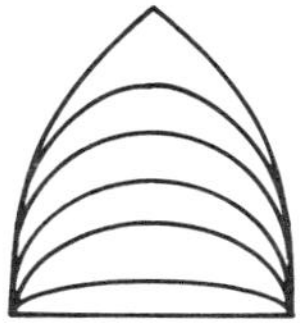
REPRESENTATIONAL FORMS	sun, moon, shell, wheel, halo, globe, bubble	whirlwind, whirlpool, coil, scroll, spiral stairway, tendrils, serpent	flame, waves, leaves, vines, serpents	cave, arbor, arch, gate, trilithon, gravestone, stone tablets
HUMAN FIGURES	crouched, in fetal position, or expansive, outstretched limbs as radii	dancing, flying, tossed about, contorted, twisted	dancing, flying, leaping, climbing, or statuesque, static	crouched, supine, re-clining

FIGURE I.

structure, the Mundane Shell, or the cranium (see [33] for an instance of the coupling of the Gothic arch with the spiral).

We should also note that two or more of these schemata may appear in a single design, sometimes to suggest contrast or antagonism between two radically different spaces or states, sometimes, by means of linking forms, to suggest transformation from one state to another, sometimes to compound and emphasize one form with another (for this last device, see, for example, "The Lamb," "The Divine Image," and "On Another's Sorrow" in *Songs of Innocence*, where the S-curve is encircled by the spiral line).

An exemplary case of the contrasting technique is plate 4 of *Visions of the Daughters of Albion* [29], in which Blake superimposes an S-curve over a basic composition of inverted U-forms (the wave which lifts the enchained Oothoon over the crouched figure of Theotormon and the stony shoreline). A literal, historical reading of the picture will see Oothoon as a chained slave drowning in a wave, while her husband (the ineffectual abolitionist?) ignores her cries for help. But the stylized character of this wave, and the unnatural way it leaps up over Theotormon's head, connects it to the "flame-flowers" which Blake uses to convey vitality and passion in *Songs of Innocence* and the Lambeth books. Theotormon's posture similarly connects him with the oppressive old men of *Songs of Experience*, the familiar lineaments of the gravity-stricken patriarch. This view of the design demands a change, however, in our "vision" of what is happening to Oothoon. We begin to see her as consumed by flames or flying up through the air rather than drowning, a view which is reinforced by a highly probable source for this design, Quarles' emblem of the earthbound soul aspiring to heaven [30].[35] Quarles' verses on this emblem could almost be the words in Oothoon's mouth:

> Great God, I spread my feeble wings in vain;
> In vain I offer my extended hands:

[35] Blake probably knew Quarles' emblems well. They went through numerous editions in the seventeenth and early eighteenth centuries, suffering one brief decline from 1736 to 1777, and they were, as Freeman points out, "enthusiastically admired for their religious teaching by eighteenth century evangelical ministers" (*English Emblem Books*, p. 117), a fact which would have commended them to Blake the radical Christian. Another analogue to the soaring, chained figure appears in plate 16 of Blake's engraved designs for Young's *Night Thoughts*; in *America* 3 the chain is broken.

I cannot mount till thou unlink my chain;
I cannot come till thou release my bands.

Oothoon's cries are directed, however, not toward a sky god, as in Quarles' emblem, but toward her "god-tormented" lover Theotormon, whose code of chastity prevents Oothoon from attaining sensual or spiritual fulfillment.

Blake's system of schematic forms allows him to produce much greater metaphorical complexity than Quarles with much simpler iconographic means (note that Blake does not need to restate his theme in a background detail, as Quarles does in the image of the tethered hawk; the variation on Blake's theme is implied in the lineaments which connect it to other compositions). The stylized quality of the wave form produces a kind of sensory oxymoron: Oothoon is felt to be either hot or cold, depending on how the wave is seen. And the striking contrast of this form with the rest of the design evokes related conflicts between forms of motion and stasis, expansion and contraction in Blake's pictorial corpus. Later we will see this theme expressed not primarily as an emblem of the relation of the sexes as it is here, but as a vision of the relation of an individual to his own suppressed emotional life ([75], and below, p. 158).

Not every design in Blake's illuminated books will be found to contain a clear or explicit variation on one of the four forms he associates with the senses. But the presence of these configurations is so pervasive and, what is more important, so essential a part of Blake's most striking, characteristic designs, that it must be a central feature of whatever we mean by his style. Like the vortex in Turner, the point of light in Rembrandt, the line of beauty in Hogarth, these forms, although they do not appear in every design Blake produced, create a context in which exceptions or marginal cases take on a different meaning than they would have in the *oeuvre* of a different artist. The play of light through verticals, horizontals, and diagonals is the structure of reality for a Piranesi; to Blake they are reductive distortions of the free curvatures of "living form," and are therefore to be passed through and left behind, not contemplated as "eternal visions." Blake would probably have been struck by the appropriateness of Piranesi's style to his subject. *Carceri* or prison houses are best rendered as labyrinths of indefinite verticals and horizontals. But for Blake, there is always a golden string to lead us out of the rationalistic maze: the traveler can pass through the trilithon or dolmen which embodies "Druidical Mathematical proportion of length bredth & highth" (Blake illustrated this moment of passage in *Milton* 6 and *Jerusalem* 70). The necessary vertical and horizontal structure dictated by the iconography of the crucifixion can be transformed into a dance of liberation, as it is in *Jerusalem* 76 [103].

If pictures are like sensory openings or perceptual structures, then looking at them is like putting on a new pair of spectacles or (more precisely) like opening your eyes. In other words, Blake's style, like that of any great artist, affects our vision: we start seeing vortices and arches and wave forms everywhere, in and out of Blake's pictures, just as we learn to see dark interiors from Rembrandt and storms from Turner. Thus, Blake's exceptional compositions, the ones that do not contain a fairly obvious rendering of one of his schematic forms, frequently *imply* these forms by means of gestures which convey invisible lines of force. The position of a hand, turned up or down, feels so crucial in Blake's pictures because we see these hands emanating all sorts of energies (lightning, plagues, vegetative fibers) in other compositions, and thus tend to feel those energies as invisible presences in pictures where they are not represented.

Plate 2 of *Europe* [31], for instance, does not contain any explicit rendering of the four basic forms, and yet the downward thrust of the inverted U-shape is implied in the shoulders and arms of the central figure who strangles his compatriots, and the S-curve is implied in the extended contours of the figure fleeing at the upper right. The distortion of the trio at the bottom is accomplished, moreover, by a curiously paradoxical device. Despite the group's appearance of wild, frenetic struggle, all the limbs, whether extended or contracted, are constructed as verticals, horizontals, and diagonals, with the whole group rotated a few degrees askew from a "square" relation to the picture frame. The very kind of compositional device which, in another context, could suggest mathematical, rational order becomes, in Blake's visual world, the epitome of self-destructive chaos. The slight "skew" from the perpendiculars of the picture frame creates the sense that this rigidly composed group is falling (reframe the group in a squared setting to see how stable it becomes), and thus introduces the ironic moral of the design: by the time the central figure (Pitt strangling his political opponents?) has finished off his victims, he will be about to hit bottom himself. The escaping figure above still reflects his participation in the grisly wrestling match, clutching at his own head. But his body suggests an affinity with the flying, hovering figures of the S-curve family, especially in the elongation of the leg. Figures with this kind of duality, bodies expressing dancelike kinesis coupled to shoulders, arms, and heads which convey just the opposite feeling of contraction, pain, and stasis, become in themselves a significant bodily leitmotif, a compound of closed forms like the U and O with the S and the spiral.[36]

Despite their lack of inherent iconographical significance (especially innate moral value), Blake's schematic forms do seem to evoke a definite range or spectrum of meanings. The circle and inverted U are frequently associated with images of contraction and with emotional states of self-absorption, fear, pain, and isolated entrapment. The spiral and S-curve, on the other hand, tend to appear in expansive, dynamic contexts, conveying emotional states of passionate abandon and ecstasy. The basic point of these forms, however, is not to allow us to make *a priori* judgments about the significance of images, but to perceive the subtle connections between all sorts of different visual experiences. This point is best demonstrated by examining the use of one of Blake's forms in some detail.

V. METAMORPHOSES OF THE VORTEX

The spiral or vortex form is one of Blake's most pervasive and protean schemata, appearing in his earliest illuminated books, usually as a subordinate, ornamental detail such as a vine, scroll, or serpent, and steadily growing in importance to become a major compositional structure which can dominate the entire space of a design. The connotations of this form range from the imagery of dissolution, annihilation, and disorientation ("a whirlpool fierce to draw creations in") to images of dialectical interaction or conflict (a dance of lovers, as in the title page of *Thel* [37], or a "yin-yang" composition such as *The Angel Michael Binding the Dragon* [32] to designs which suggest epiphany or visionary breakthrough into a new level of consciousness (the "spiral ascents to the heaven of heavens" [33] or the vision of God in the whirlwind [34].

Although particular designs may emphasize one of these versions of the spiral, Blake thinks of them as metaphorically connected: epiphany or revelation depends upon the process of "Self-annihilation"; the "breakthrough" may look, from our perspective, very much like a "break up" of stable notions of self or society. Epiphany and Self-annihilation depend, in turn, upon the vigorous interaction

[36] See similar forms in plates 6 [54], 14 [69], and 27 [84] of *Urizen*.

of contraries, between the two halves of a divided psyche, or between persons—the "Mental Warfare" which Blake describes as the essence of imaginative activity. Blake's pervasive intellectual contrariety is what dictates his choice of the vortex as the configuration of "progression" or breakthrough. Vortexes occur in nature as the focus of the encounter between conflicting forces; whirlpools arise from the interaction of conflicting currents, and an electron introduced into a cyclotron will accelerate in a widening spiral as a result of the alternate flow of current through positive and negative poles.[37]

But the physical analogy must be carried one step further: the vortex is not simply the product of two equal and opposite forces. The result of that situation would be static equilibrium, or (given some initial momentum) an endless circle. The vortex depends upon a third element to give progression to the cycle of contraries, to bring it to a critical point with a conical apex like the point of the Gothic arch. In nature this third element is gravity, friction, or changes in the intensity or direction of the contrary forces. For Blake, I would suggest, the third element is Imagination, the force which gives direction to the interaction of contraries, and which continually adjusts their intensity or reverses their polarity. Despite his commitment to equal and opposite forces freely interacting, Blake continually takes highly partisan positions. His writing never equivocates. If his culture has unduly emphasized "angelic" virtues such as prudence, restraint, and reason, Blake will side with the devils and advocate unbounded energy and spontaneity. But his position never quite becomes a mere reaction or reflection of the force he opposes: he is essentially a dramatic artist, never totally identified with any of the persons in his poems. And no matter how evil or mistaken he may think some character, he always envisions a divine comedy of forgiveness, reconciliation, and transformation at the end of the vortex.

Blake's fullest description of the vortex is the difficult and justly famous passage in *Milton*:

> The nature of infinity is this: That every thing has its
> Own Vortex; and when once a traveller thro' Eternity
> Has passd that Vortex, he perceives it roll backward behind

[37] For a discussion of the relation of Blake's vortex to Newtonian and Cartesian physics, see Donald Ault, *Visionary Physics: Blake's Response to Newton* (Chicago, 1974), especially Chap. V. Unfortunately Ault has little to say about the vortex as a graphic image, dealing primarily with its role in "transformations of perception" (p. 158).

His path, into a globe itself infolding; like a sun:
Or like a moon, or like a universe of starry majesty,
While he keeps onwards in his wondrous journey on the earth
Or like a human form, a friend with whom he livd benevolent.
As the eye of man views both the east & west encompassing
Its vortex; and the north & south, with all their starry host;
Also the rising sun & setting moon he views surrounding
His corn-fields and his valleys of five hundred acres square.
Thus is the earth one infinite plane, and not as apparent
To the weak traveller confin'd beneath the moony shade.
Thus is the heaven a vortex passd already, and the earth
A vortex not yet pass'd by the traveller thro' Eternity.
(*M* 15:21-35, E 108-109)

The difficulty with this passage arises from the description of eternity and infinity (concepts which we generally assume to be beyond or antithetical to space, time, and finite things) in terms of travel through space and time and the encounter with finite things. *Jerusalem* opens with a related paradox, a "passage through/Eternal Death," which suggests that Blake does not see eternity as something endless or "Indefinite," but as something which can be passed through, experienced in time and space, not beyond it. "Infinity" is a way of perceiving finite things, not as indefinitely extended or boundless, but with a special kind of intensity, particularity, and empathy. Frye suggests that entering the vortex of a book is like trying to read the book from its own point of view;[38] similarly, "passing the vortex" of a thing, whether a stone, a flower, or a person, involves an entry into the interior life of that object, a recognition of its inherent "genius." (Note that words such as "essence" or "genius" could be substituted for "vortex" very easily, though with a great loss in complexity, in the statement that "every thing has its/ Own Vortex.")

Blake describes the passing of the vortex in a series of similes, a suggestion that the experience occurs in phases or distinct levels. The first phase is the recognition of the object as a world with its own unique laws and form ("a globe itself infolding," like the "world in a grain of sand"); the second phase is a recognition of the object as something that has relations with things outside itself, a transmitter and receiver of light "like a sun:/ Or like a moon"; the third phase

[38] *Fearful Symmetry* (Princeton, 1947), p. 351.

is to see it as a "universe," that is, not just an irreducible unity like a globe or atom, but a system which contains numerous subworlds within itself (cf. "The Vegetative Universe, opens like a flower from the Earths center:/ In which is Eternity. It expands in Stars to the Mundane Shell/ And there it meets Eternity again"; *J* 13:34-36, E 155-56).

In the fourth phase of vision the object is seen not just as a self-contained world or a universe but as a human form, a center of consciousness as complex as the perceiver himself, "like . . . a friend with whom he livd benevolent." This is, of course, a radical anthropocentrism which claims not just that everything in the universe is alive and holy ("every particle of dust breathes forth its joy"; *E* iii:18), but that everything is potentially conscious of itself, and thus deserving of what Buber would call an "I-Thou" relationship with human consciousness. But Blake does not employ the anthropocentric notion in the service of an all-devouring egotism of the species or the self. His strategy seems closer to that of Keats with his nightingale, to affirm a simultaneous sense of intimacy and otherness as the nature of "infinite" perception. Blake uses the word "vortex" rather than "genius" or "essence" because he wants an image that suggests both convergence toward a center or apex (the "inner being" of the object) and doubleness, the interaction of contrary forces. A thing is what it is, and what we see it as: Blake is saying that we can never abolish one of these modes of existence as an illusion and elevate the other to reality. What we can do is intensify the dialectic between them until we comprehend the thing, and feel ourselves comprehended. That is why the view of a thing when we have passed its vortex is both intimate and personal, like a friend, and vastly alien and impersonal, like a universe of starry majesty. Vision does not travel in a straight line, but oscillates between contrary forces, converging on a moment of illumination. Thus, "Fear and Hope are—Vision!" (*GP*, E 263).

"Thus is the heaven a vortex passd already," because we see it as a majestic universe full of worlds like our own, encompassing us. The earth is "a vortex not yet pass'd" because we do not yet see all the worlds and universes in the "Minute Particulars" of our immediate environment, "spread in the infinite microscope" (*VDA* 4:16). Blake is like a visionary astronaut who has gone beyond the realm of "the weak traveller confin'd beneath the moony shade" only to turn his gaze back to the earth and see it in a new light, as a field for infinite perception and creativity, "One infinite [*not* indefinitely extended] plane."[39]

This digression on the vortex would seem to bring us a long way from the loops and spirals of Blake's pictorial style, but it is, I think, the context in which those forms need to be viewed. The tiny coil at the end of Newton's scroll [22] is quite literally the "end-point" of the two-dimensional world in which he creates abstract forms. When he has persisted in his heroic folly long enough, "Creating many a Vortex fixing many a Science in the deep" (*FZ*, 72:13, E 342), he will become wise, all his abstract reductions rolling up in a prophetic scroll, a living spiral absorbing the conic section (circle and triangle) that he is inscribing. The circle will then be squared or made "fourfold" not by being enclosed in a box, but by coiling into a vortex which leads to a new level of perception. In a similar way the coiling serpent into whose vortex the headless tyrant falls in *America* 5 [35] is a figurative suggestion that once the tyrant has passed through the point of the cone he will be consumed in the flames which leap up from the bottom of the page and undergo a rebirth (the fact that there are seven coils in the spiral, Blake's consistent number for creative and apocalyptic completion, reinforces this impression). Blake's use of the coiled serpent as an emblem of revolution is his way of saying that revolutions need not just "revolve" in an endless cycle of oppression and reaction: they can take us somewhere, to a new phase in the cycles of history. This does not eliminate, of course, the threatening feeling of this particular vortex, nor does it rule out the possibility of the image being used to suggest an endless torment of whirling disorientation, as in *Dante* 29 [36], or an endless struggle which traps both combatants (note that in [32] Michael is entangled in the chain with which he binds Satan). In general, however, the vortex serves as an image of the gateway into a new level of perception. At maximum it embodies the opening into infinity, a Jacob's Ladder spiraling into the heaven of heavens [33].

It is, of course, entirely consistent with Blake's pictorial style that

[39] The Mental Traveller, one suspects, is *not* the visionary astronaut he is often made out to be, insofar as he remains obsessed with circularity and compulsive repetition ("And all is done as I have told") rather than envisioning the infinite plane, full of unique moments and particulars. Like some of the narrators of *Songs of Experience*, he can "see" all too clearly, his knowledge only producing despair, doubt, and alienation.

he render the infinite in terms of a finite image rather than the indefinite, mysterious, "sublime" vistas which are the usual embodiment of this concept in Romantic painting (see, for examples, the landscapes of John Martin or Gustave Doré). For Blake the infinite does not reside in an obscure, transcendent realm at the "vanishing point" of three-dimensional space, but is located immanently in the intense, dialectical perception of immediate "minute particulars," a process which is symbolized and embodied in the vortex.

We must return now to our initial question. If the schematic forms which recur so frequently in Blake's designs do not mean anything in the iconographical sense, as representations or symbols, then what is their function? Marshall McCluhan seems to me very close to the mark when he says that Blake's "bounding line of sculptural form" produces an "interplay among experiences," a kind of "tactility" or "synaesthesia": "The Romantic poets fell far short of Blake's mythical or simultaneous vision. They were faithful to Newton's single vision and perfected the picturesque outer landscape as a means of isolating single states of the inner life."[40] But Blake's "synaesthetic" pictorial style is not simply produced by linearism per se, but by the construction of specific linear motifs in accordance with what Blake understood as the structural dynamics of our sensory openings. The senses do not perceive his pictures: they are imbedded *in* the pictures. Thus, we look at reality *through* his pictures, as if they were stained-glass windows constructed to fit our sensory openings. In formal terms, then, the function of Blake's schematic forms is to give structural consistency to his style; in expressive terms, it is his way of conveying his "Fourfold Vision"—the world as sensed through *all* the gates of the body, not merely the eyes; and in rhetorical terms, it is a way of improving the sensual enjoyment of his spectators, designing visual illusions which continually demand and imply all the other senses in their structures.

To summarize: Blake's pictorial style, like his poetic form and the total form of his composite art, is organized as a dramatic, dialectical interaction between contrary elements. His poems present the drama of consciousnesses interacting with themselves, with others, and with a malleable, nonobjective environment. His pictures present the dramatic interaction of bodies with one another and with the im-

[40] *The Gutenberg Galaxy*, pp. 265-66.

mediate, multisensory elements of existential (not visual) space. The total form or aesthetic "presentation" of his composite art is thus a dialectic of dialectics, a doubleness doubled, which may be one reason he so often referred to it as "fourfold art." Despite the vigorous contrariety and rivalry between the two elements of his composite art, however, the total design of his illuminated pages continually reaffirms the ultimate identity of poem and picture by displaying a continuity between the most abstract linear patterns and the most representational forms. At one extreme, visual form is constructed in accord with what is, from the point of view of the visual arts, a completely arbitrary, abstract, nonsensory system (language); at the other extreme, the picture is designed as an immediate, synaesthetic presentation of primitive sensory elements.[41] The union of these two concepts of form is embodied, appropriately enough, by the word "marriage" on the title page of *The Marriage of Heaven and Hell* [8], which unites the abstraction of typography with the flowing, organic forms of Blake's pictorial style.

Blake's dialectic is obviously much more than an aesthetic principle governing the relationship and internal dynamics of the two components of his composite art. The aesthetic implications of the theory of contraries are best seen as a by-product of Blake's deepest ethical and metaphysical convictions. The mutual independence, lively interaction and conflict between Blake's poems and pictures is his way of enacting his vision of a liberated social and psychological order, the world of imagination as "Mental Warfare." Blake is not a Hegelian dialectician, pushing us toward an abstract realm of pure spirit where conflict, and thus the dialectic itself, ceases to operate. Nor is he simply presenting another version of the venerable code of *concordia discors*, which posits a mysterious order or harmony behind the apparent conflicts of our world. Blake's dialectic pervades his entire cosmology, rendering it as a continuous process which never attains a final resting place. One major use of the dialectic is to dramatize the vertical discrepancy between the world of imaginative desire and the fallen world of "reality." Although Blake frequently treats this discrepancy as a matter of fallen "illusion" versus imagina-

[41] A promising avenue of investigation in Blake's style would be his use of "folk" forms in the visual arts, not just graphic or pictured forms, but semi-dramatic or ritualistic forms such as the pantomime, which became an important part of London life in the eighteenth century. See John Adlard, *The Sports of Cruelty* (London, 1972), for an excellent study of Blake's use of verbal folk traditions.

tive "reality," he recognizes, with Shakespeare, the vitality of illusion: "What seems to Be: Is: To those to whom/ It seems to Be" (*J* 32:51–52, E 177). On the other hand, it is his way of organizing the horizontal conflicts of that fallen world, not by imposing "One Law" from above, but by allowing each particular of experience to express its own essence. Thus, "one portion of being, is the Prolific. the other, the Devouring. . . . These two classes of men are always upon earth, & they should be enemies; whoever tries to reconcile them seeks to destroy existence" (*MHH* 16-17, E 39). Similarly, the two sides of Blake's composite art may not be reconciled as the daughters of one Nature; they insist upon a contrarious interaction to draw the spectator into their vortex of mental progression.

There is a place, however, where the contraries are equally true and live in peace, the land of sexual harmony which Blake calls Beulah in the late prophecies, Innocence or the Vales of Har in the early works. Blake sees human life as beginning in this integrated state and falling into Experience, the world of division where the contraries are at war. *The Book of Thel* (1789) is an account of this harmonious world and the way it disintegrates. *The Book of Urizen* (1794) is Blake's explanation of the various causes and manifestations of disintegration, and *Jerusalem* (1804-18) is his attempt to reorganize the divided world into a new personal and cosmic unity. These three works, then, adumbrate not only the full range of Blake's career as a creator of illuminated books, but also the mythic drama conveyed by those works. For that reason, they allow us to develop answers to two questions which I have so far managed to avoid.

The first is the question of development. It is obvious that neither Blake's style nor his symbolic system sprang fully-armed from his forehead while he was writing *Songs of Innocence*. The spiral form cannot have meant as much to him in 1789 as it did in 1824. I do not subscribe to the theory, however, that Blake's life can be divided into separate compartments in which he repudiates the ideas and styles of earlier work. Blake's development seems to me much more a matter of growth, maturation, and expansion—in a word, he gets deeper as he gets older, but it is not the kind of depth which grows out of the negation of earlier achievements. This continuity does not release us from the question of development, but it does suggest that the "phases" in Blake's career cannot be inferred simply from the external events of his life and times, but must be based upon a close analysis of stylistic developments in the total form of his illuminated books, i.e., poem, pictures, and the manner in which they are related.

This brings us to our second neglected question, the problem of stylistic differences among his various books. I have so far presented a general picture of Blake's style, but it is clear that there are many important differences among his various books. The "style" of *Urizen*, for instance, is unique in Blake's corpus, and yet its pictorial splendor has made it an attractive basis for generalizations about Blake's illuminated books. What I am suggesting is that we cannot really say very much of substance about Blake's development until we have examined the formal characteristics of all his illuminated books taken individually. The present study is a modest start in this direction, consisting in the chapters to come of close readings of text and design in three different works from what are commonly assumed to be the three different "periods" in Blake's life, containing three distinct, but continuous thematic ideas: the loss of Innocence (*Thel*), the state of Experience (*Urizen*), and the comic resolution (*Jerusalem*). I could have chosen other works (especially as alternates for the first two), and I do not mean to suggest that these somehow disclose the one true pattern in Blake's development. They do provide a finite beginning, however, which one hopes will be either provocative or provoking enough to stir up the investigation of other lines of development, and to improve the sensual enjoyment of the works under consideration.

Chapter Three

THE FORM OF INNOCENCE

Poetic and Pictorial Design in *The Book of Thel*

The Book of Thel is Blake's first illuminated prophecy. Chronologically, it comes between *Songs of Innocence* and *Songs of Experience*,[1] and thematically, it provides a bridge between these two groups of lyric poems describing the "Two Contrary States of the Human Soul." It is thus an especially appropriate vehicle for focusing on the critical moments in Blake's management of the symbolism and iconography of Innocence. *Thel* represents Blake's attempt to explore the limits of Innocence and to define its relationship to more complex psychological conditions. It is, in a sense, the only prophecy of Innocence, and as such demands a central position in any consideration of the development of Blake's prophetic art.[2]

I. STRUCTURING READER RESPONSE: *CLARITAS* AND *DIFFICULTAS*

The relationships of text and design in *Thel* seem relatively straightforward when compared with the complex, obscure illustrative devices of Blake's later books. Most of the designs illustrate a

[1] Scholars agree that the date 1789 on the title-page "probably corresponds to the time of composition rather than execution of the plates" (Nancy Bogen, *The Book of Thel: A Facsimile and Critical Text* [Providence, 1971], p. 3). The final state of *The Book of Thel* was the result of several years' work, possibly begun as early as 1787 and finished in 1791. This is also the period when Blake, having written most of *Songs of Innocence*, was beginning to work on *Songs of Experience*, although one should not make the mistake of supposing that these two groups of lyrics were composed in strict sequence. Several of the *Experience* poems appeared in the 1789 edition of *Songs of Innocence*.

[2] I use the word "prophecy" here in a loose sense to refer to Blake's dramatic or epic nonlyrical illuminated poems. *Thel* is also a "prophecy of Innocence" in a stricter sense, in that it explores the *ends* of Innocence, that is, both its future and its purpose.

specific scene in the text, their arrangment follows the narrative order, and their compositional qualities, the delicate coloring and flowing lines, seem completely in tune with the evanescent imagery and languid verse of the text. There are exceptions, however, to this general clarity of surface. We open most copies of the book, for instance, not to the relatively literal title-page illustration of Thel watching the courtship of Cloud and Dew [37], but to a verbal, emblematic puzzle, "Thel's Motto," which is not only mysterious in itself but has no clear and obvious relation to the poem it introduces. The text of the poem itself is similarly framed by pictorial enigmas: the first "chapter" is introduced by a group of human forms [38], and the poem concludes with a picture of three children astride a serpent [44], neither design calling up a clearly appropriate caption from the text. Blake seems to have fractured the close, rather literal unity of text and illustration at the beginning and end of his poem, framing the relative simplicity and clarity of his book in a context of complex obscurity.

It could be argued, of course, that the relative obscurity of the first and last plates is not purposeful, but merely a symptom of the different stages of composition.[3] The lettering style of plates i ("Thel's Motto") and 6 [44] indicates a later date of execution, and the similarity of their contents (enigmatic rhetorical questions) suggests that they were added to the poem at the same time, either as replacements for canceled plates or as new additions.[4] But Blake did

[3] Anne Mellor suggests in "Blake's Designs for *The Book of Thel*," *Philological Quarterly* L (April 1971), 201, that "the obvious ambiguities and obscurity of the final plate of the poem are the predictable result of Blake's not very successful attempt to fit new conceptual material into an already established but no longer adequate plot-line and illustration." As will become clear in what follows, I think the attempt to assimilate new material was successful.

[4] See D. J. Sloss and J.P.R. Wallis, *The Prophetic Writings of William Blake*, 2 vols. (Oxford, 1957), II, 267, and E 713 for discussion of the dating of plates i and 6. The verbal similarity of i and 6 is no accident. In a canceled passage from *Tiriel* we find language much like that of Thel's Motto and the voice of sorrow uttered by a single voice in a single, connected speech:

Dost thou not see that men *cannot* be formed all alike
Some *nostrild wide* breathing out blood. Some *close* shut up
In silent deceit, *poisons inhaling* from the morning rose
With daggers hid beneath their lips & *poison* in their *tongue*
Or *eyed* with *little* sparks of Hell or with infernal brands
Flinging flames of discontent & plagues of dark despair
Or those whose mouths are graves whose teeth the gates of eternal death
Can wisdom be put in a silver rod or love in a golden bowl

(E 736; italics mine)

choose to integrate these elements into a single book, and we must at least test the hypothesis that these later additions, in spite of their apparent incongruity with the rest of the book, have an organic relationship to it.

Why would Blake want to frame his relatively straightforward poetic drama with a pair of plates which exhibit both verbal and iconographical obscurity? We might note first that the placing of simple, direct illustrations in a context of complex, indirect illustrations is structurally analogous to the psychological state of the main character of the poem. Thel's world, the Vales of Har, is a state of innocence and pastoral unity where human beings can converse directly with natural creatures that see no conflict between life and death. And yet Thel perceives this state of harmonious unity, as must the reader, in the context of her own state of alienated, divided consciousness. She can converse with the Lilly, the Cloud, the Clod of Clay, and feel an emotional affinity with them, but always with a reservation: she is unlike them in that she does not know the purpose of her life, or the meaning of her death. For her the state of Innocence exists only in the context of Experience, just as for the reader the clarity and harmony of the main body of *The Book of Thel* must be seen in a context of obscurity and ambiguity.

It seems, then, that Blake's placement of relatively obscure poetic and pictorial elements, some of them late additions, in such a way as to "frame" his book has a rhetorical as well as a formal function. The effect of his strategy is to undercut any attempt by the reader to pass judgment on Thel from some fixed perspective. By subjecting the reader's imagination to a vicarious analogue of Thel's experience, Blake encourages us to identify with Thel, or at least to refrain from passing externally derived value judgments on her behavior. One of the major problems with commentary on *Thel* has been a tendency to ignore Thel's role as a surrogate for the reader, and to see the poem as either a satire on Thel's adolescent inability to come to terms with life or a panegyric on her good sense in fleeing this rough world for a realm of spirituality. The poem can be made to support either reading, but neither one seems adequate, and both involve the imposition of external values. The fact that the poem can be made

---

The italicized words are also spoken by the voice of sorrow in *Thel.* There are, of course, many other stylistic and thematic parallels between the two passages, both of which depict the senses as treacherous aggressors or victims of aggression in a broadside of rhetorical questions.

to support two apparently contradictory interpretations seems to me a strong suggestion that Blake is trying to subvert this sort of univocal judgment, and to confront us with a human dilemma that eludes any fixed moral stance.[5]

II. AMBIGUITIES OF PLOT AND THEME: SOME VERSIONS OF THE PASTORAL

The first problem facing the reader of *Thel* is to decide just exactly what is happening in the poem. The "plot" seems simple enough: Thel, the youngest of the "daughters of Mne Seraphim," leaves the pastoral society of her sisters to "fade away" from her mortal day. She asks the various creatures of her garden world to explain to her why all living things are "born but to smile & fall," and receives a series of answers, all variations on the basic idea that everything is interdependent, and death is only a part of the larger pattern of life. When Thel sees that this interdependence extends even to the lowliest beings, the Clod of Clay and the infant Worm, she accepts the invitation to explore the underworld of death. At her own grave plot she hears a "voice of sorrow" asking terrible, frightening questions about the senses, sexuality, pain, and death, and she flees back to the Vales of Har.

It has not seemed obvious to all commentators that this is primarily a story about dying. The Neoplatonic school of Blake criticism reads it as a story of birth (or, more precisely, abortion). The Vales of Har are equated with a Platonic realm of preexistence like that depicted in Wordsworth's "Intimations" ode and the underworld becomes a symbol of this temporal, material world. Thel is thus an unborn soul descending from the world of spirit into matter, and very sensibly rejecting it.[6] Biblical typologists tend to read *Thel* as

[5] A related problem in criticism of *Thel* has been a tendency to transfer attitudes toward its heroine onto the poem itself. David Erdman calls it a "mystery play for adolescents" consisting largely of "a series of Barbauldian moral hymns" (*Prophet*, pp. 132-33). Northrop Frye suggests that the poem comes perilously close to the "namby-pamby," and is scarcely able to bear commentary at all (*Fearful Symmetry*, p. 233). I would not deny that the poem elicits these responses (especially from male readers), but I hope to show in the following pages that it also subverts them, in effect inviting us to pass judgment, only to set a trap for the position from which we judge.

[6] George Mills Harper, in *The Neoplatonism of William Blake* (Chapel Hill, 1961), states the case most directly: "Thel is privileged to examine the frightfulness of earthly life and then return to the bliss of her eternal existence"

a displaced allegory of the fall: the Vales of Har is a type of the Garden of Eden, the underworld the postlapsarian world of sorrow, and Thel a timorous Adam waiting for judgment from "the voice/ Of him that walketh in the garden in the evening time" (an echo of Genesis 3:8).

Two other, somewhat more remote analogues suggest themselves. If not a source, Johnson's *Rasselas* is obviously a spiritual ancestor of *Thel.*[7] Both Thel and Rasselas find themselves out of tune with a pastoral world of natural perfection, and both engage in a series of unsatisfactory dialogues in order to understand their dilemmas. Both leave their "Happy Valleys" in order to explore the larger world of experience, and both make an apparently circular journey to "a conclusion in which nothing is concluded." *Thel* seems further to owe a good deal of its structure and language to the Book of Job.[8] Thel, like Job, undergoes isolation and trial, and after consulting three "comforters" who try to explain her experience for her, she receives instruction from a mysterious prophetic voice whose words have a major impact on her.

Blake's palette was filled, in other words, with a rich and eclectic spectrum of traditional versions of the pastoral. It is one thing, however, to recognize the presence of an external context or allusion; quite another to understand the compositional unity into which it has been assimilated. What should be understood, at a minimum, is that no single one of these parallel "plots" provides an adequate account of what happens in *Thel.* The Neoplatonic version is certainly there in some sense, but not at the primary, literal level. Even the reading of the poem in terms of Blake's own system, as a parable of the passage from Innocence to Experience, is only implicitly there, and given the date of 1789 we certainly cannot assume that it was very clearly articulated for Blake himself. What is primarily there is the story of a young woman who questions her own usefulness and purpose in a world where everything dies or fades away, and who is given the opportunity to explore death in order to come to her

(p. 66). Not all the Neoplatonists take such a one-sided view of the poem. Kathleen Raine, for instance, sees *Thel* as a debate between the Neoplatonic (antimaterialist) and alchemical (materialist) philosophies, rather than an endorsement of a realm of disembodied, immaterial idealism. See her *Blake and Tradition*, 2 vols. (Princeton, 1968), I, Chap. IV.

[7] Raine, *ibid.*, I, 112-14, elaborates this parallel in some detail.

[8] Robert Gleckner, "Blake's *Thel* and the Bible," *Bulletin of the New York Public Library* LXIV (1960), 573-80, notes the verbal parallels.

own conclusions. Read metaphorically, with an awareness of its implicit contexts, *Thel* is a story of dying as growing up as being born.

Thel's response to her fate may remind us of e. e. cummings: "dying's fine, but death o baby, that I wouldn't like." Given the choice between the hell of pain and terror she encounters in the underworld and the pastoral evanescence of the Vales of Har, Thel's choice is simple, and needs no Neoplatonic explanation. Those who judge Thel as a failure, a suicide, or a weakling should put this choice to themselves in the literal terms the poem provides. We do need to ask, however, if Thel's flight is to be seen as a solution to the problems the poem has raised.

The answer to this question depends on what it is that Thel is returning to when she flees back into the Vales of Har. One clue is provided in the first lines of the poem: "The Daughters of Mne Seraphim led round their sunny flocks,/ All but the youngest. she in paleness sought the secret air./ To fade away like morning beauty from her mortal day. . . ." After her journey to the underworld perhaps Thel will no longer feel useless and alienated in the Vales of Har, but will join her older sisters in the pastoral life. Her departure and return would thus be a kind of initiation ritual, a temporary separation from her community as a preparation for full participation in its life. But it is not entirely clear how highly Blake wants us to regard this accomplishment. Are we to associate the "Daughters of Mne Seraphim" with "a realm of spirit" distinct from the Vales of Har, as Bogen advises?[9] Or are we to see these beings as dwellers in a land of infantile regression, daughters of ineffectual memories (Mnemosyne) rather than inspiration?[10] Has Thel passed through the realm of Experience to a Higher Innocence, or has she fled from Experience, refusing, in the light of the three symbolic plots we have noted, to die, to be born, or to grow up? The textual crux, "Mne Seraphim," does not, it seems to me, provide a definitive perspective. On the contrary, it tends to keep the meaning of Thel's return ambiguous, and it may even be a reflection of Blake's own uncertainty about the thrust of his poem. It tends, in other words,

9 Bogen, *The Book of Thel*, pp. 17, 23, 24.

10 This is the more widely accepted interpretation. See Joseph H. Wicksteed, *Blake's Innocence and Experience* (New York, 1928), p. 132, and Hagstrum, *Poet and Painter*, p. 87n. Cf. Blake's Preface to *Milton* (E 94) predicting a new art in which "the Daughters of Memory shall become the Daughters of Inspiration."

to return our attention to Thel's dilemma rather than offering a solution for it.

The enigmatic emblems which frame *The Book of Thel* serve, in a similar way, as foci for the tensions in Thel's dilemma rather than resolutions. The tailpiece emblem of three children astride a serpent [44], for instance, admits of at least two possible relationships to the text, as well as two antithetical meanings in itself. It may be an emblem of "Higher Innocence," a fusion of the images of Innocence and Experience analogous to the Christian iconographical tradition of dove and serpent.[11] Or it may be an emblem of infantile regression and flight from Experience, the serpent of energy (cf. Orc in the political prophecies and the curbed "youthful burning boy" of Thel's grave) bridled by a virgin who takes the younger children back to the world of Innocence. Blake reverses the serpent's sinister direction and gives him a gentler face in *America* 11 (E 54), a plate in which Boston's Angel "indignant burning with the fires of Orc" rejects the tyranny which "keeps the gen'rous from experience." The internal ambiguity of this emblem in *Thel* is compounded by its problematic relation to the text: as an image of "Higher Innocence" it may depict the successful completion of Thel's initiation, or it may allude to a mastery of experience she failed to achieve when she fled from the underworld. As an emblem of infantile regression, it may be a comment on Thel's escapism, or an ironic image of a fate which she rightly avoided. It is highly unlikely that any reader will find all of these permutations equally convincing, but it seems just as unlikely that any one of them can prevail exclusively.[12]

[11] Matthew 10:16, from which this tradition derives, might well serve as an epigraph for Thel: "Behold, I send you forth as sheep in the midst of wolves: be ye therefore wise as serpents, and harmless as doves."

[12] Although it does not resolve the ambiguity of the serpent emblem, the ultimate source for Blake's image is probably the representations of dolphins and sea serpents on Roman sarcophagi. The Cupids and Nereids depicted riding on the backs of these creatures, often with bridle in hand, were symbols of "the happy dead . . . carried safely over the waves on the backs of friendly, frolicsome sea-lions, sea-bulls, sea-horses, sea-griffins, sea-centaurs, Tritons, dolphins and other Ocean-born creatures" (see Jocelyn Toynbee, *Death and Burial in the Roman World* [London, 1971], p. 38). As a maker of books and print dealer Blake would also have been aware that the coiled serpent was a conventional tailpiece in French rococo book illustration, a tradition which derived from the ancient practice of ending a manuscript with a curved stroke or flourish of the pen. Ernst R. Curtius notes a particularly apt example of this tradition in the *Greek Anthology*: "I, the koronis [colophon] the faithful

Like the tailpiece emblem, "Thel's Motto" (plate i) resonates with secondary questions and contradictory answers, rather than pointing to a clearly correct set of responses.[13] Does the eagle know what is in the pit? The answer is no if you are using common sense, yes if you take the eagle to be a symbol of wisdom and clear-sightedness.[14] Wilt thou go ask the mole? Yes, again, in terms of common sense, but no if you consider the mole a symbol of blindness and ignorance. The answer becomes even more equivocal if we note that the question does not necessarily imply that the mole "knows" what is in the pit, only that *going to ask* the mole (and thus, like Thel, entering the pit yourself) may be more instructive than the eagle's knowledge from a distance. We should also note at this point that the Motto's questions raise a prior question about the validity of metaphor and symbol. If we take the questions metaphorically, then we side with the eagle's wisdom at a distance; if we take them literally, we choose the immediate, "tactile" knowledge of the mole.

The second pair of questions in the Motto is calculated to tease the reader out of whatever certainties he has managed to win from the first two. "Can Wisdom be put in a silver rod?/ Or Love in a Golden Bowl?" Literal-minded moles have the fewest problems with this question, having rejected symbolism. Hierophants and exegetes will have to quarrel over whether the silver rod and golden bowl are "appropriate," decorous symbols for wisdom and love in the same way that the mole and eagle may be. Many readers who will accept a knowing eagle cannot accept a wise rod, usually on

---

guardian of the written pages, announce the final boundary stone. . . . And I, curved round like a snake's back, am placed at the end of this pleasant work" (*European Literature in the Latin Middle Ages*, tr. Trask, p. 307).

13 A tendency in commentary on *Thel* has been, however, to translate these questions, like those of *The Tyger*, into statements. See Bogen, *The Book of Thel*, pp. 64-65, for a survey of the best-known answers.

14 The answers to the questions of "Thel's Motto" would thus be self-evident for an empiricist who prefers the "objectivity" and clarity of visual knowledge to the relative darkness of the other senses. Blake may be echoing Locke's use of the eagle and mole to make precisely this distinction: "The ignorance and darkness that is in us no more hinders nor confines the knowledge that is in others, than the blindness of the mole is an argument against the quicksightedness of an eagle" (*An Essay Concerning Human Understanding*, ed. A. C. Fraser, 2 vols. [Oxford, 1894], II, 214). The "common sense" principle invoked here is the assumption that a place is known best by its own inhabitant (thus, the eagle knows of light and air, the mole knows the subterranean darkness). This sort of propriety of place is consistently assumed by Blake in his "Proverbs of Hell" (see *MHH*, E 35-37).

the basis of some antimaterialistic sense of decorum, or a preference for nature over art.[15] The point of all this is that the further we push the questions of "Thel's Motto," the more we encounter the same fundamental ambiguities expanded into wider fields of reference. How *do* we know or love things? At a distance, through symbolic mediators and created forms such as eagles, bowls, and rods? Are some mediating forms appropriate and others not, and how do we know? Or do we know things and love them immediately, sensuously, blindly probing like the mole? Is knowledge a process and a probe, or a product and a point of view?

These are not academic questions for someone like Thel, for whom knowledge of what is in the pit, not to mention wisdom and love, is a matter of immediate concern. To her credit, Thel does try both ways of investigating the meaning of her death, first by asking others to explain it for her, and then by descending into the pit to find out for herself. The two procedures produce antithetical answers: the Lilly, Cloud, and Clod of Clay tell her that death is the gateway to "eternal vales," "tenfold life," and "a crown that none can take away." They assure Thel that even if her only use is "to be at death the food of worms," that is a great blessing. When Thel investigates her death at firsthand, however, she finds it full of sorrow, pain, and frustration. The two modes of knowledge offered in the Motto lead, then, to apparently irreconcilable visions of life and death. Mediated, abstract "eagle knowledge" produces a vision of the pit that is desirable, but apparently false; immediate, sensuous "mole knowledge" discovers the apparent truth, but this truth is

[15] Commentators have read the silver rod and golden bowl as symbols of authority (scepter and chalice), of sexual organs (phallus and vulva), or simply of materialism. Another possible analogue is the silver cord and golden bowl of Ecclesiastes 12:6, traditionally associated with the spinal cord (sensuality) and brain pan (intellect). *Annotations Upon All the Books of the Old and New Testament*, 3rd ed., 2 vols. (London, 1657), I, s.v. Ecclesiastes 12:6, provides a typical exegesis. The silver cord and golden bowl are seen as symbols of "Vital parts of the body," the former representing "the marrow or *pith of the* back, continued from the brain as it were in a cord or string. . . . for the white color of it, compared unto silver." The golden bowl is understood as "the Meninx or skin wherein the brain and vital powers thereof are contained as in a bowle." It is important to note that the clarification of these correspondences between the artifacts of "Thel's Motto" and the organs of the body does not clear up the mystery of the motto's meaning, but simply extends it into a new context: Can wisdom be found or put into the nervous system? Does love reside in the brain? Exegesis does not answer the questions of the motto; it only recasts them in a new form.

intolerable. The question is whether the poem offers any escape from this dilemma, or whether Thel is inevitably condemned to vacillate between realms of irrelevant idealism and intolerable realism. For Samuel Johnson, I am assured by my Augustan colleagues, there would have been no problem: he would have told Thel to "get on with it." But then Johnson gives Rasselas an escape from a similar dilemma by hinting at a "future state" in which all the insufficiencies of this life will be remedied. By making Thel's journey include an exploration of her own "after-life," Blake removes this escape, forcing us to decide whether Thel's dilemma is soluble in concrete, human terms, or is simply an unavoidable element in human nature. One thing seems clear at this point: the tantalizing ambiguities of the poem, and especially of its "framing" elements, are a very effective device for preventing the reader from sitting in easy, secure judgment on Thel. If she says no to life, our task is not to condemn her, but to form a yes out of elements of her experience.

III. RESOLUTION, INDEPENDENCE, AND NOTHINGNESS: THE USES OF SELFHOOD

In one sense the answer to Thel's dilemma is quite clear. All she has to do is submit herself to the process Blake was later to call "Self-annihilation" (*M* 41:2, E 141), and yield herself willingly to death, experience, and sexuality.[16] Thel's problem is that she lacks the faith, spontaneity, and selflessness of her comforters, and insists on clinging to her present identity. Mary Lynn Johnson states the case with admirable clarity: "Thel . . . wishes to surrender nothing, risk nothing. Her virginity is a physical sign of her psychological self

[16] I recognize the anachronism involved in using a concept Blake did not employ until much later. It seems to me that the use of the idea here is nevertheless justified simply because it is so useful in focusing the issues raised by the poem. This is not an argument for an ahistorical assumption that Blake had the concept of "Self-annihilation" in mind fifteen years before he used it in a poem. On the contrary, the *absence* of any name for the way out of Thel's dilemma is an important feature of the meaning of the poem. On the one hand it is a very effective way of drawing the reader into Thel's dilemma, and preventing a detached labeling of her predicament. On the other hand, from Blake's point of view the lack of this concept was simply a reflection of how much more imaginative exploration he would have to engage in before a way out could be articulated. *The Book of Thel* is, in other words, a seed for the later poems, raising problems which Blake could solve only by writing more poems, and which the reader can solve only by reading on through the illuminated books.

enclosure. . . . Thel chooses memory over inspiration, striving for the knowledge that puts two and two together rather than accepting wisdom that grows out of love."[17]

The only problem with this formula is that it sounds just a little too easy. If Thel will only stop asking questions and learn to live and love without thinking, everything will work out. But it is precisely Thel's insistence on asking questions and striving for knowledge which identifies her as the only fully human character in the poem. Self-annihilation is presented as an easy, natural mode of being for her comforters, not something which requires or permits "pondering": "when I pass away,/ It is to tenfold life," the Cloud assures her; "But how this is sweet maid, I know not, and I cannot know," says the Clod of Clay. "I ponder, and I cannot ponder; yet I live and love."

The difficult question which the poem raises, then, is whether Thel's pondering, her rational, skeptical attitude and her related feeling of alienation from the spontaneous life of nature, is in itself the cause of her problems. Blake's reputation as the arch-foe of rationalism would seem, at first glance, to answer this question. We need to remind ourselves, however, that Blake never advocates Dionysian mindlessness, that Urizen is one of the four faculties of consciousness to be redeemed, not expelled, and that "sweet Science" and "Intellectual Battle" are his names for the highest activities of human consciousness. We should remind ourselves also that Thel's alienation from nature, her doubt that its lessons apply to her, may have made some sense to the poet for whom "There Is No Natural Religion." We cannot assume that Thel's skepticism and alienation are the causes of her problem. The poem challenges us, in fact, to find a way of differentiating the alienation which Thel feels as a mark of her humanity from the alienation which cuts her off from the fulfilled existence enjoyed by her comforters. The only alternative is to conclude, as Freud did, that the human instinct to go beyond nature is itself the cause of neurosis, and that a spiritual sickness is therefore the unavoidable human condition. In order to avoid this conclusion, the reader must be able to locate the primary error or "original sin"—other than self-consciousness itself—which leads Thel into the fallen world outside the Vales of Har, rather than the "eternal vales" which her comforters promise.

[17] "Beulah, 'Mne Seraphim,' and Blake's *Thel*," *Journal of English and Germanic Philology* LXIX (April 1970), 266, 269-70.

The traditional sin of disobedience is, of course, completely absent from Thel's moral universe, and there can be little doubt of Blake's contempt for the orthodox doctrine that man might have lived forever if he could have suppressed his desire for God's property. In Blake's view, the god who plants a garden with forbidden fruit is not worthy of worship; he is Satan, the tempter and accuser, or Jehovah, the selfish, arbitrary judge. If the Vales of Har are to be seen as a type of the Garden of Eden, then, an important qualification must be made. There is no implication that a different kind of behavior on Thel's part would save her from the fate endured by all the creatures in her garden world. Adam is faced with death only *after* he commits his original sin; Thel's premonitions of mortality *precede* her vague allusions to the approach of a judge whose mercy must be implored ("gentle may I lay me down . . . and gentle hear the voice/ Of him that walketh in the garden in the evening time"; cf. Genesis 3:8). The moral framework of *The Book of Thel* might be described, then, as an inversion of the values of Genesis: man does not die when he falls from grace; he falls from grace when he fails to learn how to die.

It is significant, however, that the first manifestation of Thel's failure to learn how to die is not, as we might expect, an impossible wish to live indefinitely and preserve her individual consciousness. She has, after all, "*sought* the secret air./ To fade away . . . from her mortal day" (italics mine), and the refrain of her prayer to the deity of the Vales of Har is not a wish to live forever, but to "gentle sleep the sleep of death." Her reaction to the threat of annihilation is not struggle or resistance, but a regressive wish for a painless, unconscious Nirvana—in Freudian terms, a return to the womb. Mary Lynn Johnson is probably correct in saying that Thel wishes to "risk nothing," but certainly wrong in supposing that she wishes to "surrender nothing": Thel is eager to surrender everything, if only she can find a conqueror who will be gentle about it. It is ironic that she prays to the "voice/ Of him that walketh in the garden in the evening time" to accept this surrender, for—if we can import the context of the Genesis echo—this is precisely the kind of voice which commands departure from the womblike garden. In a negative sense, this mysterious voice is a projection of Thel's doubt and fear: she senses an impending crisis which she can explain only by reference to a transcendent father, an invisible accuser-judge whose mercy must be begged. In a positive sense, the voice is a projection of her human instinct to quit the Vales of Har, like Rasselas leaving the Happy Valley to seek the meaning of human life in a realm beyond the "perfection of nature."[18]

Thel's original sin, then, is not her restless striving for knowledge, nor her desire to go beyond nature, but rather her impossible wish to return to nature and give up the double-edged gift of self-consciousness. Her failure to learn how to die arises, paradoxically, from her wish for death. Since this wish to regress into oblivion cannot be directly or literally satisfied in Thel's available universe (she seems condemned to exist, if not really to live, in the Vales of Har) she tries to satisfy it in indirect ways. She uses her reasoning powers to retreat from and evade experience, and instead of finding herself she creates what Blake was later to call the "Selfhood" or "spectre," an "abstract objecting power" which reduces the contraries of life to negations, and objectifies the human self to itself (*J* 10:14-15, E 151). Thel's reduction of contraries is manifested in her inability to understand paradox, particularly the paradoxical interdependence of life and death experienced by her comforters. Her self-objectification is exhibited in her frequent references to herself in the third person (also a sign of infantilism), and in her tendency to define the pathos of her situation in terms of hypothetical observers for whom she will "objectively" cease to exist: "I vanish from my pearly throne, and *who shall find* my place"; "I pass away. yet I complain, and *no one hears* my voice"; "*all shall say*, without a use this shining woman liv'd" (italics mine). Since Thel's world is defined as constant flux, however, any particular objectification of the self is doomed. Blake was probably thinking back to Thel's problem when years later he wrote in *Jerusalem*, "In Selfhood we are nothing, but fade away like morning breath" (*J* 40:13, E 185).

The matron Clay hears Thel's sighs and questions flying over her roof, and calls them down into her oracular underworld where Thel can hear them translated into their most extreme form, as they will sound in the earth, the world of Experience. The "voice of sorrow" (Thel's own voice, really, since it comes from her grave),

[18] Blake treats the "voice of him that walketh in the garden in the evening time" with a similar ambiguity in the opening poems of *Songs of Experience*. The "Introduction" to *Experience* presents the "Voice of the Bard" who has heard and is identified with or transmits the "Holy Word/ That walk'd among the ancient trees/ Calling the lapsed Soul/ And weeping in the evening dew." What the Earth hears, however, is not the Bard calling her to rise up, but the "Selfish father of men" who accuses and punishes ("Earth's Answer," E 18).

expresses her general alienation from nature in the more narrow, radical form of a protest against the condition of her own little piece of nature—her body, its senses and sexual drives. The senses are seen as breaches in the defenses of the self through which beguiling, destructive forces may enter, or as offensive weapons designed for the entrapment and destruction of others. Male sexuality is seen repressed by "a tender curb," and female sexuality is shrouded in mystery by "a little curtain of flesh."

But Thel's "voice of sorrow" asks *why* all these things must be so, and challenges us to answer—or to flee like Thel back to our own realms of secure thoughtlessness. If these things are simply a consequence of Thel's human tendency to ponder and question and to seek her destiny beyond nature, then they are no more avoidable than the death which Thel questions in the Vales of Har. The "moral" of the poem is then that human beings, cursed with the attribute of an alienating, individualizing self-consciousness, are inevitably cut off from the spontaneous acceptance of life as a unified process. But if, as I have argued previously, Thel's tendency to question and her creation of a doubting Selfhood are seen as ambiguous symptoms rather than root causes of her problems, then the questions are not merely rhetorical complaints, but genuine inquiries into her condition.[19] Thel's shriek and flight back to the Vales of Har may then be seen not as a failure to face life, but as the sign of a revelation.

What is it that Thel has learned from the voice of her own "buried self"?[20] We can answer this best by looking back at the hypothesis she was testing when she decided to enter the underworld

[19] If we again look ahead to Blake's concept of Selfhood in his later poems, we find it treated not as an unambiguous source of evil but as a necessary part of the structure of consciousness. "Self-annihilation" does not mean the permanent abolition of Selfhood; it is the prelude to the creation of a *new* Selfhood which will serve the imagination. Blake's rhetoric can be misleading on this point. His insistence on putting off the Selfhood "alway" (*M* 40:36) and "ever and ever" (*M* 38:49) should be read in the sense of continuity, not finality. Milton descends "to teach Men . . . to *go on*/ In fearless majesty annihilating Self" (*M* 38:40-41, *E* 138; italics mine). Ultimately the Selfhood and his brethren, the Spectre, the Elect, Urizen, and Satan, are to be "reclaimed" (*M* 39:10), and compelled to assist the artist in his work (see *J* 8:14-15: "thou my Spectre art divided against me. But mark/ I will compell thee to assist me in my terrible labours").

[20] Mary Lynn Johnson applies this phrase very aptly to the voice of sorrow ("Beulah, 'Mne Seraphim,' and Blake's Thel," p. 271).

in the first place. Thel's doubts are not put to rest by any of the promises of "eternal vales" or "tenfold life" given her by the Lilly and Cloud. It is the matron Clay's speech that changes her mind:

> . . . he that loves the lowly, pours his oil upon my head.
> And kisses me, and binds his nuptial bands around my breast,
> And says; Thou mother of my children, I have loved thee.
> And I have given thee a crown that none can take away.
> (5:1-4, E 5)

Somehow, this clears everything up (at least momentarily) for Thel:

> The daughter of beauty wip'd her pitying tears with her white veil,
> And said. Alas! I knew not this, and therefore did I weep:
> That God would love a Worm I knew, and punish the evil foot
> That wilful, bruis'd its helpless form: but that he cherish'd it
> With milk and oil. I never knew; and therefore did I weep. . . . (5:7-11, E 5)

Thel's relief depends, however, upon either a misunderstanding or an evasion of what the Clod of Clay is saying. She translates the account of God's relation to his creatures as a fruitful marriage into the relation of parent to infant. Where the Clod of Clay sees God as a husband, Thel sees him as a father. Her previous understanding of God as a judging patriarch who manifests his love by punishing evil is not substantially changed, merely qualified to make this deity a benevolent father who "cherishes" his creatures with milk like helpless infants and singles them out for special favor by anointing them with oil. Thel's evasion of the matron Clay's point is signaled, in fact, by her insertion of "milk" into the list of God's gifts. The ritual of anointing with oil was a traditional sign of consecration, the calling to a special mission as a "charismatic" warrior or prophet. Thel figuratively dilutes the heroic implications of anointing with the milk of infantile dependency.[21]

[21] Anointing with oil is a traditional ritual of consecration, often performed upon a person who has been selected for some high mission. As John L. McKenzie explains, "anointing brings the spirit of Yahweh upon the person and impels him to some extraordinary deed . . . anointing made the person a charismatic officer whose mission could be executed under the impulsion of the spirit" (*Dictionary of the Bible* [Milwaukee, 1965], p. 35).

Thel enters the earth's household, then, with the assumption that her fate is in the hands of a just and merciful deity. She discovers there what she had only suspected throughout her dialogues with her comforters, that this god does not exist. The "voice/ Of him that walketh in the garden in the evening time" is conspicuously silent, existing only as a manifestation of Thel's wishful (or fearful) thinking. Her shriek at the end of the poem may be a cry of pain at this basic discovery, or it may be something more, a recognition that the vision of repressed, destructive sexuality she has just witnessed is not "a world she never made," but a product of her reliance on that father-god. It may have occurred to her, for instance, that if our highest image of spiritual or sexual fulfillment is defined in terms of the parent-infant relationship, then later stages in human development will be seen as degenerations from this ideal. Adult sexuality between equals will seem inherently destructive, unstable, or corrupt in comparison to the purity and stability of parent-child relations, and will be seen as a diversion from a "higher," more spiritual love, generally for some abstraction at the top of an invisible hierarchy. "Love! sweet Love!" as Blake was to complain in "A Little Girl Lost," will be "thought a crime" (E 29).

But it will be a sweet crime nevertheless. While this love destroys its victims, it also showers "fruits and coined gold," and impresses the senses with "honey from every wind" (*Thel* 6:15, 16). It will be, in other words, romantic love, that curious combination of pleasure and pain, guilt and idealism, with its constant identification of Eros with disease, madness, and death, and it will produce "prisoners of sex" who need a dash of guilt to spice their lovemaking, or "star-crossed lovers" who can unite only in death.

Blake fills the "voice of sorrow" with the love-language of Donne, Shakespeare, and the Petrarchan sonneteers to stress the larger cultural and historical implications of Thel's private sorrow. But Renaissance protests against the pathological character of love never take on the exaggerated anxiety we feel in Thel's voice of sorrow. They do not ask "Why a tender curb upon the youthful burning boy?" because they think they know the answer. Lust, sex, even love are diseases of the soul which are inseparable from our nature as fallen beings. This disease can be tolerated, laughed at, even enjoyed because there is a future escape, a disembodied spirit-realm outside the fallen world presided over by a perfectly just and merciful parent. Carefully sublimated sexual love may even lead us up a Platonic ladder to that ideal realm. Thel flees in terror from the world of fallen Eros because that parent with his vague "eternal vales" turns out not to be there, or anywhere else, and because she sees that the belief in this illusory deity was at the root of the problem all along.

But now that this god has disappeared, what is left? That is perhaps another thing Thel has to shriek about. Her Last Judgment is only half over. She has "rejected error," but what truth must she embrace? The image of the way out is clearly before her in the life patterns of her comforters: offering yourself up as food for another, being consumed—and improved—by love, uniting with God as an equal. When stated in this way it becomes clear that the way out is, translated into human terms, the life of Christ.[22] Thel must be willing to give up her Selfhood or ego and construct a new self. She must be willing to offer up her body, literally as fertilizer, symbolically as a Eucharistic sacrifice for others, sexually as a shameless offering to another, and just possibly as a martyr for love or principle. The world in which she must thus offer herself is not the pastoral retreat of "eternal vales," but the "Furnaces of Affliction"—the world, in

[22] The imagery which describes the fulfilled lives of the Lilly, Cloud, and Clod of Clay might best be described as a threefold system of Christological "consummation." First, all the creatures consume or are consumed, literally, as food. The Lilly is "fed with morning manna," a typological prefiguration of the Eucharist (I Corinthians 10:3), and in turn donates her own body to nourish the lambs, recalling Christ's injunction to "feed my lambs . . . feed my sheep" (John 21:15-17). The fact that the Lilly's body is medicinal, curing "all contagious taints" further links her to the tradition of Christ as the "good physician." We might note parenthetically that the reference to "morning manna" may have further significance, given Thel's fear of becoming the "food of worms": when the Israelites tried to hoard manna beyond the morning "it bred worms and stank" (Exodus 16:20). For Thel, the implication is that she will become the "food of worms" one way or another. If she flees from the Worm as a symbol of sexuality or mortality by clinging to her virginity or Selfhood, she will be consumed anyway, by the worms of corruption.

Like the Lilly, the Cloud and Clod of Clay have Eucharistic roles, nourishing other creatures with their bodies. For them, however, the sexual meaning of consummation is most prominent. The Cloud is a bridegroom, the type of Christ in the Song of Solomon, and the matron Clay is linked with the Madonna, a new Eve who is given "a crown that none can take away."

The overriding meaning of all these consummations is the union of the human and the divine. Blake adopts the traditional imagery of food and sexuality as metaphors for God's relation to his creatures, but with an important difference. Traditionally God is the masculine force in the encounter of human and divine, and he is the one who supplies food or other gifts to his passive creatures. Blake subverts this hierarchical concept of consummation by diffusing the divine role among all the creatures of the Vales of Har; God "acts & is" in each one of them, in their relations with their fellow creatures.

other words, of Oothoon, the heroine of *Visions of the Daughters of Albion* who loves without shame and is rewarded with rape, enslavement, and ostracism.

Given these conditions, it is very difficult to judge Thel a coward for returning to the Vales of Har. Her return is, in the first place, quite ambiguous, and could as well be the sign of success as failure. But even if we see Thel's flight as a negation of her search for a meaningful life, it is only the logical extension of several small, almost imperceptible negations which are scarcely distinguishable from the basic human acts of pondering and questioning. Are Thel's questions only a series of evasions which prevent her from growing and learning? Or are they part of a dialogue, and a dialectic, which lead her to the edge of revelation? Has she persisted in folly long enough to become wise? What should be clear, at any rate, is that Blake is not criticizing Thel's use of reason per se: the mistaken assumption she carries with her into the underworld is based in the failure to make a distinction between herself and the infant Worm, and in the failure to understand clearly what the matron Clay is saying. Thel needs to reason better, not give up thinking. Whatever is in the pit, we will need both eagle and mole knowledge to comprehend it.

But the most fundamental reason that we cannot judge Thel a coward for fleeing her grave is that Blake has stripped away all the superior vantage points from which we might pass judgment. The moral structure of the poem is implicitly based on the process of Self-annihilation. Thus only someone who has undergone this process has a right to judge Thel. But anyone who *had* submitted to Self-annihilation would be capable only of forgiving her, not judging. The absence of any finite moral norm in the poem provides the reader with an analogue to Thel's experience of the absence of God. The reader is thus lured into sharing Thel's dilemma vicariously, continuously creating and then discarding the moral systems evoked by the interlaced plots of the poem. Perhaps that is why this simple, transparent little poetic drama has teased generations of readers into some of the most enduring controversies in Blake criticism, and why it will remain, like the Grecian urn it resembles, a "friend to man."

IV. THE ILLUSTRATIONS: STYLE AND STAGING

It should be clear by now that *The Book of Thel*, like most of Blake's poems, is a perfectly adequate, self-sustaining text which does not need the accompanying illustrations to make it a successful work of art. To what extent are the designs similarly self-sufficient? The major illustrations correspond directly and obviously to the important scenes in the poem, so there is very little of the metaphorical "density" we will encounter in the iconography of the later prophetic books. The question is, do the designs have anything of significance for us to *see*, or must we return to the texts to which they refer for meaningful forms?

It seems to me that this question is simply a way of restating the challenge Blake must have felt as soon as he began selecting his subjects for the *Thel* illustrations. The problem was to design a series of plates whose relationship to the text would be unproblematic (in keeping with the poem's ostensible clarity), and yet to give those plates compositional qualities which would in themselves disclose meaning, and not simply send us back to the text. In practical terms, this meant he had to devise strictly visual ways of conveying the rich sense of paradox and ambiguity latent in the apparent clarity of the poem, both in its overall tone and in the specifics of the dramatic unfolding of action.

The style of the *Thel* illustrations is clearly a response to the problem of tone. Art historians have noted that *Thel* reflects many features of the late eighteenth-century classical revival, including an emphasis on pure, sculptural form, a tendency to linear abstraction, and composition which favors balanced, frontal arrangement of figures.[23] But if this were an adequate description of the style of *Thel*, we could scarcely distinguish it from a work by Flaxman. Blake departs from the neoclassical linear style in two important ways: first, and most obviously, he fills his composition with delicate watercolor washes which are more or less independent of the delineated figures; second, the figures themselves are not, as in Flaxman, drawn entirely in clear, spare outlines. Instead, lines frequently thicken into shadows or break off, interrupting the sense of sculptured volume. The method is more like sketching or drawing on copper than sculpting out what Blake called "firm and determinate outline" (*DC*, E 540).

The total effect of this pictorial style is to create a sense of continuity rather than contrast between the elements of line and color. The figures, like Flaxman's, look as if they belong in an archaic bas-relief, but instead of being incised from stone they seem to have

[23] Rosenblum, *Transformations*, Chap. IV, describes this movement in detail, especially in relation to the art of Flaxman.

condensed from the shimmering, incandescent atmosphere which surrounds them. Blake's familiar equation of color and shading with the mutable and "lineaments" with the permanent and eternal need hardly be invoked for us to see that the style of *Thel* embodies a world of evanescence and flux, a world in which the figures probably represent transitory "states of the soul" rather than the permanent "identities" which pass through those states. These "classical" figures are, in other words, not Keats's foster children of "silence and slow time," frozen motionless forever on a Grecian urn, but "children of the spring . . . born but to smile & fall" (*Thel* 1:7).

A second problem Blake had to deal with was one of staging: how to arrange his figures to depict the drama of Thel's dialogues with her comforters, giving some strictly visual sense of their complex and paradoxical relationships. Since the comforters are all presented in human form, their differences from Thel had to be indicated by their placement in the composition rather than by emblematic or representational cues. Blake could have stressed the nonhuman character of Thel's comforters more literally, by blending their human forms with natural ones (see, for instance, the Preludium to *America*, where a torso is visible in the subterranean tree roots, or *Milton* 19, copy D, where a face of stone and a man sprouting branches emerge from the ground). But the Lilly is simply a smaller version of Thel herself, the Cloud a flying youth, and the matron Clay a reclining nude. If we were relying solely on literal representation to give us an idea of Thel's relation to her comforters, the problem of the poem would seem to disappear: Blake depicts them all as "Human Forms identified" (*J* 99:1, E 256), and their mode of being is apparently not essentially different from Thel's.

But compositional features, especially the dynamics of staging and background, tell a more complicated story. The most comprehensive rendition of Thel's relation to her comforters is presented in the title page [37], the one full-page design in the book. Thel is depicted standing apart from a world of exuberant vitality and movement like an archaic Greek statue, her columnlike form harmonizing with the trunk of the willow tree that frames the left border of the design. Her posture is, of course, an utterly conventional contrapposto, but in the context of a work where bodily positions are so consistently symbolic it cannot be dismissed as a mere convention. The position of her body suggests a simultaneous attraction to and withdrawal from the scene at the right, her upper body drawn back while her lower body curves toward the center of the design. This ambivalence renders not only Thel's uncertainty about her relation to the scene of fulfilled love which she beholds, but also her role as a mediator between the viewer and the interior life of the picture. In theatrical terms, she occupies the position of an induction, standing toward the front of the stage, part of the play and yet a detached observer or commentator on the action. The energy and significance of the design thus resides in the tension between Thel's literal closeness to the action and her imaginative, figurative distance from it. Blake reinforces this sense of distance by making the narrow space between Thel and the embracing figures of the Cloud and the Dew a gulf between antithetical kinds of linear form. In the most abstract terms we might map out the composition as the opposition between a vertical and a spiral, with the two compositional ideas connected by the long, gentle curve of the tree which embraces the entire design (see fig. 2). In expressive terms, this opposition can be described as

FIGURE 2.

stasis versus movement, detachment versus involvement, antitheses which reflect the basic nature of Thel's withdrawal from the spontaneous life around her into a passive, ambivalent Selfhood. As in the text, however, Thel's relationship with her world is presented as a paradoxical fusion of identity and alienation. It seems as if she could simply reach out and touch the dynamic figures in the center of the design, as if her difference from them were nothing more fundamental than the difference between the unopened blossom by her knee and the opened blossoms which coil like vegetative flames around the Cloud and Dew. And yet Blake's careful manipulation of depth of field makes Thel's actual distance from the scene and the relative scale of the figures very ambiguous. She could be a considerable distance into the foreground, as the shadow behind her suggests, and any direct sweep of the eye from Thel to the center of the design must cut across lines and traverse empty spaces. The indirect route provided by the arching curve of the tree, on the other hand, is not only uninterrupted, but also resolves the ambiguity of depth by coming into direct contact with the coiled foliage that surrounds the Cloud and Dew. The total effect of the design is to render Thel's alienation from the world of exuberant vitality around her at the same time it indicates essential, if extremely indirect connections between her and that world.

Even Blake's handling of the typography of the title page seems calculated to reflect this relationship. Thel's name is written in block letters (cf. the letters of the title page of *The Marriage of Heaven and Hell* [8]), which look, in copy O, like pillars overgrown with moss. The coiling vines and the naked human figures (whose activities range from the passive reading of the "angel" seated on the L to climbing, leaping, and even flying) are antithetical to the typography of Thel's name in the same way that the figures of the Cloud and the Dew are antithetical to the figure of Thel. The opposition between rectilinear and curvilinear becomes, in this portion of the design, the juxtaposition of symbolic, abstract, artificial forms with representational, concrete, natural or living forms—one is tempted to call it a juxtaposition of the letter and some spirits! The formal purposiveness of Blake's typography is demonstrated by his choice of a completely different style on the same page for the word "Book," printed in slanted letters which harmonize rather than contrast with the vegetative forms around them. The contrast between the two styles of lettering may be seen as a charmingly literal way for Blake to tell us that even if Thel is incapable of resolving the dualities of experience, the "Book" which tells her story may contain an implicit resolution.

The possibility that Thel is not inevitably condemned to the sterile abstractness embodied in the lettering of her name is indicated on the first page of the text [38], where Blake writes her down in vibrant script letters that not only harmonize with vegetative forms (as the word "Book" does) but even *become* those forms. Again we find her name surrounded by human figures engaged in a complete range of activities from repose to flight, this time with an additional overtone of aggressiveness suggested by the figure pursuing the eagle (or hawking?) at the left, and the warrior at the right. The activities of war and hunting are, for Blake, deeply ambivalent. As metaphors for search and struggle in the realms of imagination, they can be seen as images of the "Mental Warfare" of eternity ("the two Sources of Life in Eternity, Hunting and War"; *J* 43:41). They can also become symbols, however, of "Corporeal Warfare," the battle of the sexes, or the war between soul and body—the situation described in *Thel* by the "voice of sorrow," which sees the body as an armed camp "Where a thousand fighting men in ambush lie" (6:14). We should note, however, that Blake balances these militant images with figures of innocent love just below Thel's name, and then frames the scene, as he did the title page, in the gaze of the detached observer reclining on the leaf below. This figure is presented in what we might call the posture of the "awakening Adam" (cf. *MHH* 21 and the naked figure above Death's Door in the engraving for Blair's *Grave* [88]), which Blake probably borrowed from engravings after Michelangelo's Sistine ceiling. This Adam's emergence from unconscious vegetative life is depicted as an encounter with contrary images of love and aggression, Innocence and Experience, the contraries that Thel leaves unresolved. As an Adam figure, Thel (so far as we know) never goes beyond a vision of human fulfillment as merely a state of innocence and infantile dependency. The observing figure in this design, on the other hand, is not detached compositionally from the curvilinear forms he observes, and thus this design, like the emblem of the children riding the serpent, may suggest a resolution for her dilemma.

If the title page presents a comprehensive view of Thel's relation to her comforters, stressing her essential alienation from them even as it hints at circuitous connections, the remaining plates dramatize her attempt to step directly into the world of her comforters, and thus stress not her alienation but her close similarity to them. In spite of Thel's sense that she is unlike any other creature in the Vales of Har, the comforters all serve as metaphors for her condition: the Lilly is an emblem of her virginity, she is explicitly compared to "a faint cloud kindled at the rising sun" (2:11), and like the matron Clay, she may be the "food of worms" (3:23). Her role as virgin is most clearly analogous to that of the Lilly, and so the illustration of their dialogue [39] shows them in very similar poses. The static verticality of Thel's pose on the title page is modulated into a gentle S-curve which imitates the curtsey of the Lilly. For the moment of the design, both figures seem like delicate humanized flowers, the rumpled drapery of their skirts harmonizing with the coiled vegetation on the ground. Blake employs a similar kind of visual "rhyming" when he makes Thel's gesture of astonishment over the worm at her feet a cruciform posture analogous to the pose of the departing Cloud [40]. Her gown is pressed against her body to make it seem as if she is gently pushed toward the left by the same breeze that carries the Cloud. Finally, in the illustration of Thel's interview with the Clod of Clay and the Worm [41] her posture becomes contracted and her garments are spread out flat to blend her figure with the ground. Proportions are altered, and the flowers and leaves which formerly curled at Thel's feet now bend over her, as if she had shrunk in scale in order to converse with the lowliest creatures. Viewed as a unified series, the three designs present the human figure in postures of moderate expansion, full expansion, and contraction, a sequence of images that Blake may have recalled when he wrote the following passage in *Jerusalem*:

> Let the Human Organs be kept in their perfect Integrity
> At will Contracting into Worms, or Expanding into Gods
> . . . for tho we sit down within
> The plowed furrow. listning to the weeping clods till we
> Contract or Expand Space at will: or if we raise ourselves
> Upon the chariots of the morning. Contracting or Expanding Time!
> Every one knows, we are One Family: One Man blessed for ever (*J* 55:36-37, 42-46; E 202)

Thel, of course, lacks precisely that very difficult "will"[24] which recognizes the flexible nature of perception. She is looking instead for an escape from this kind of freedom, and would prefer to be like just *one* of her comforters, with her nature and destiny mapped out for her. To be human in Blake's universe, however, is to contain all possibilities, and so whenever Thel denies her likeness to any one of her comforters, she simultaneously affirms her likeness to some other creature in the Vales of Har. She is not like the Lilly because she is "like a faint cloud"; she is not like the Cloud because like the

[24] Thel's name may be derived from the Greek word for "will" or "wish." One is tempted to see her book, then, as the first in a series of psychological prophecies which includes a book of reason (*Urizen*) and a book of imagination (*Los*). Peter Fisher develops the "will" theme very interestingly in his *Valley of Vision*, ed. Northrop Frye (Toronto, 1961).

Clay she may be the "food of worms." She is not like any particular creature, in other words, because she, with her ambivalent gift of self-consciousness, reflects the nature of her entire cosmos, "Like a reflection in a glass. like shadows in the water" (1:9).

Thel's decision to enter the grave of experience occurs only after she has contracted her perspective sufficiently to identify herself with the Worm, an image of man as helpless, dependent infant. But this contraction of her imagination violates the "perfect integrity" and flexibility of consciousness when it becomes a permanent escape from human nature rather than a restful preparatory phase before the "Mental Warfare" of imaginative existence ("Rest before Labour"). We must note, however, that Blake does not depict this regressive attitude visually, as he did in the previous plates, by making Thel's pose resemble the particular creature whose perspective she is adopting. Instead of showing Thel becoming like a tiny infant form, he presents her as a mother figure, her crouched posture and draped garments providing a protective enclosure around the naked bodies of the matron Clay and the infant Worm. The composition is strongly reminiscent of a nativity scene with Thel as Madonna, the Worm-infant as Jesus, and the naked figure of earth as John the Baptist. It is, to be sure, not the typical treatment of the Virgin with child on her lap or in a cradle, but an echo of a somewhat more specialized theme, the *adoration* of the infant Jesus [see 42, 43].[25] This allusion becomes highly ambiguous and ironic in the context of *The Book of Thel.* The cruciform pose of the infant could suggest an image of potential awakening for Thel, a hint that "God is in the lowest effects as well as in the highest causes for he is become a worm that he may nourish the weak" (Annotations to Lavater, E 589). On the other hand, Thel's worshipful pose and her attitude of self-clutching contraction suggest that this image may be lost on her. Her identification with the Madonna may be a sign not that she wishes to care for the Worm-infant like the matron Clay, but that she wishes to preserve her virginity. This possibility is enhanced by the contrast between Thel's heavy clothing and the nakedness of the worm's real mother. Her adoration of the infant, then, is not a

[25] Blake would have known this theme as a fairly common one in Christian iconography, if not from Francia's treatment [42], then perhaps from Raphael or Dürer [43]. The textual sources and pictorial history of the theme of adoring the infant are traced in meticulous detail by Gertrud Schiller in *Iconography of Christian Art*, 2 vols. (Greenwich, Conn., 1971), I, 77-85.

recognition of its divinity, but a desire to *be* the worm, to be cherished and nourished passively rather than to "nourish the weak."

The text, in other words, stresses Thel's infantilism directly, while the illustration makes the same point indirectly through the image of adoring maternalism. Perhaps Blake is suggesting that these roles are interdependent (overprotective mothers *need* dependent children, and vice versa), or even manifestations of a single regressive psychic formation. In any event, Thel's position in this plate was, like her S-curve curtsey and cruciform gesture, a crucial "seed-image" in Blake's developing iconography. The crouching, contracted figure with heavy garments obscuring the lineaments of the body was to become Blake's consistent emblem of parentalism, especially in the figures of Vala and Urizen. Thel's posture is thus an omen of what her sympathies will become if they serve as a refuge from existence. The infant Worm, "image of weakness," will grow into the "burning boy," a phallic Orc-serpent who will be at war with woman, and who will thus have to be repressed even more subtly, perhaps by a "tender curb" like the bridle in the hands of the demure virgin who rides the serpent on the final plate [44].[26]

The background of the design illustrating Thel's dialogue with the matron Clay and the Worm reflects the ominous lineaments of her form. The stems of the flowers are no longer coiled with resilient energy as they were in the earlier designs, but are weighted down by their overripe blossoms, producing a series of rounded arching forms which echo the curve of Thel's form and anticipate Blake's consistent portrayal of Urizen in settings involving the barrel arch, the gravestone, and the tablets of the law. The obscuring of Thel's form by her garments is also reflected in the setting by an increasing obfuscation of outline by color.[27] It is not simply that the color is

[26] An ironic premonition of the conflict between the Worm and Thel is her allusion to the peace between them which is imposed by the deity of the Vales of Har. Whoever "bruises the helpless form" of the worm is punished by this deity. In the state of fallen Experience, on the other hand, the deity puts enmity between the woman and the serpent, compelling it to bruise her heel while she bruises its head, a symbolic version of the sexual warfare which Thel finds in her grave. The phallic quality of the serpent tailpiece becomes clearer if this emblem is compared, as Hagstrum suggests, with the Priapian symbol of cupid astride a phallus, a figure which appeared in *Le Antichita di Ercolano Esposte* (Naples, 1757). See Hagstrum, *Poet and Painter*, p. 89 and pl. XLIXA.

[27] These remarks are based on copy O, and would have to be qualified in other copies. In copies N and I, for instance, the emergence of complex color

darker than in the previous plates, but that the whole system of color relationships has become more complex and ambivalent. In the first four plates translucent zones of primary watercolors lend a certain incandescence to the space of the design, but in this plate the primaries are replaced by intermediate hues. Moreover, color assumes a life not simply independent of but antagonistic to form in this plate. The streaked blue and brown shadows in the foreground bear no relation to a rational light source. The dark yellow area along the horizon conforms to no imaginable topography. The stems of the plants bear black streaks which we might conjecture to be caterpillars, but which nevertheless remain simply areas of color which interrupt linearity. Thel's descent into a perspective of contracted opacity is thus embodied not only in the crouched posture of her body and its obscuring garments, but also in the structure and atmosphere of her setting.

The backgrounds of the other designs similarly reinforce the drama of Thel's exploration of perspectives. The tree which frames the composition of the title page, for instance, is systematically altered to reflect the stages of Thel's search. On the title page she seems to be staying close to it as if it were a guarantee of security, a fixed point in the world of flux which surrounds her. Like the protective arbors of *Songs of Innocence*, it embraces the scene, creating a secure enclosure. As Thel's pictorial drama unfolds, however, she not only moves away from the tree, but the tree itself begins to look bare and sere like the trees in *Songs of Experience*. By plate 5 [41] it has almost completely disappeared, except perhaps for the dark hint of a trunk on the left side of the picture. The framing, enclosing function of the tree is taken over in this plate by the bowed arches of vegetation.

Thel's progress through the three "interior" designs of the book, then, could be described as a movement from a protective, closed space, to an open, expansive space, to a new, more sinister kind of closed space. The placement of the designs in relation to the text reinforces this sense of a closed-open-closed squence, the two "closed" designs placed beneath the text, the "open" one above.

Thel, like the other children of the spring in the Vales of Har, is "born but to smile & fall," opening and closing like the flowers around her. But she, unlike the other creatures, must *will* the meaning

effects and cloudy, opaque backgrounds begins in Thel's encounter with the Lilly and the Cloud.

of that natural cycle rather than passively receive it. Thel's attitude of abstracted passivity, manifested either as an exaggerated alienation from nature or, contrarily, as a wish to substitute the unselfconsciousness of nature for "Mental Warfare," transforms the dialectics of nature (life and death, sexuality) into the "Corporeal Warfare" of mutually destructive "Negations"—life against death, the battle of the sexes. The title page depicts the courting dance of the Cloud and Dew as a whirling vortex of pleasure, but to Thel's Selfhood the erotic awakening of the senses is inseparable from the threat of annihilation, and so she sees only "a whirlpool fierce to draw creations in" (6:17). In the precariously balanced world of the Vales of Har, Thel's connection with the vortex of nature is still maintained by the protective willow tree, symbol of paradisal innocence. Like the children in Wordsworth's *Lyrical Ballads*, her connections with nature have not yet been broken. In the world of Experience, however, the bond is broken, and the vortex may appear without mediating links to more stable forms, as in the illustration of Dante and Virgil observing the fate of sexual offenders in *The Inferno* [36]. Like Thel, Dante and Virgil stand at the edge of a whirlpool which seems to threaten and beckon simultaneously, but there is no compositional bridge between their statuesque detachment and the whirling forms they observe. The design displays the human form in attitudes of absolute opposition, a vision of the world of Experience where man is divided from himself and others. The fact that the victims in this whirlpool, Jacopo Rusticucci and his comrades, were sexual offenders, must have reminded Blake of his early vision of the sexual union of the Cloud and the Dew, and strengthened his conviction of the internal consistency of his visions.

The rich interrelations between the poetic and pictorial symbolic systems of *The Book of Thel* extend even to the minutest particulars, such as the vines which coil around the margins. Thel's movement away from the tree to a momentary posture of maximum expansion in plate 5 is echoed by the vine behind her, which seems also to be casting itself off from the tree, just as in the title page her attachment to the tree is paralleled by the vine clinging to it. The vine is, of course, a pictorial and metaphoric relative of both the serpent and the worm, and it participates in the same world of symbolic ambivalence. The vine of the pastoral realm may grow into the "vegetable world" of Experience, "where the fibrous roots/ Of every heart on earth infixes deep its restless twists" (6:3-4), or it can be the "true vine," an image of Christ. Similarly, the worm symbolizes both birth and death, and metamorphoses into a serpent which can symbolize either Satan or Christ.

The most trivial details of text and design, then, even as they embody the harmonious innocence of the Vales of Har, divulge subtle tensions which threaten to become the polarized divisions of Experience. The language of the poem unfolds images of a paradoxical harmony between life and death, time and eternity, and yet mediates these images through a perspective which sees life as antithetical to death, time as the ruins of eternity. The illustrations similarly depict a world of essential continuity between human and natural images, a world where the lineaments of permanence and identity flow into the color, light, and shade of change and mutability. And yet the choreography of the human figures reveals a tension between the natural and the human which achieves only a very ambiguous resolution in the emblem of the children astride a serpent, and the harmonious continuity of outline and color, figure and drapery is complicated in the closing plates by the presence of heavy, obscuring drapery and the blots and blurs which disrupt linearity.

Finally, the total form of *The Book of Thel* involves the placing of clear, direct relationships between text and design in a context of obscure and indirect relationships. The internal drama of Thel's passage from psychological unity to division is thus embodied in the elements of the mediums in which it is presented, and the reader's imagination is subjected to an initiation analogous to the one he observes. The form of the illuminated book leads us, in other words, to experience our own versions of the paradox and ambivalence which torment Thel. We are continuously tempted to judge Thel's actions and form a moral for her story, and yet both text and design subvert any moral stance we adopt. We are similarly invited to take the apparent clarity and simplicity of the book as an index of its intellectual complexity, and yet this simple little artifact continues to tease us into thought, forcing us to ponder issues which may ultimately defy all pondering.

One thing seems clear: *Thel* is the kind of work of art which propels us far beyond a relaxed contemplation of its formal artistry. The themes and images of this book lead us, as they obviously led Blake, beyond the world of pastoral simplicity and ideal unity with nature, toward the epic of human nature, the earth from which Thel flees, and on which we must dwell.

Chapter Four

THE HUMAN ILLUSION

Poetic and Pictorial Design in *The Book of Urizen*

I. THE VOID OUTSIDE EXISTENCE: *URIZEN* AND THE PROPHECIES OF THE LAMBETH PERIOD

BLAKE continued in the early 1790s to descend into the "hollow pit" in order to contemplate the dangerous world from which Thel fled. The *Songs of Experience* and the Lambeth books are all explorations of a world of slavery, warfare, and the more subtle terrors of "mind-forg'd manacles." But these works are not mere catalogues of contemporary outrages. There is a steady pressure in Blake's art to seek an explanation for the nightmare of history, and to envision an awakening from it. This pressure for resolution is disclosed most explicitly in *The Marriage of Heaven and Hell* with its continuous affirmation of the possibilty of transformation, and in the endings of the political prophecies, *America*, *Europe*, and *The Song of Los*, all of which promise an imminent end to the era of empire and priesthood. In the later Lambeth books (*Urizen*, *Ahania*, and *The Book of Los*), however, Blake seems to be moving into a new thematic and stylistic period, characterized superficially by increasing irony and pessimism and by poetic forms which end not with a promise of resolution but with a note of apparent despair. At the end of *The Book of Los*, the work of Los (and Blake) is summarized:

> . . . a Form
> Was completed, a Human Illusion
> In darkness and deep clouds involvd.
> (5:55-57, E 94)

This is not the first time that Blake has seemed to step outside of his work and find it less than good. In the Preludium to *America* the Bard is "asham'd of his own song" and smashes his harp; the

Bard's call to the Earth to awake from slumber in the "Introduction" to *Experience* is heard by the Earth as the voice of "the Father of the ancient men/ Selfish father of men/ Cruel jealous selfish fear." Before we take these self-critical ironies too literally, however, it might be well to put them in context. For Thel the exploration of the underworld means facing a world of corrupted sexuality; for the artist it means confronting a world of corrupted creativity and facing the possibility of misunderstanding and meaninglessness. The nightmare cannot be understood or dispelled from outside; it must be entered into and internalized.

The image which Blake consistently associates with this nightmare is the void or indefinite abyss, and the work of the artist is to fill it with substance and form, even if it is only a "Human Illusion." In order to render this world Blake moves beyond the topical, historical framework of the political prophecies and into the realm of myth, a movement which can be seen even in the political prophecies as a steady expansion of frame of reference: *America* deals with the events surrounding the American Revolution; *Europe* places contemporary revolutions in a context of 1,800 years, beginning with the birth of a "secret child" in the year one; *The Song of Los* goes all the way back to Adam. *Urizen*, then, is the logical culmination of the developmental process disclosed in the political prophecies, moving completely into the realm of myth, pushing back to the very origins of time and space, when "Earth was not: nor globes of attraction" (3:36, E 70).

Blake's movement toward a more cosmic perspective in his poetry is accompanied by the increasing elimination of orienting contexts in his pictures, and—what might be seen as a contradiction of his larger temporal scope—an intensification and narrowing of pictorial perspective. Probably the most distinctive feature of the late Lambeth books is the monolithic quality of the compositions: there are fewer groups of figures, and the isolated human figure tends to appear in rigidly frontal, symmetrical poses. Iconographical content is drastically simplified, with an absolute minimum of "literary" devices such as emblematic attributes, narrative sequence, and allusions to contemporary history. If Blake was a topical satirist, a "Gillray of the infinite" in the political prophecies, he is now more like a Michelangelo of the infinite, saying everything with the human form in a simplified background.

Many of the tormented, crouching figures of *Urizen* can be found in earlier books, of course, but there they are surrounded by more open settings and are not presented in isolation. The figures falling into the flaming abyss of *America* 5 [35] are balanced and explained by the figures on the clouds above; *Urizen* 6 [54] shows us only the falling figures, leaving unexplained why or from whence their fall takes place. The crouched, subterranean figure of *America* 1 is seen in relation to a scene above the ground; no such perspective is provided on the figures buried alive in *Urizen* (see plates 9 [62] and 10 [63]; cf. *BL* 2). The figure in chains in *Europe* 13 [65] seems to be crying for pity to the departing jailer; the chained figures in *Urizen* 11 [64] and 22 [78] have no one to appeal to. In *Urizen* Blake has "zoomed in" on the tormented figures that appeared in his earlier books, concentrating his vision and eliminating the relief provided by a larger perspective. The emotional atmosphere of the *Urizen* illustrations is one of absolute isolation, cut off from all normal reality in a claustrophobic enclosure or adrift in a bottomless void. Plates which do show more than one human figure tend to show these figures isolated from one another or united only by their common anguish. Fear, pain, and sorrow are presented in *Urizen* as radical conditions of the human soul, not as states which are caused by or related to other conditions. The effect of this pictorial strategy is to place the human figure in a void like that described in the poem, a space that has no perceivable boundaries (other than the picture frame), and no relationships or orientations beyond itself. Blake depicts the void not literally, as a vast inner space receding toward a vanishing point, but metaphorically and sensuously, by allowing us to experience the vertigo, disorientation, and isolation of the figures that inhabit his pictures.

This stylistic congruence between text and design in *Urizen* is not accompanied, as it was in *Thel*, by clear and direct illustrative or iconographic relationships. The fact that both text and design have been rendered in such abstract, schematic modes tends to multiply the number of possible intersections between them. Every character in the poem acts like Urizen at one time or another, and Urizen insists on playing all the roles imaginable in a cosmogony. Hence the identification of figures is often problematic, and the assignment of a design to a particular episode in the narrative is frequently impossible. It seems clear, moreover, that the pictorial dimension asserts a more vigorous independence in *Urizen*: ten plates out of the twenty-eight have no text at all, whereas there are no plates without some pictorial elements, and about seventy percent of the total space on the copper plates is devoted to pictorial expression, far more than in any other illuminated book. Blake's pictorial invention seems to leap ahead of his poetic capability, the text of *Urizen* seeming more like a sketch or outline of a longer poem which will expand between and beyond the lines of the present one. The designs, on the other hand, are all fully realized, and Blake did not find words adequate for some of them until he wrote *The Four Zoas.*

But the most notable feature in the physical relationship of text and design in *Urizen* is the absence of the free interpenetration of poem and picture which characterized the earlier Lambeth books. Blake now tends to divide his plate into distinct areas of text and design, interlinear and marginal decoration is less adventurous, less likely to sprout into a coherent scene, and the text is no longer placed within a pictorial context. The earlier Lambeth books placed the text on a cloud, a wall, amid flames, under a sea, or surrounded the text with pictorial forms in some way. In *Urizen* the only concessions to pictorial form in the textual area are tiny interlinear forms of vegetation, punctuated by occasional animal and human forms, but these forms are generally not connected to the larger scene on the plate, and their shapes are bent to accommodate the text rather than a pictorial scene.

This increasing separation of textual and pictorial space is heightened by the subdivision of the text into two columns, a procedure which Blake employs only in *Urizen*, *Ahania*, and *The Book of Los.* This format may be dictated partly by Blake's adoption of a shorter three- or four-stress line in the late Lambeth books, but it seems to be partly a matter of visual design as well. Blake employed the single-column arrangement in *The Song of Los* even with the shorter line, and achieved a corresponding freedom of interpenetration of picture and text (see [45]). The two-column format leaves less room for this kind of interpenetration, and when it is coupled with the introduction of chapter and verse numbers in the text (which appear for the first time in the late Lambeth books), it gives the inescapable impression that Blake is trying to keep his two forms more distinct at a basic sensuous level, emphasizing the text as a strictly verbal, nonpictorial form and reducing the "literary" elements in his designs to a minimum. Considered as a total symbolic presentation, then, *Urizen* is designed with many more dividing, compartmentalizing elements than we find in the earlier Lambeth books. Iconographical relationships are more attenuated and problematic, and the physical structure of the page appears as a grid with vertical and horizontal dividing lines. Certainly this seems an appropriate style for telling Urizen's story, an account in nine chapters of how "times on times he divided. & measur'd/ Space by space in his ninefold darkness" (3:8-9, E 69). It is notable that the one plate on which the text is *not* divided into two columns (the Preludium plate [48] with its statement of theme and invocation to the muses) is also the only plate where text interpenetrates design (vegetative flames burst out from the letters to fill the bottom half of the plate) and the only plate where human figures make positive contact (the woman touches the child at the top of the plate). All this suggests that the physical relationship of text and design is a metaphor for other relationships—or lack of relationships—within the poetic and pictorial forms which comprise *Urizen*. To substantiate this hypothesis, however, we must first investigate the constituent forms in themselves more extensively.

II. WIT, HUMOR, AND REVOLUTIONARY EPIC

Readers who love Blake for the *Songs* and *The Marriage of Heaven and Hell* may wonder where the humor and tenderness of those works have gone. Blake's movement away from epigrammatic wit and lyric immediacy into the rarefied atmosphere of cosmology and sacred history was clearly a risk in several senses. First, it involved the possibility of losing touch with his audience, however small. It is one thing to issue a tongue-in-cheek declaration that "the cherub with his flaming sword is hereby commanded to leave his guard at [the] tree of life" (*MHH* 14, E 38) so that mankind may reenter paradise. It is another thing to sing solemnly "Of the primeval Priests assum'd power" (*U* 2:1, E 69). The increasingly high seriousness of Blake's tone, his obsession with grand mythical patterning, risked a loss of touch with history and a flight into sublime egotism which, unlike Wordsworth's, is not tempered by any apparent acknowledgment of personal limitations.

But the more closely one examines the late Lambeth books, the more evident it becomes that Blake has not taken leave of wit or humor but has simply shaped them to the demands of a new poetic form. The terse wit of the "Proverbs of Hell" is now occupied with the development of a new verbal form, a line of "epic wit" which creates complex textures of ambiguity, paradox, and typological condensation from the materials of the Christian epic. We tend to think of the line of wit as the "other tradition" in English poetry, somehow alien to the sublime aspirations of Milton, Spenser, and the Romantic poets. But the epic, prophetic strain, as Blake understood it, is a tradition of continuous revolution: Dante must surpass Virgil and Milton must soar above the Aonian Mount. One of the chief methods for accomplishing this continuous regeneration of epic form and values is the witty adaptation of conventions, machinery, and diction to new contexts. For Blake this new context is the epic of consciousness which supersedes and absorbs the epic of empire, personal quest, and providence.

Let us examine a "Minute Particular." When Milton describes the Holy Spirit "with mighty wings outspread/ Dove-like . . . brooding on the vast Abyss" (*Paradise Lost* I: 20-21),[1] we must read "brooding" primarily in terms of its immediate context: the Holy Spirit is incubating or fertilizing the abyss. The other sense of "brooding," having to do with solitary, introspective intellectual activity, is suppressed by the context. When Blake describes Urizen as "unknown, abstracted/ Brooding secret" (3:6-7, E 69) and "unprolific!/ Self-closd, all-repelling" (3:2-3), our primary reading of the word is in its mental, introspective sense. But what happens to our reading of the word when we go on to find that Urizen's solitude is immediately populated "with shapes/ Bred from his forsaken wilderness" (3:14-15)? Urizen's "unprolific" solipsism, his uncreative brooding, immediately "breeds" a world of "beast, bird, fish, serpent & element" (3:16). We are confronted, not just with a pun, but with a one-word oxymoron: "brooding" has been defined by its immediate context as both a prolific, creative activity and an unprolific, destructive force. Urizen's "brooding," moreover, evokes both the divine and demonic contexts of *Paradise Lost*: Urizen is Father (law giver), Son (creator of form), and Holy Spirit (fertilizing agent), but he is also their demonic parodies, Satan, Sin, and Death (see especially the description of Sin, "With terrors and with clamors compasst round/ Of mine own brood"; *PL* II-861-62). If Milton subverted the classical epic by giving Satan the martial virtues of Achilles and Ulysses (courage and cunning), Blake subverts the Christian epic by giving his Satanic figure the attributes of Milton's deity. It begins to look as if there is more than one way of marrying heaven and hell, that the nuptials may occur in epic as well as satiric form.

But Blake's wit is not applied exclusively to the task of ironically overturning the values of his Miltonic model; the irony is also directed at himself. The potential egotism and megalomania of the

[1] Text quoted here and below is that of *Milton: Poetical Works*, ed. Douglas Bush (London, 1966).

prophetic, bardic role is continually tempered by Blake's portrait of the artist as Los, a self-portrait which sees the "Eternal Prophet" not as a self-assured cosmic spectator, but as a tormented figure, afflicted by internal divisions and fettered with a "Chain of Jealousy" (see *Urizen*, Chap. VII). Even Urizen is conceived to some extent as a self-portrait. Blake depicts him in the political prophecies mainly as "Priest & King," caricaturing him in *Europe* 11 [26] as a composite figure of the Pope and George III. In the title page of *Urizen* [46], however, we see a portrait of Urizen as Blake himself, the isolated creator of books writing his poems with one hand and illustrating them with the other.[2] Urizen's sublime egotism, his isolation, his attempt to see the whole universe as subject to "one Law," and his production of mysterious books full of the "secrets of dark contemplation" (4:26, E 71) must have been for Blake a constant reminder of what could become of the role of prophet and sublime allegorist. This element of self-satire is Blake's way of moderating and humanizing the godlike point of view he must adopt to write a poem like *Urizen*, and it points to one of the more interesting aspects of his development. In spite of the fact that *Urizen* is more cosmic and epic in scope than the political prophecies, it is also more personal, and begins the process by which Blake will connect his vision of an entire universe to his own particular grain of sand: "I write in South Molton Street, what I both see and hear/ In regions of Humanity" (*J* 34:42-43, E 178).

If Blake's wit has been sublimated in *Urizen* in elaborate subver-

[2] I am less confident now about identifying Urizen's writing tools as a quill pen and burin or other engraving tool than I was in my essay "Poetic and Pictorial Imagination in Blake's *The Book of Urizen*," *Eighteenth-Century Studies* III (Fall 1969), 84. (See Erdman, *TIB*, p. 183, who accepts this identification but does not clarify which hand holds which tool in which copies.) A clearer detail is the different grip which Urizen uses on each tool, his left hand coiled in a thumb-forefinger writing grip, his right hand lying flat on the tablet, perhaps resting or sketching and shading the composition. While these details remain uncertain, the basic point is clear: Blake is trying to convey the reduction of distinct activities to a symmetrical similitude, and satirizing the literal implications of allowing "one Law" to govern two different art forms, the programme of *ut pictura poesis*. An even more compelling reading of the picture is provided by Leslie Tannenbaum, who sees Urizen as God the Father writing the names of the saved and the damned at the Last Judgment. ("Blake's Art of Crypsis: *The Book of Urizen* and Genesis," *Blake Studies* V [Fall 1972], 161). This interpretation heightens the sense of the design as a self-portrait, an image of the trap an apocalyptic artist must avoid. For further discussion of this design see Morris Eaves, "The Title-page of *The Book of Urizen*," in *Essays for Damon*, ed. Rosenfeld, pp. 225-30.

sions of the Christian epic and in the ironic treatment of both self and history, his humor must be seen as displaced into the realm of possibility. The last lines he engraved in the Lambeth books evaluate his own achievement as a prophetic artist by 1795: "a Form/ Was completed, a Human Illusion/ In darkness and deep clouds involvd" (*BL* 5:55–57). Some critics have read this as an expression of Blake's pessimism and nihilism in the mid-1790s, his way of saying that human life is invariably a nightmare of compulsively repeated mistakes.[3] If so, one wonders what the point was in calling it an illusion. The word inevitably evokes its contrary, pointing to the possibility of creating a "real" human form, perhaps *by means of* as well as in spite of the prevalence of illusion. Blake may have had no clear idea in 1795 of how this form was to be created, but it exists in the works of that period, as it did in *The Book of Thel*, as an implicit imperative, a direction or faith continually suggested by the experimental, open-ended quality of the Lambeth books and by the continual emergence of "pangs of hope" (*U* 11:19, E 75) in the most dismal episodes. The commitment to write a "Bible of Hell" entailed a promise not just to subvert Milton and the Bible and prove that creation never should have happened, but to discover a new ethical and cosmic scheme in which a comic resolution to history might be envisioned.

III. TRANSVALUING VALUES: THE PARODY OF MILTON

Blake's movement toward a more comprehensive vision is implied in the very form of the Preludium to *Urizen*, which, for the first time in his illuminated books, employs the epic formula for statement of theme and invocation of the muses:

> Of the primeval Priests assum'd power,
> When Eternals spurn'd back his religion;
> And gave him a place in the north,
> Obscure, shadowy, void, solitary.
>
> Eternals I hear your call gladly,
> Dictate swift winged words, & fear not
> To unfold your dark visions of torment.
> (2:1-7, E 69)

[3] See Anne Kostelanetz Mellor, *Blake's Human Form Divine* (Berkeley, 1974), p. 100. For a more detailed critique of this argument see my review of Mellor in *Blake Newsletter* VII: 4, no. 32 (Spring 1975), 117-19.

This opening seems to promise a poem structured around moral antagonisms like those which inform *Paradise Lost* and Genesis: the "primeval Priest" has taken over Satan's role as the "prime evil," acting as a rebellious usurper who upsets the eternal order, and the Eternals play the role of God as judge and punisher, spurning the rebel and casting him into a dark, lonely prison. The Eternals also serve, like the Holy Spirit of *Paradise Lost*, as the muses, dictating the verse ("swift winged words") and the illustrations ("dark visions of torment") which are to follow. The Preludium invites us to expect a rather simple parody which mirrors and inverts the roles and values of *Paradise Lost*, Blake reading black where Milton reads white, and Los (like Milton's Adam) caught in between.

Readers have always been disturbed, however, that the Preludium gives a somewhat misleading picture of what will happen in the poem. Sloss and Wallis point out, for instance, that "though the Eternals inspire Blake's prophecy, it is to be noted that the myth does not represent them as a beneficent providence."[4] There are vague hints even in the Preludium that all is not perfection with the Eternals. If Blake thought of them as traditional muses who comfort and enlighten the poet, why would he have to comfort and reassure them in his invocation, telling them to "fear not" to unfold their "visions of torment"? What do they have to fear, and whose torment do they see? Is it Urizen's tormented isolation or their own?

When we proceed into the poem with these questions in mind, no clear answers emerge. The Eternals seem to be trying to act, if not like a "beneficent providence," at least like an unfallen remnant of the prelapsarian condition. All their efforts are directed at avoiding any contact with the detestable "shadow of horror," Urizen. First, they delegate Los "to confine/ The obscure separation alone" (5:39-40, E 72), and stand as "wide apart" from Urizen's world "As the stars are apart from the earth" (5:41-6:1, E 72). Then, as Los begins to be entangled in Urizen's world, they abandon him as well: " 'Spread a Tent, with strong curtains around them/ Let cords & stakes bind in the Void/ That Eternals may no more behold them' " (19:2-4, E 77). It is very difficult to know what to make of these actions, whether to see them as attempts to preserve a last bastion of the original visionary perfection, or as frightened reactions which do nothing to heal the "wrenching apart" of the eternal order, and which may even worsen the schism by ratifying and imitating Urizen's initial act of withdrawal. Certainly there is something absurd about having Los "confine/ The obscure separation alone," since

[4] *Prophetic Writings*, I, 86.

Urizen has already done this to himself, first enclosing himself in "self-clos'd, all-repelling" solitude, and then, when the Eternals reject his laws, fleeing and enclosing himself in "a womb . . . like a black globe" (5:30-34, E 72). The desertion of Los by the Eternals and their erection of the "Tent of Science" have a similarly ambiguous quality. Perhaps Los is at fault for having succumbed to pity for Urizen, but he has already been sickened by the task the Eternals have imposed on him and has "suffer'd his fires to decay" (13:44, E 76) before he falls into the trap of pity. And the creation of a Tent of Science which will prevent any intercourse between the fallen and unfallen world is a curious way of dealing with Urizen's abuse of rationalism. When Urizen becomes disenchanted with his creations, he acts in a way suspiciously similar to the Eternals, wandering "on high" over the cities of the world, covering them over with the Net of Religion (see Chap. VIII). The ultimate result of the two actions is the same: when the Eternals finish the Tent of Science, "No more Los beheld Eternity" (20:2); after Urizen spreads the Net of Religion, mankind shrinks up from existence and its members "forgot their eternal life" (27:42).

I am not arguing that there is no moral distinction to be made between the activities of Urizen and those of the Eternals, but that this distinction is not reducible to absolute good versus absolute evil. It seems clear that while Blake has inverted the roles of *Paradise Lost*, he has not simply inverted the *values* which Milton associated with those roles. The Eternals are not treated as a benign, just, merciful Providence;[5] and Urizen's "crime" of seeking "a joy without pain,/ . . . a solid without fluctuation" (4:11-12) may be mistaken or misguided, but it can hardly be equated with the self-conscious malice, ingratitude, and hypocrisy that Milton attributes to Satan. Urizen's attempt to impose "one Law" on existence, like Thel's attempt to

[5] The closest the Eternals ever come to playing this role in Blake's poetry is in *The Four Zoas*, where they make up a "Divine Council" or "Great Solemn Assembly" that deputizes the "Seven Eyes of God" to enter into and redeem human history. The first six "Eyes" fail to provide humanity with insight because they insist on behaving like wrathful, jealous, bloodthirsty gods. The Seventh Eye, Jesus, is more successful, but even his message is immediately absorbed into mystery religion and holy war. In *Milton* Blake satirizes the detachment of the Eternals from history and makes the central redemptive act Milton's rejection of their false heavens and his return to earth. The Eternals then coalesce into a multitude called "Ololon" which follows Milton's example and returns to earth. For further discussion of the Eternals see my essay "Blake's Radical Comedy: Dramatic Structure as Meaning in *Milton*," *BSA*, pp. 284-85, 300-305.

rationalize her personal existence, is a "crime" which is all too human for us to categorize it in terms of moral absolutes. For us to judge Urizen as "the author of all our woe" is to fall back into the same ethical trap which Blake saw in *Paradise Lost.* Milton's mistake, in Blake's view, was not that he identified himself with the wrong side in the war in heaven, but that he assigned all the "moral virtue" to one party and suppressed his sympathy for the other. Milton's poetic instincts were more complex than this: he "wrote in fetters when he wrote of Angels & God, and at liberty when of Devils & Hell . . . because he was a true Poet and of the Devils party without knowing it" (*MHH* 5, E 35). Blake does not mean that the "true Poet" will simply invert the conventional moral scale, treating his devils as angels and vice versa, but that he will instinctively resist the reduction of his conflicts and contraries to "what the religious call Good & Evil" (*MHH* 3, E 34). Milton seems to be "of the Devils party" because this is the side of the imagination which has been suppressed, and which the true poet will instinctively seek to release.

The schematic, allegorical surface of Blake's prophetic books can mislead the moral imagination of the unwary reader. We are conditioned to read allegory as a parade of moral virtues and vices thinly disguised with human or natural imagery, and we tend to associate moral complexity with the "thickness" of the mimetic disguise.[6] Spenser's Artegall is one of the more "human" knights in *The Faerie Queene*, and we are therefore at pains to decide in specific episodes whether he is acting as a personification of justice or simply as a "just man" in a fallen, historical world. Blake does very little to clothe his personifications in realistic human dress: Urizen is not a man "representing" reason, or a man dominated by the faculty of reason; he *is* reason, a particular mode of consciousness. Blake's peculiar genius was not in dramatizing the social, human behavior associated with mental and emotional states, but in exploring the activities of various modes of consciousness *as such.* Hence the paradox that while Blake's poetic form minimizes the "realistic" social dimension with its extraordinarily abstract, schematic allegorical surface, the moral issues in his poetry approach the complexity of the ironic "novels without heroes" that were beginning to be written

[6] Hence, as Frye points out, modern critics have preferred ironic and low mimetic modes because there are fewer constraints by the author on the direction of interpretation, and thus more opportunities for the analysis of complex, ambiguous, unsystematized material (*Anatomy of Criticism*, [New York, 1969], p. 90).

in his time. Blake combines Miltonic sublimity with a Shakespearean relativism in questions of ethics and epistemology.

The Book of Urizen, then, is rather like the poem Milton would have written if he had eliminated the absolutist notion of a transcendent, perfect God from *Paradise Lost* and accepted Satan's claim that the angels are coeternal with God. It might also be compared to a world of Homeric deities in which human social reality is seen from an extremely distant, abstract perspective, and in which the deities are cosmic projections of human desires, thoughts, and powers rather than moral virtues and vices. The point is that all the machinery of myth, epic, and romance is being mobilized to embody a world defined as a human mind. Urizen cannot ultimately be "cast out" or confined alone because he does not really exist in a spatial world. Any attempt to dispense with him simply perpetuates the cosmic schizophrenia he has caused.

Blake's characters, then, are not related to one another in terms of the moral antitheses and hierarchies of allegory, romance, and myth: they are, despite the abstract surface, more like the complex matrices of intersubjectivity we find in the novel, without the novel's controlling dimension of low mimetic realism.[7] Characters are parts of one another, capable of becoming one another, or at least metaphors for one another. They are capable of change, conversion, degeneration, transformation, mutual absorption or repulsion, and indefinite subdivision and differentiation. That is why "Sublime Allegory" addressed to the "Intellectual Powers" is so much more demanding of its readers than mere "Fable or Allegory" addressed to the "corporeal" intellect which wants to see virtue rewarded and vice punished in a confirmation of its own righteousness. "The Last Judgment is not Fable or Allegory but Vision," and the Last Judgment occurs, according to Blake, "when all those are Cast away who trouble Religion with Questions concerning Good & Evil" (*VLJ*, E 544).

Blake dramatizes the complexity of the relations among his characters and subverts the expectations of moral allegory in the first

[7] In this dissolution of the social, realistic dimension of character (as distinguished from its "moral realism") Blake is converging from a different direction on one of the fundamental developments in the way modern fiction treats character: the movement, as John Bayley describes it, from fictions of "character" to fictions of "consciousness." See Bayley's "Character and Consciousness," *New Literary History* V (Winter 1974), 235: "this may be the condition to which the novel ultimately aspires, not to take over the world but to unify it into *Geist*, one indivisible solution of consciousness."

encounter between the antagonists of his poem, Urizen and the Eternals. When Urizen announces his "Laws of peace, of love, of unity" (4:34) he also mentions that he has discovered several violations of these laws: "terrible monsters Sin-bred:/ Which the bosoms of all inhabit;/ Seven deadly Sins of the soul" (4:28-30). The Eternals react immediately:

> . . . Rage siez'd the strong
>
> 2. Rage, fury, intense indignation
> In cataracts of fire blood & gall
> In whirlwinds of sulphurous smoke:
> And enormous forms of energy;
> All the seven deadly sins of the soul
> (4:44-49, E 71)

This is hardly the calm detachment of a superior justice, or of an "unfallen remnant" secure in its paradise. Far from providing an alternative to Urizen's vision, the Eternals seem to be absorbed in it, or, to paraphrase the formula Blake was to develop later, "they become what they behold."[8] This does not mean that they become indistinguishable from Urizen: their relationship is, for the moment, that of lawgiver and lawbreaker. But the question arises, if the "primal crime" in *Urizen* is the promulgation of law and tyranny of reason, is the primal redemptive act the violation of that law? Presumably Urizen has discovered that deep in "the bosoms of all" we are proud, lustful, envious, angry, slothful, covetous, and gluttonous. It is a measure of Blake's prophetic insight how positive, or at least normal, some of these sins will sound to modern ears, attuned to the values of Freud and Nietzche. Perhaps the Eternals are just trying to remind Urizen by means of active resistance that there was a time when the deadly sins were not so deadly:

> 3: O Times remote!
> When Love & Joy were adoration:
> And none impure were deem'd.
> Not Eyeless Covet
> Nor Thin-lip'd Envy
> Nor Bristled Wrath
> Nor Curled Wantonness
> (*BL* 3:7-13, E 89)

[8] Blake employs this epithet frequently in his later poems to summarize an encounter of adversaries. See especially *J* 32.

Dorothy Plowman argues that Blake is endorsing the reaction of the Eternals: "What Urizen calls the 'seven deadly sins of the soul' are no more than exclusive assertions of individuality. The Eternals, or elemental forces of life, have been forced into a narrow channel by Urizen's passion for objectifying. He has 'condensed' all things—fire, winds, waters, earth—and it is this very restraint which actually calls sin (the bursting of restraining bonds) into being."[9]

But the breaking of a bad, oppressive law, while it may be a necessary condition for liberation, is hardly presented as sufficient. The release of pure energy and emotion as a response to Urizen's rule of "one Law" can have disastrous consequences:

> Raging furious the flames of desire
> Ran thro' heaven & earth, living flames
> Intelligent, organiz'd: arm'd
> With destruction & plagues.
>
> (*BL* 3:27-30, E 90)

The division of Urizen and the Eternals is not to be seen (except ironically) as a division into fallen and unfallen realms, but rather as the splitting of the one mind which contains the world of the poem into realms of reason and emotion. This split cannot be healed by either of these opposing forces, but requires a mediator, a role played by Los, the personification of imagination. Thus, Los continually finds himself "in the midst" of the conflict, "in the void between fire and fire" (*BL* 3:30, 44), occasionally drawn into one of the opposing camps as an ally of the Eternals or of Urizen, his divided loyalty manifested by his literal division into sexual forms.

It should also be clear what a difficult poetic and intellectual task Blake has set for himself. He has defined the artistic role as a mediation between conflicting psychological forces, neither of which has any claim to moral certitude or providential insight. Since one of these forces has been suppressed or has withdrawn itself from the world (the "life-forces" or Eternals), it is his duty as a "true Poet" to bring about its return without loosing mere anarchy on the world. Since the Eternals dictate the poem, Blake puts himself in the position of having to be critical of his own muses at the same time he accepts their call. (He shows a similar ambivalence toward the muses of *Milton*, the "Daughters of Beulah," who "inspire the Poets

[9] "A Note on William Blake's *Book of Urizen*," in *The Book of Urizen*, facsimile ed. (London, 1929), p. 19.

Song," but whose realm is described as a place of "soft sexual delusions"; *M* 2:1, 3, E 95). *The Book of Urizen*, then, is in large measure the story of how difficult it is to be a prophet when there is no absolute divine order to refer to, only the vague memory (or perhaps it is only, as Blake says, a "sick hope") of a time when "The will of the Immortal expanded/ Or contracted his all flexible senses./ Death was not, but eternal life sprung" (*U* 3:37-39, E 70).

But that is not the only moral to the story. Blake is also criticizing the history of the prophetic role and suggesting that if the task is difficult without a transcendent deity or a "fiction of the absolute," it is surely impossible with one. When Los treats the Eternals as his masters and tries to "confine/ The obscure separation alone" to keep them safe from Urizenic infection, he only manages to worsen the wrenching apart of eternity, close himself in with Urizen, and divide into sexual forms in a reenactment of the initial schism. Once he is enclosed in Urizen's world he begins to act the part of Urizenic prophet, foreseeing nothing but the usurpation of his own power. Thus he imitates the actions of those whose "inspiration" serves only as a jealous, fearful (and futile) attempt to ward off the future, adopting the role of Abraham sacrificing Isaac, Jupiter chaining down Prometheus, or Laius exposing Oedipus:

> They took Orc to the top of a mountain
> . . . .
> They chain'd his young limbs to the rock
> With the Chain of Jealousy
> Beneath Urizens deathful shadow
> (20:21-25, E 79)

This critical view of the prophet in history, tracing the abuse of imagination to its obsession with moral (or, in the case of the Eternals, amoral)[10] absolutes, is a way of developing a new concept of the prophet as an explorer of human possibilities: the prophet as mediator, not between man and God, but between the conflicting claims of human nature; the prophet not as "Arbitrary Dictator" but as one who, like Moses in his best moments, seeks to make all the Lord's people into prophets.[11]

[10] I call the Eternals "amoral" because they seem to represent a kind of reservoir of libidinal energy which is beyond categories of good and evil.

[11] Blake continually sought to distinguish the authoritative voice of the inspired prophet from the authoritarian role: "a prophet is a Seer, not an Arbitrary Dictator" (Annotations to Watson, E 607).

IV. TRANSFORMING FORMS: THE CRITIQUE OF TIME AND SPACE

Blake's transvaluation of the value structures associated with Christian epic necessitated, as we might expect, a transformation of formal structures as well. If the artist has been thrown back on his own wit and imagination as the final judge of value, he must also reinvent form, and Blake will later argue that he must even remake the language: "English, the rough basement./ Los built the stubborn structure of the Language, acting against/ Albions melancholy, who must else have been a Dumb despair" (*J* 36:58-60, E 181). Joseph Wittreich has argued that Blake's formal innovations are, paradoxically, an integral part of the epic-prophetic tradition, especially as it was practiced by Milton and analyzed by such critics as Hayley, Cowper, and Lowth.[12] For Blake the epic tradition is a mode of continuous revolution in form and values reflecting the evolution of mankind toward a liberated social and intellectual order—this, in contrast to the neoclassical view of the epic tradition as a history of decline from energetic originals to increasingly imitative, derivative copies. I can not do justice to these rich traditions here, nor identify all of Blake's debts to and departures from them. But it is possible to examine the structure of *Urizen* in itself and in relation to its primary model, *Paradise Lost*, in order to gain a general view of Blake's formal modifications of the epic tradition.

It seems obvious that *Urizen* was written by a man who knew *Paradise Lost* and perhaps even the Bible by heart.[13] This is not simply a matter of numerous echoes, allusions, and parallels, but a function of the ontological status of the illuminated books. One suspects that Blake saw *Urizen*, like *The Divine Comedy* and Milton's poetry, as an extension of the one holy book whose writing has been in progress since the beginnings of sacred literature. The fact that *Urizen* is in part an attack on the sacredness of this tradition, a mock Genesis in a parodic "Bible of Hell," does not detach it from the

[12] See "Opening the Seals: Blake's Epics and the Milton Tradition," *BSA*, p. 26.

[13] Thomas Minnick has demonstrated rather convincingly that Blake knew at least *L'Allegro* and *Il Penseroso* from memory. Minnick's collation of Blake's inscriptions for his illustrations to these poems with editions of Milton that were available to him suggests that it is highly unlikely that Blake copied them from any edition of Milton's works, all the evidence indicating that Blake remembered his inscriptions almost verbatim. See "On Blake and Milton," Ph.d. diss., Ohio State University, 1973, pp. 30-31.

tradition but is a necessary characteristic of Blake's evolutionary notion of prophecy. *Urizen* is a part of the Bible and *Paradise Lost*, and they in turn are absorbed, criticized, and reevaluated in the new context of the Bible of Hell, just as the Book of Revelation absorbs both Old and New Testaments into a new critical and symbolic framework.

The general structure of *Urizen* is modeled after the three-phase time sequence which lies behind the narrative of *Paradise Lost*. Milton begins his poem *in medias res* with the devils already imprisoned in hell, but we can reconstruct the implicit chronology of his poem as follows: (1) a "pre-creation" state in which God creates heaven and a host of angels, some of whom rebel when God appoints his Son as vice-regent, causing the war in heaven and the fall of the rebels into hell; (2) the "creation" phase, when God creates earth and mankind to replenish the heavenly host; (3) the fall of man, his exile from the garden, and the beginnings of human history with its promise of a redeemer and a consumate episode, the apocalypse. *Urizen* follows this general pattern rather closely. The first three chapters describe a time before the creation of the world ("earth was not"; 3:36) in which a heavenly war breaks out between Urizen and the Eternals; the next three chapters (IVa and b through VI) describe Los's creation of a body for Urizen, the creation of Enitharmon, and the birth of the first human child, Orc. The last three chapters are concerned primarily with the postlapsarian world of early Biblical history, describing the first human sacrifice, the beginnings of religion, the degeneration of mankind, and a flight from captivity. Probably the most noticeable modification Blake imposes on his model is his presentation of the fall of man as a *fait accompli* at creation. There is no unfallen Adam in *Urizen*, and the Garden of Eden is mentioned only in passing, as a "garden of fruits" which Urizen plants after the human sacrifice has already occurred. It is tempting to label all this a Gnostic version of Genesis which identifies creation with fall and treats the entire created world of matter, time, space, the body, and the sexes as illusory and evil, but let us resist this temptation until we have examined the poem more closely.[14]

When we attend to the details of imagery and action in *Urizen* we find that Blake's apparent imitation of the time scheme of Genesis

[14] Leslie Tannenbaum in "Blake's Art of Crypsis" treats the Gnostic view of Genesis in considerable detail. See also Clark Emery's introduction to *The Book of Urizen*, University of Miami Critical Studies No. 6 (Coral Gables, Fla., 1966).

and *Paradise Lost* is continually subverted and dislocated by the local textures of the poem. Chapter I begins with Urizen's withdrawal into solitude, an episode that recalls Satan's withdrawal into the northern sector of heaven to muster his rebellion (*PL* V: 685-710). But Urizen's withdrawal insofar as it involves a creative, brooding introspection is also a parody, as we have noted, of a much earlier event in Milton's time scheme, the "brooding" of the Holy Spirit who "from the first/ Was present" to make the vast abyss pregnant. And as we look more closely at the imagery of Urizen's isolation in Chapter I, we detect echoes of a situation which arises some time *after* Satan's withdrawal to the north, namely, his imprisonment in hell, "The dismal Situation waste and wild/ A Dungeon horrible on all sides round" (*PL* I: 60-61). The final verse of Chapter I, moreover, evokes the scene of Satan calling up his legions in hell, his review of his armies prior to the war in heaven, and, in a closing simile ("like thunders of autumn/ When the cloud blazes over the harvests"; 3:35), the apocalyptic harvest. Urizen's withdrawal into introspective solitude resounds, in other words, with echoes of widely disparate events in the temporal and spatial structure of *Paradise Lost*, touching on all the regions of Milton's cosmology (heaven, earth, hell, and chaos) and alluding to several distinct phases in his picture of sacred history (creation of life by Holy Spirit, war in heaven, Satan in hell, Satan traversing chaos, and the apocalypse). Blake suggests that Urizen's withdrawal is, in some sense, all of these events, and occurs in (or creates) all these places.

Chapter II dramatizes Urizen's emergence from his solitude, his description of what he has endured, and his declaration of "one Law." As Urizen emerges, the echoes of apocalypse continue to be heard ("The sound of a trumpet the heavens/ Awoke"; 3: 40-41), and the war in heaven seems imminent: "myriads of Eternity,/ Muster around the bleak desarts" (3:44-4:1). Urizen's review of his solitary experiences continues to evoke Satan's journey through chaos, and the creation of life by the Holy Spirit is alluded to once again in Urizen's account of his "self-balanc'd" hovering over "Natures wide womb" (4:17-18). The major focus, however, shifts to Milton's dramatic, oratorical moments. Urizen now seems like the Satan of Book V in *Paradise Lost*, assembling his myriads in the North after he has brooded secretly over his planned revolt to persuade them to join the rebellion against God. But then this analogy takes a curious turn. Urizen is not counseling the Eternals to rebel; he is declaring a new ethic based on the concept of absolute unity under law, and his language echoes God the Father announcing the reign of his Son, under whom all shall

> . . . abide
> United as one individual Soul
> For ever happy: him who disobeys
> Mee disobeys, breaks union, and that day
> Cast out from God and blessed vision, falls
> Into utter darkness
>
> (*PL* V:609-14)

Blake even goes back to the source of Milton's concept of "the unity of Spirit in bond of peace" in St. Paul ("There is one body, and one Spirit, even as ye are called in one hope of your calling; One Lord, one faith, one baptism. One God and Father of all"; Ephesians 4:3-6) to find a rhetorical model for Urizen's declaration of

> One command, one joy, one desire,
> One curse, one weight, one measure
> One King, one God, one Law.
>
> (4:38-40, E 71)

If Urizen's initial withdrawal from Eternity identifies him as both a brooding, plotting Satan and a fertilizing deity like the Holy Spirit, his reemergence to declare his laws identifies him with both Satan the political tyrant and God the Father.

This fusion of divine and demonic roles is, as we might expect, transferred in the next chapter to Urizen's antagonists, the Eternals. From one point of view the Eternals play rebellious, devilish angels to Urizen's role as God the Father; from another they are the loyal angels who rally in defense of God's kingdom against Urizen's Satanic plot. From either perspective, the main source of imagery is now Milton's war in heaven, but the echoes of creation continue to resound. Urizen frames "a roof, vast petrific around . . . like a womb" (5:28-29) which recalls his brooding over "Natures wide womb" in his initial withdrawal. This womb is also "like a black globe" (5:33), which suggests that he is creating the earth and possibly other "globes of attraction," and "like a human heart" (5:36), which anticipates the creation of a human body. Los now appears for the first time, keeping watch "for Eternals to confine/ The obscure separation alone" (5:39-40), which suggests that he, too, is to be a godlike creator, forming a hell to enclose Urizen.

But this implication is immediately distorted: Los acts not like the powerful creator preparing a place like the one "Eternal Justice had prepared" in *Paradise Lost*, but more like a tormented victim, "for in anguish,/ Urizen was rent from his side" (6:3-4). In the eighth verse of Chapter III we see Los as the creative agent of an eternal order which stands "wide apart/ As the stars are apart from the earth" (5:41-6:1); in the ninth verse he is reduced to the status of creature, an Adam giving birth to Eve. These two roles control the structure of the middle triad of chapters, Los appearing as a cosmic creator in Chapter IV, as a tormented Adam in Chapters V and VI. His prominence as a central character ends with the birth of his son Orc at the end of Chapter VI, his only appearance after that occurring at the chaining of Orc "beneath Urizens deathful shadow" (20:25).

Although the second and third sections of the poem (Chapters IV-VI and VII-IX) disclose a progressive movement based on Milton's sequence of creation, fall of man, and beginnings of history, they too contain numerous elements which complicate the sense of linear order. Milton describes the creation of Adam's body as an event which occupies the latter part of the sixth day of creation; from God's point of view, the whole week of creation is but a mere instant: "I . . . in a moment will create/ Another world, out of one man a Race/ Of men innumerable" (*PL* VII: 150, 154-56). Blake inverts this time sense, treating Los's creation of a body for Urizen as the work of "Seven Ages," one age required for the completion of each bodily organ, and each age containing more "ages on ages" of time. The size of Urizen's body is correspondingly expanded in space, described as a cavernous, cosmic form which fills up the "vast abyss" of Milton's cosmos. When Blake comes to treat the theme of the shrinking and degeneration of mankind in the historical section of the poem, however, he treats this process not as a gradual, long-term historical sequence,[15] but as the work of the week of creation:

> 3. Six days they shrunk up from existence
> And on the seventh day they rested
> And they bless'd the seventh day, in sick hope:
> And forgot their eternal life
>
> (27:39-42, E 82)

[15] The traditional view of human history as a long process of physical shrinkage and moral degeneration may be seen in Donne's *Anatomy of the World* and in the "Proem" to Book V of Spenser's *The Faerie Queene*.

The creative act of one day in Genesis is expanded to include a vast historical process, and the range of human history since creation is compressed into the week of Genesis.

Our sense of conventional "objective" time sequence is even more drastically disrupted when we find Los in Chapter VII playing the roles of Abraham, Laius, and Jupiter to Orc's Isaac, Oedipus, and Prometheus. As we read on into the subsequent episode we might expect one of these allusive contexts to take priority, but instead Blake fuses them into a new context: Orc becomes a Christ-child like the "secret child" that Blake adopted from Milton's *Nativity Ode* in *Europe* (3:1-4, E 60), and his voice awakes the dead, including Urizen, evidently. If we try to locate our progress in the narrative at this point (laying aside the allusions to Oedipus and Prometheus) we find ourselves witnessing the sacrifice of Isaac as the Crucifixion as the Nativity. When we go on to examine Urizen's reaction to this complex of events, we encounter another radical disruption of sequence: Urizen "explores his dens" (see Chaps. VII and VIII) like the fallen angels in hell (*PL* II: 570-628) and gives them form. Not, however, the form of Milton's infernal regions, but the celestial workmanship of God the Son:

7. He form'd a line & a plummet
To divide the Abyss beneath.
He form'd a dividing rule:
. . . .
He formed golden compasses
And began to explore the Abyss
And he planted a garden of fruits
(20:33-35, 39-41; E 79-80)

Why is it necessary to "explore the Abyss" if one is capable of encompassing it? Satan is the only explorer in *Paradise Lost* (Adam is warned not to explore too curiously the secrets of the Almighty, and God's omniscience makes exploration irrelevant for him). Blake fuses the roles of God and Satan into one identity at the same time he collapses Milton's chronology, presenting the creation of the world as, in some sense, a consequence of the first human sacrifice! This can make sense only if we see creation not as an event which occurred in the remote past, but as something which continually recurs in time, as if the cosmos were being redesigned with each passing moment.

The more closely we examine *Urizen* the more it becomes evident that it does not conform very strictly to the three-phase temporal pattern of *Paradise Lost.* The poem is more like an elaborate counterpoint of intertwining narrative lines, the three-phase sequence of pre-creation, creation, and history a major governing pattern but clearly not the only one. The nine chapters (perhaps a reflection of Blake's developing interest in Young's *Night Thoughts* with its nine nights) are surely another way of organizing Urizen's "ninefold darkness" (3:9) into even more specialized phases. From a broader point of view the poem divulges a two-part structure, the dividing line or crisis coming in the middle or fifth chapter as Los completes his creative work and shrinks from his task, apparently defeated: "And now his eternal life/ Like a dream was obliterated" (13:33-34). The graphic structure of the plate on which this occurs [67] certainly suggests that this is a major "dividing moment": the design shows a figure floating in space pushing apart two cloud banks, and Blake places this scene in the middle of the page, framing it with text above and below, the only use of this arrangement in *Urizen.*

Blake's purpose in employing contrapuntal structures and episodes that conflate widely disparate moments in the conventional picture of cosmic chronology is surely to convey a sense of time as a simultaneous presence, a vast panorama of events which may be rearranged by the poetic imagination into any order which discloses significance. In the 1790s Blake had not yet articulated his view of creative time as the compression of "Six Thousand Years" into the "pulsation of the artery" (see *M* 28:63-64, E 126), but he did have the notion of prophetic time as the simultaneous perception of "Present, Past, & Future" ("Introduction," *Exp*; E 18). He is obviously working toward the idea of compressing all history into the vivid moment in *Urizen*, in his attempts to conflate beginnings and ends, pasts and futures in each episode of the poem.

The sense of temporal simultaneity is perhaps most subtly—and significantly—embodied in the general statement of *Urizen's* theme:

> Of the primeval Priests assum'd power,
> When Eternals spurn'd back his religion;
> And gave him a place in the north,
> Obscure, shadowy, void, solitary.
>
> (2:1-4, E 69)

Our first reading of these lines, conditioned by the obvious parallels to Miltonic narrative patterns, will read the word "when" as "until": we assume that Urizen's assumption of power, like Satan's revolt in heaven, must logically (and chronologically) precede his spurning and banishment. But our second reading, informed by an awareness of Blake's dislocations of Miltonic time schemes, will take the lines literally. The primeval priest's assumption of power can be seen as occurring before, after, or at the same time as his expulsion by the Eternals. Urizen's assumption of power over his world can be seen as a consequence of the Eternals' behavior as much as a cause of it. We are reading a story, then, not of crime and punishment, but of crime *as* punishment. If this seems too great a paradox to contemplate, we need only remind ourselves that the second chapter of the poem will imply that the primal crime is the promulgation of law, not the violation of it.

The sense that all time happens at once in *Urizen* is accompanied by a feeling that all space is here. The Miltonic cosmos with its clear boundaries between heaven, hell, earth, and chaos collapses into a single form, a consciousness or human form in which "space" has no fixed, immutable character. The heaven or "eternal life" which Urizen rejects is, from his point of view, a hell of "unquenchable burnings" (3:39, 4:14). Urizen's stable law-built heaven, which he spends so much time "dividing & measuring," is precisely the opposite of the solid, peaceful, unified utopia he had in mind. It is hell, chaos, this world—a globe rolling in voidness, englobed in a salt ocean, or a heart, a womb, an embryo populated with "horrible forms of deformity" (13:43) and "portions of life; similitudes/ Of a foot, or a hand, or a head/ Or a heart (23:4-6). Every "space" immediately begets its contrary: a boundless, indefinite void becomes a hollow shell in which all forms contract into atoms, and every globular form immediately splits in two, or divides into innumerable branches. The "place in the north" to which Urizen, like Satan, withdraws to muster his rebellion becomes his place of punishment, an "obscure, shadowy, void, solitary" dungeon, much like the "place Eternal justice had prepar'd/ For those rebellious" in *Paradise Lost.*

Containing all the collapsing, dividing, shrinking worlds of Urizen, however, is the implicit boundary of a human form. It may be asleep, having nightmares, as it is in Chapters IV through VI, it may be stirring, "stung with the odours of Nature" (20:31) as it is in the last three chapters, or it may be falling into a schizophrenic battle with itself, a cosmic psychomachy like the one described in the first three chapters, but the implicit assumption remains, that time and space are not independent realities but modifications, fragments, or distortions of this total human form. The range of possible fragments of this form is, of course, theoretically indefinite, but it does seem that Blake concentrates on a few dominant ones in *Urizen*, forms which not only appear as recurrent images but govern the structural patterns of his departures from Miltonic structures of space and time. Probably the most obvious of these recurrent images is the globe rolling in or containing a void, an image which suggests, in spatial terms, both the constricted, claustrophobic, "buried alive" feeling of much of the poem and the recurrent sense of empty isolation, vertigo, and disorientation. In temporal, narrative terms the globe is an image of rotation and cyclicity ("The eternal mind bounded began to roll"; 10:19), and governs the sense that the same action is compulsively repeated in each succeeding episode of the poem. In a spatial context the globe becomes a heavenly body (a planet or a sun "burning deep/ Deep down into the Abyss"; 11:3-4), an earthly human body with orblike organs such as the skull ("a roof shaggy wild inclosed/ In an orb his fountain of thought"; 10:33-34), the eye, the heart, the womb, or the embryo in the womb.

A second recurrent form which governs temporal and spatial structure is the imagery of vegetation and fibrousness, the "ten thousand branches" (11:6) which shoot out from each form like a labyrinth of roots, veins, nerves, or tentacles. In *The Book of Los* this form is called the Polypus, a vegetative sea creature constructed with "intricate pipes" (4:69), an "immense Fibrous form" (5:1).[16] The temporal manifestation of this form is the structure of intricate, labyrinthine interplay between various narrative lines, and the feeling that our movement through the poem is like watching the uncontrolled growth of a cancer, an explosive series of mitoses, divisions, and subdivisions, or the proliferation of genealogical "branches" from a single root.

But probably the most subtle image pattern in *Urizen*, and the one which most consistently dominates its structure, is that of the vortex, the image of simultaneous contrariety and progression (cf. *BL* 4:35-36, in which Los's fall is "measurd by his incessant whirls/

[16] For a survey of Blake's use of this image see Paul Miner, "The Polyp as Symbol in the Poetry of William Blake," *Texas Studies in Language and Literature* II (1960), 198-205. Blake seems to have grasped the essential features of the life cycle of the polyp, its ability to regenerate whole creatures from fragments of itself and its sharing of vegetable and animal characteristics. One wonders if he was aware that the polyp became a central exhibit in the attempt of eighteenth-century naturalists to argue for the materiality of the soul. See Aram Vartanian, "Trembly's Polyp, La Mettre, and Eighteenth-Century French Materialism," *Journal of the History of Ideas* II (1950), 259-86.

In the horrid vacuity"). Our movement through the poem is both linear-progressive (in imitation of Miltonic time schemes) and cyclical-recurrent, and the relation between episodes is generally one of action and contrary reaction: Urizen tries to establish peace, the Eternals react with war; Los tries to unify Urizen, and finds himself divided; Fuzon plays the liberator and becomes the tyrant. But it is not just the relations between episodes which disclose this pattern of contrariety: many individual episodes, taken in themselves, are constructed as paradoxical fusions of contrary actions and images. Urizen is both God and Satan, the Eternals are both devils and angels. Creation is fall, and the primal crime is the institution of law.

But Blake does not seem particularly interested in the mere contemplation of the fearful symmetries of paradox. Urizen's oxymoronic realm of "petrific . . . chaos" (3:26) is interesting to behold not because it fuses opposites, but because it proves the impossibility of maintaining a "solid without fluctuation" (4:11).[17] The paradoxical, contrarious structures of *Urizen* are not designed, in other words, simply to demonstrate an ironic world view in which everything is perverted into its opposite. The ironic, symmetrical futility of Urizen's world is itself the subject of satire, and the energies of paradox and contrariety continually shatter his monolithic despair with "pangs of hope." It is in this sense that Blake departs from the Gnostic view that creation is fall and the world utterly corrupt. For Blake, the redemptive energies are in this world, or must be brought into this world. There is no escaping beyond the skies to where the Eternals dwell; they must be brought back to earth, as Blake will make explicit when he has them descend *en masse* as the "multitudes of Ololon" in *Milton* (34-37).

V. NOTHINGNESS, ILLUSION, AND THE FORTUNATE FALL

When Los and Enitharmon chain Orc to a rocky mountaintop "with the Chain of Jealousy/ Beneath Urizen's deathful shadow" (20:24-25) in Chapter VII, we seem to be witnessing the absolute

[17] For a study of Urizen which elaborates the structural symmetries in great detail, see Robert Simmons, "Urizen: the Symmetry of Fear," *VFD*, pp. 146-73, which describes *Urizen* as a "house of mirrors." Simmons sees the brief glimpse of pre-creation eternity in Chapter II as the only relief from this symmetry. As will become evident below, I see many more windows in the house of mirrors.

corruption of Imagination and Prophecy, their absorption into the Urizenic mentality. But the very next verse suggests another possibility:

> 5. The dead heard the voice of the child
> And began to awake from sleep
> All things. heard the voice of the child
> And began to awake to life.
> (20:26-29, E 79)

Not all the paradoxes in *Urizen* are designed to convey an ironic sense of futile symmetry. Some of them suggest that the other side of error is revelation and redemption, or as Blake phrased it years later, "to be an Error & to be Cast out is a part of Gods design" (*VLJ*, E 551).

Echoes of the Book of Revelation resound throughout *Urizen*: the war in heaven which precipitates creation anticipates the struggle which will consume it at the end of the world; the "Seven Ages" of the binding of Urizen are like the opening of the seven apocalyptic seals; Fuzon's departure from "the pendulous earth" ("They called it Egypt, & left it"; 28:21) is an Exodus which prefigures the ascension of God's witnesses from "the great city, which spiritually is called Sodom and Egypt, where also our Lord was crucified" (Rev. 11:8).[18] The whole pattern of compulsive repetition in *Urizen* can be seen not just as a cyclic nightmare like the "all is done as I have told" of the Mental Traveller, but as a process of typological ripening, the recurrent event as prefiguration, epiphany, glimpse of liberation.

Even the "primal crime," Urizen's declaration of absolute law, is described in apocalyptic imagery:

> 2. The sound of a trumpet the heavens
> Awoke & vast clouds of blood roll'd
> Round the dim rocks of Urizen, so nam'd
> That solitary one in Immensity
> (3:40-43, E 70)

Is this simply a demonic parody, a false revelation? Or does the fact that the "heavens/ Awoke" at Urizen's call suggest that the "eternal life" he is disturbing was in some sense a sleep, a kind of

[18] Tannenbaum, "Blake's Art of Crypsis," p. 160, was the first to point out this allusion, but he stresses the ironic reading: "Through this fusion of Revelation and Genesis, Blake is representing Genesis as an inverted Apocalypse."

innocent anarchy which had no consciousness of death, nothingness, or futurity and thus no need for law? When Urizen defines the nature of his laws, it is hard not to be struck by the mixture of liberating and tyrannical elements they contain:

> 8. Laws of peace, of love, of unity:
> Of pity, compassion, forgiveness.
> Let each chuse one habitation:
> His ancient infinite mansion:
> One command, one joy, one desire,
> One curse, one weight, one measure
> One King, one God, one Law.
>
> (4:34-40, E 71)

The first four lines in this passage are generally ignored in estimates of Urizen's character, or dismissed as hypocrisy or self-deception. But there is no evidence in the poem that Urizen promulgates his laws with selfish motives. The passage can be read as Blake's attempt to conjure up some "sympathy for the devil" in his readers, a sympathy which will be dramatized later when Los pities Urizen.[19] In this case, the sense that an action has occurred already in some other frame of reference is a way of foreshadowing the "promised end." Urizen's fall into error is also a revelation, if not for Urizen, for the reader. The first event in time, the "primal crime," is, if read imaginatively, an image of the last event in time, the apocalypse of forgiveness and infinite perception described at the end of *Jerusalem*. This does not mean that Blake had the complete plan of *Jerusalem* in his head when he wrote *Urizen*. It does mean that he conjures with the imagery of apocalypse long before he knows how to dramatize it as an episode in his epic, that he sees from the first that a "Bible of Hell" will have

[19] Commentators have generally regarded Los's pity for Urizen as a mistake on the grounds (1) that Urizen is not worth anyone's pity; (2) that pity does not help Urizen anyway; (3) that it hurts Los by dividing him into sexual forms. If it is a mistake, I would argue that it is the one genuinely fortunate fall in *Urizen*. Los's alternative to pity at this point in the story is the withdrawn indifference and fear of the Eternals, and his division into sexual forms is a way of guaranteeing that the prophetic role will be fruitful and multiply, bearing an "enormous race" to provide imaginative alternatives to the societies bred by Urizen. If we are looking for negative instances of pity, we can find one in Chapter VIII, when Urizen's tears over his deformed creation turn into a "spiders web, moist, cold, & dim" which divides heaven like a dungeon and is named "The Net of Religion." But even this hypocritical pity (like hypocritical charity) may have beneficial side effects, as Blake will suggest in *Milton* 23:39-41.

to conclude with a Book of Revelation, and the implicit promise of this consummate episode will govern all the earlier actions.

Blake undoubtedly got the idea of fusing Genesis with Apocalypse from Milton's use of a similar device to compare the rebellion and fall of the angels to the war in heaven described in Revelation.[20] But Milton's allusion works as a reinforcing parallel: the dragon defeated by Michael and his angels is "that old serpent, called the Devil and Satan" (Rev. 12:7-8). Blake's allusion, on the other hand, unites the antithetical meanings of fall and revelation. Urizen's fall into the "stony sleep" of his world of "one Law" is couched in the rhetoric of millennial proclamation and accompanied by the imagery of apocalyptic awakening. This can be read ironically, as Leslie Tannenbaum suggests, as an "inverted Apocalypse" which depicts the "victory of Justice over Mercy,[21] but it can also be read as a premonition of a genuine apocalypse, one in which peace, love, unity, pity, compassion, forgiveness, and the infinite capacity of the individual (all the values invoked by Urizen) would not be corrupted by being attached to a notion of absolute, abstract law. Presumably the genuine apocalypse would not involve a simple return to the prelapsarian state when "earth was not" but rather the assimilation of what Urizen has discovered, an awareness of death, nothingness, and time. Urizen's mistake is in trying to create *through law* a world like the one he has fallen from, a world where "Death was not"—or at least not perceived. The Eternals' mistake is that they refuse to contemplate and absorb what Urizen has discovered.[22]

If we push our sympathy for Urizen's plight far enough we can read his book as the story of a "fortunate fall," a mythic account of the passage from Innocence to Experience of the cosmic mind. Urizen's fall into nothingness is fortunate because without it human life would not exist, or to state the inverse in the words of Sartre, "Man presents himself . . . as a being who causes Nothingness to arise

[20] See *PL* IV:1-3.

[21] Tannenbaum, "Blake's Art of Crypsis," p. 160.

[22] Blake's apparent inconsistency on the matter of death in Chapter II seems designed to dramatize this difference in perspective. He first describes the pre-creation state as one in which "Death was not, but eternal life sprung" (3:39), then has Urizen ask "Why will you die O Eternals?" (4:12). This contradiction suggests that there was death in eternity, but the Eternals, like the natural creatures of *Thel*, do not perceive it as such—or at least not until Urizen shows it to them ("What is this? Death"; 7:9)—and they are determined to have nothing to do with it.

in the world."[23] The concept and experience of nothingness, the void which Urizen explores, becomes the ground of being for human consciousness. The problem with calling this a "fortunate" fall is that Blake concentrates so exclusively on the anguish that follows from it, and it is certainly *not* fortunate in the traditional sense of allowing God, through Christ's sacrifice, to manifest even more sublime wisdom and love than he would have without Adam's sin. But it is fortunate in the sense that it must be a part of, not excluded from, any restoration of the eternal order, just as all the history that follows from it, the nightmare of human experience, will not be negated or forgotten, but preserved by the imagination: "all things acted on Earth are seen in the bright Sculptures of/ Los's Halls" (*J* 16:61-62, E 159). Without this consciousness of Nothingness, in fact, Blake's ultimate moral and visionary act—the act of Self-annihilation—becomes meaningless and unnecessary. We may reply that Urizen should have stayed out of the void of subjectivity, but this is like telling Thel to stop asking questions and live spontaneously. It is good advice for those who can take it—flowers, clouds, clods of clay.

One of the major purposes of Blake's rendering his episodes in repetitive structural patterns, then, is to convey the sense that Urizen's fall is reenacted throughout history, not just because he "started it" (cf. Adam's "original sin"), but because we are human. Our lives repeat, as ontogeny recapitulates phylogeny, the mythic tale of fall from a state of undifferentiated unity, unselfconsciousness (remembered as the womb, infancy, childhood—ultimately, any stage we remember as simpler and unproblematic) into a state of division, self-consciousness, doubt, the state of the "Human Illusion." We can no more circumvent this fall into Urizen's "place in the north" than Thel can avoid entering the "Northern Gate" into the wintery, polar realm of Experience. Urizen's fall is a given, like the crime of

[23] *Being and Nothingness*, tr. Hazel E. Barnes (New York, 1956), p. 24. Sartre goes on to suggest that the concept and experience of Nothingness gives rise to our notions of freedom, transcendence, and time, all of which arise in Urizen: his wish to be a totally free, autonomous subject, his desire to transcend everything in a realm of the absolute, and his obsession with dividing "times on times." I would not argue, of course, that Blake "anticipates Sartre"; one could find similar parallels in Heidegger or Kierkegaard. The point is that Blake dramatizes the experience of nothingness in a strikingly modern way, and he seems to see it as a necessary phase in the growth of consciousness. We can no more return to a phase when "Death was not" than we can make the earth and globes of attraction disappear by being energetic, spontaneous, and unselfconscious.

the Ancient Mariner; what is not given is the nature of our response to it.

In spite of Blake's apparent adoption of the Gnostic view that fall is creation, and that both are totally unfortunate (and thus matter, the body, the senses, sexes are all irredeemably evil), it seems clear that he ultimately regards the fall as necessary and inevitable, if not fortunate. The task of the imagination, faced with Urizen's void and the material world, is not to fly from it in search of some transcendent, spiritual realm, but to enter into the fallen world, giving it form and illumination. Urizen cannot be abandoned: he is "rent from Los's side" like Eve from Adam, and must be recovered before any restoration of unity is possible.

If Los is the mediator between the conflicting values of reason and energy in the moral allegory of *Urizen,* he is also the mediator between conflicting senses of time, one structured as an ironic or tragic sense of continuous loss, the other as a comic and romantic vision of renewal and recovery. Imagination or vision depends upon the continuous interaction of both these views of time. When one view dominates—say the "pangs of hope" for recovery—the mind "labour[s] upward into futurity" (E 662) toward a consummate episode to end all episodes—revolution, utopia, apocalypse. We tend to identify this labor with Blake, the revolutionary, utopian prophet. But in *The Book of Urizen* this role is assigned to Urizen, who seeks a utopian "joy without pain," acts as a revolutionary, assuming power and issuing new laws, and ushers in his own apocalypse by insisting on what Wallace Stevens would call "a supreme fiction," the fiction of an absolute. For Blake, imagination is the supreme fiction, but it is not an absolute because it is conscious of itself as a fictive, fabricating activity, a maker of illusions. This suggests that in structural terms Blake's problem in the later poems will be to devise an apocalyptic ending which does not foreclose the possibility of continued evolution, possibly even new "falls" into error.

Blake was evidently not ready to write this consummate episode in 1794. He was capable, however, of constructing a coherent epic form with beginning, middle, and intimations of an end, structured around a dialectical concept of moral values and narrative structure. The focus of this dialectic is the figure of Los, the tormented prophet whose artifacts embody his ambivalence:

> The Eternal Prophet heavd the dark bellows,
> And turn'd restless the tongs; and the hammer

Incessant beat; forging chains new & new
Numbring with links. hours, days, & years
(10:15-18, E 74)

Is Los's time a chain that binds us down from eternity or links us to it? Are the links the nightmarish circles of compulsive repetition, or the division of the night into "watches" for a possible dawn? Blake's purpose at this point in his work was not to answer these questions, but to involve his readers in their full complexity

. . . till a Form
Was completed, a Human Illusion
In darkness and deep clouds involvd.

VI. "DARK VISIONS OF TORMENT": *URIZEN* AS PICTURE GALLERY

1. *Narrative and Antinarrative in the Sequence of Plates*

If narrative or sequential structure is difficult to discern in the text of *Urizen*, it may seem impossible to find in the illustrations. The designs do not provide the kind of direct visual translation of the narrative that we find in *Thel*. Some pictures do not refer to any episode in the text, and many seem to refer to several different episodes at once. The fact that over a third of the plates are movable full-page designs without text, and that their order is different in each of the seven known copies of *Urizen*, suggests that this atemporal, antisequential quality is a deliberate formal device, a way of augmenting the antinarrative elements disclosed by the text.

But *Urizen*'s picture sequence is not in a state of absolute flux: certain plates (title page, Preludium, and the sixteen plates containing text) keep the same relative order in every copy, providing a stable framework within which Blake could rearrange his movable plates. The total form of *Urizen*'s pictorial presentation is rather like that of a mobile sculpture which rotates and transforms itself while adhering to a carefully designed central structure. If one considers only the "fixed stars" in the firmament of *Urizen*, the plates containing text, it seems much more orderly, revealing a structural progression which, while it does not illustrate the narrative progression of the text, provides a kind of parallel to it. The *Urizen* designs are arranged as a journey through three rather distinct settings which correspond roughly to the three major landscapes of *Paradise Lost*: hell, heaven, and earth. The opening group of plates (3-11 [49, 51, 53, 54, 60-64]) places us in a hellish, subterranean realm filled with dark flames and human figures burning or buried alive. Around the middle of the book, however, we encounter a change of key. The crushing, claustrophobic confinement of the first section gives way to a feeling of unbounded space, the void of outer space or the starry night revealed by Enitharmon in plate 13 [67], and the imagery of earth and fire gives way to water and air. This middle section of the book terminates at plate 18 [74], where we encounter Los with his hammer amid flames and blocks of stone, a scene that takes us back to the earth and fire imagery of the first section, but with a twist. The flames now seem less tormenting, more like the creative medium in which Los works, and Los's position is much freer. He no longer has to struggle for space in which to live and work, but is able to rest in an expansive, unfettered posture. This third section (plates 18-28 [74-82, 84, 47]) is the most realistic in the book, placing most of its human figures in firm relation to the ground or the horizon rather than underground or in the sky. No particular set of elements seems to dominate as is the case in the first two sections, and in fact we see all four being born on plate 24 [80].

We should hasten to qualify this account of the different landscapes in *Urizen* by noting that there is a pervading air of anguish and isolation which prevents the various sections from seeming like radically distinct worlds. The "heavenly" middle section is not filled with pleasant fields or a celestial city, but with a void that may be more terrifying than the condition of burial alive depicted in the opening sequence. All the pictures in *Urizen* place us in hell in some sense. A second qualification is that this order is dislocated slightly in some copies by the different position of some full-page plates. In copy B, for instance, the full-page picture of Urizen buried alive is moved from its normal location in the first section and placed after plate 13 in the middle of the book. The structure I have outlined is most obvious in copy D (British Museum), the version which I have chosen as my standard for plate sequence, interpolating the plates lacking in this copy (4, 16) to create an ideal copy of *Urizen*.[24]

[24] The reproductions in this text are not from the British Museum *Urizen*, however, but from the Morgan Library and Rosenwald copies. This "ideal copy" corresponds to the one devised by Keynes in his *Census of the Illuminated Books* and followed by Erdman in *The Illuminated Blake*. Although this involves basing the discussion on a partly nonexistent copy, the practical advantages of following the standard arrangement are overwhelming. Further

In this copy the full-page designs seem to be arranged in closest conformity with the imagery of the fixed textual plates, and it therefore serves as a relatively stable framework against which variations and transformations may be seen.

All this concern with the sequence and potential narrative dimensions of the *Urizen* designs should not distract us from the intrinsic qualities of the compositions taken individually. *Urizen* is surely the most spectacular picture book Blake ever designed, each composition stating its own case eloquently in the minute particulars of line, color, and formal arrangement. The pictures resist any attempt to see them purely in narrative terms, as panels in a mural or as illustrations of the verbal narrative. Blake was reaching the first of several pinnacles in the development of his graphic genius (the 1795 color prints were imminent), and his designs tend to draw the reader into their own vortices—certainly a number of the illustrations deserve separate study, so rich and suggestive are their stylistic and iconographic properties. Blake's talent for invention, the condensation of numerous iconographic traditions into strikingly original syntheses, is never displayed to better advantage than in *Urizen*, and his visual rhetoric, the manipulation of sensuous pictorial effects, is the most masterly in the entire canon of illuminated books.

Two stylistic features of the *Urizen* designs are especially prominent: pictorial synaesthesia and the imaginative use of symmetry. The pictures are a whirlwind of elemental forms which are transformed one into another with dazzling rapidity. Explosions of flame shoot out like waves of vegetation or fibers of blood, nerves, and lymph. Stone becomes cloud, hair becomes rain or a cataract of frozen flames, producing visual ambiguities and oxymorons which augment and complicate the iconographical syntheses. The symmetry produces a related effect. Psychologically, a symmetrical form is more susceptible to ambiguity. Slight adjustments of visual cues can change the thrust (in, up, down, across, motionless) of a design, and hence its meaning. Many designs seem almost like inkblots or mandalas, inviting the reader to contribute a wide range of associations, and the binary structure of symmetry invites dualistic, divided, con-

---

study will no doubt disclose other structural possibilities in other copies, but it is surely an exaggeration to expect seven really distinct pictorial narratives. In two copies (A and E) we do not have firm information as to the order Blake intended, and one must assume that the title page, Preludium, and sixteen text plates always remained in the same sequence.

trary, dialectical reflections. Most important, the necessary frontality of symmetrical forms poses an almost threatening address to the viewer. The pictures in *Urizen* "come at us" directly. We are not allowed to view them as detached voyeurs who spy on a scene which betrays no awareness of our presence. The isolation of the figures, their frontal arrangement, and the fact that many of them look directly out of the picture make it clear that their primary relationship is not with a larger world or landscape in which they exist but with us, their viewers. The ultimate effect of Blake's symmetry, in other words, is to draw the reader into it, or what is the same thing, invite the reader to incorporate the pictures into himself.

The meaning of any particular plate in the *Urizen* illustrations (or in Blake's other books, for that matter) is thus a function of the interplay between three contributing factors: (1) the relation of the design to scenes or events in the textual narrative; (2) the placement of the design in the sequence or gallery of plates around it; (3) the intrinsic visual properties of the design, including its compositional dynamics and its tendency to allude, in a nonsequential, nonnarrative fashion, to any number of other compositions in and out of Blake's work. With these three considerations in mind, let us explore the pictorial gallery which is half the experience of *Urizen.*

2. *Framing Elements: Title page, Preludium, and Final Plate*

The interplay between narrative and antinarrative elements in the illustrations of *Urizen* may be seen most dramatically in the relationship between two of the most securely fixed designs in the pictorial gallery, the first and last plates. These two pictures convey the basic peripeteia of Urizen's story: he begins, as seen in the title page [46], by creating books or tablets of law and assuming a godlike power over creation; he ends, as seen in plate 28 [47], by being trapped in the Net of Religion he has created. The first and last plates, then, would seem to correspond rather precisely to the narrative progression of the poem, working as a summary of plot.

When we attend to the compositional qualities of the two designs, however, a slightly different effect may be observed. The final plate is constructed as a kind of mirror image of the title page, repeating some elements directly and subjecting others to symmetrical reversals. The presence of the rounded-arch structure and stone tablets in both pictures, and the reversal of the protruding foot from left to right suggest a literal mirroring. More pervasive, however, is the sense of metaphorical reversal: in the concluding plate Urizen's eyes are open instead of closed, his hands are at rest instead of working, his frail, unfettered body has become a muscular physique, the tablets of law have become tombstones, and Urizen's intense inward concentration has become a passive air of defeat, with a note of receptivity to outward stimuli. It is almost as if Blake were saying that the end of Urizen's story may be seen by holding a mirror up to its beginning. The relation of beginning and end is not so much in their terminal positions in a linear sequence of cause and effect as in a kind of display at the end of the implications which reside in the beginning. Urizen's entrapment in his own creations is implicit, in other words, in the very act of making those creations. The gravestones are implied in the tablets of the law, and the enclosing net is implied in the labyrinth of tree branches which surrounds Urizen.

The inevitability of the final plate is so strongly implied in the title page that we tend to forget, I suspect, that neither design really illustrates the text, and that both contradict the narrative in important details. Urizen is never described in the poem as trapped in the Net of Religion; he wanders over the "aged heavens" leaving the net behind him to enclose the human race. The final episode of the poem presents an image of liberation from this web (Fuzon and his followers leaving the world), not entrapment in it. A similar problem arises if we try to see the title page as a literal illustration of Urizen in Chapter II writing "in books formd of metals/ . . . the secrets of wisdom" (4:24-25, E 71). The design corresponds much more closely in its details to a scene described in Chapter III of *The Book of Ahania*, an episode which takes place after Urizen has struck down his son, Fuzon, and long after he writes his first books in the pre-creation world.[25] And none of the textual episodes which can be linked with the title page accounts for one important feature of the picture: although Urizen is consistently described as the original author of all his writings, producing them alone from his self-absorbed contemplations, Blake presents him pictorially as a copyist who transcribes the contents of the book he sits on (he evidently keeps his place in the text with his toe). The Jehovah who carves his words in stone and metal in the text becomes a mere scribe or exegete in the design, making books out of other books rather than

[25] In *Ahania* Urizen sits on a rock and the "Tree of Mystery" springs up over his head, roofing him in (as shown in the title page) and taking root in the ground again on the other side. The text of *Urizen* provides none of these background details, describing Urizen's writing of his first books as occurring in the void of his solitude.

out of his imagination. In this light, we may be seeing not Urizen but Rintrah or Palamabron, one of the "children of Los" whose hands are employed by Urizen to "give his Laws to the Nations" (*SL* 3:8, E 65), or a portrait of the artist as literary—and literal—interpreter.

The first and last plates of *Urizen*, then, while they at first appear to be mere illustrations of opening and closing episodes in the textual narrative, are more precisely understood as the framing elements of an independent pictorial statement. If we read them as the beginning and end of a pictorial narrative they tell us a story with many more overtly satiric elements than we find in the text. Urizen is diminished and ridiculed in the distorting mirror of satire, and his ironic entrapment in his own snare becomes much more explicit than it is in the text alone. This is not the case with most of the designs. Many of them will depict Urizen as a heroic, titanic figure engaged in a cosmic struggle. By introducing his gallery with an ironic portrait Blake creates an ambiguous context in which satire and epic will be very difficult to disentangle: we will be alternately tempted to laugh at Urizen and to see him as a tragic figure.

The most general function of the title page, then, is to prepare us for the paradoxical and ambiguous world of intertwined contraries that we are about to enter. We encounter on this first plate a satire on the wisdom figure, a parody of the philosopher worthy of Rochester's diatribes against the rational animal. This by way of introduction to what is certainly not a mock epic in the Augustan sense (a cry of outrage or despair at the decline from epic values), but rather a mock epic in the revolutionary sense, an epic which attacks the values of previous epics and posits new values to replace them. We also encounter at the entrance to our gallery a picture which ostensibly sets the tone for what is to follow and which apparently illustrates a particular text fairly closely. Both of these impressions are contradicted by what follows. The title page presents a unity which is ready to fly apart at the seams.

The energies which will shatter the monolithic caricature-world of Urizen are not long in coming. We turn the page to a Preludium [48] whose words explode with waves of vegetative flames and sinuous curves of drapery. Before we look at this design in itself it might be well to note that the strong contrast between its sinuous asymmetrical forms and the rigid symmetrical structure of the title page serves as a simplified preview of the contrary forces which will govern the remaining compositions. Many of the plates render the human form in emotional extremes which are conveyed by exaggerated contraction or expansion of the body, by centripetal and centrifugal spatial dynamics, and by extremes of brightness and darkness. A substantial number of plates constructed on the schemata of the circle and rounded arch convey a primary feeling of intense contraction, withdrawal, and enclosure (plates 4, 7, 8, 9, 11, 16, 17, 22, 28 [51, 60-62, 64, 72, 73, 78, 47]). Some, constructed around the S-curve and spiral, convey a more expansive, open feeling (plates 2, 3, 6, 13, 14, 18 [48, 49, 54, 67, 69, 74]). But equally characteristic is Blake's technique of synthesizing contrary forces in a single composition. Sometimes this will take the form of a contracted human body in an explosive, expansive space (plates 16, 22 [72, 78]), or of an expansive human body in a crushing contracting space, as in plate 10 [63]. Sometimes a single human form will disclose both expansive and contracted lineaments, coupling long, sinuous curves in the lower body with a cramped, compressed feeling in the shoulders and head.

We discussed the general significance of these "pulsative" dynamics earlier as an embodiment of Blake's understanding of form as governed by the life of the body—internally in the systole and diastole of the heartbeat, externally in the dilation and contraction of sensory openings, and we saw them used in *The Book of Thel* as a way of illustrating the exploration of perspectives. Pictorially, Urizen begins where Thel left off, in a posture of self-absorbed contraction, and explores the consequences of the attempt to impose that kind of form and perception on the world. The most obvious consequence is ironic reversal: Urizen's search for a "solid without fluctuation" is like trying to cap a volcano; it merely serves to build up pressure so that the inevitable outbreak of energy is more violent and destructive.

Blake sometimes presents the reaction to symmetrical order as mere chaos (as in plate 5 [53], where Urizen opens his book of wisdom to reveal only a riot of disorganized colors like the ones which symbolize spiritual blindness in *Albion Rose*),[26] but more often he displays some version of "living flames/ Intelligent, organiz'd: arm'd/ With destruction & plagues" (*BL* 3:28-30, E 90). "Flame" is, of course, a metonymy for all sorts of sinuous, energetic forms. Even in his moment of purest self-absorption and contraction, expansive, asymmetrical forms threaten to shatter Urizen's solidity: on the title page his own name writhes and coils, beginning with a vortex and concluding, suggests Erdman, with whips.[27] The rigid lines of Urizen's own body are broken by the sinuous flow of his

[26] See Chap. II, note 23, above.

[27] *TIB*, p. 183.

beard, a flow which may evoke the "cold floods of abstraction" which he pours into his book, but which, if warmed by the imagination, will consume that book: "His snowy beard . . . streams like lambent flames down his wide breast" (*A* b:16, E 57).

What we want, clearly, are intelligent, organized flames without the plagues, which is exactly what Blake provides in the plate that follows the title page [48]. Above the asymmetrical burst of flames a female guardian angel guides a cautious-looking baby over the tongues of fire. The S-curve formed by the woman's body and gown makes her a humanized, moderated version of the more violent energy forms beneath her (her moderation further implied by the modest coiffure), and links her with the scroll-like lineaments of the Bard who introduces us to *Songs of Experience*. The child, accordingly, may be associated with the cherub astride the Bard/ St. Christopher in the frontispiece to *Experience* [1], the child on the cloud in *Innocence* [2], and the children riding the serpent at the end of *Thel* [44]. The iconography of the Preludium does little to narrow these associations to specific names and places: Blake allows us more play for our imagination in this plate than in any other in the book. This seems only fitting when we note that the purpose of the design, as Blake was to suggest when he reprinted it for the *Small Book of Designs*, is to "Teach these Souls to Fly" (E 662) with their own wings, not to carry them all the way. So the baby is the reader, or the child he must become to participate in prophetic vision, and the woman is a visionary reader's guide, a sign that the monolithic symmetry of the previous plate is not the whole story. On another level, the child is Blake himself and the woman is his muse, one of the Eternals whose "swift winged words" will teach *his* soul to fly. Blake's invocation, however, offers comfort to his muses at the same time it requests their aid. In that light, the woman may personify the maternal, guarding and guarded dimension of Blake's imagination (later called Enitharmon), ushering a newborn Eternal into the fallen world, telling him to "fear not" to unfold his visions. The child, then, is like the inspiring cherub of *Experience* who must be carried through the world; in the immediate context of *Urizen* he is a newborn Orc (cf. [76]) or Fuzon, a revolutionary who "flames up" at birth but who burns out without some help from the imagination. The woman is certainly the feminine half of the imagination seen (as she is described in the text) "encircled . . . / With fires of prophecy," not "*from* the sight of Urizen and Orc" (22:42-44; italics mine), but as a guide for Orc, an alternative to

Urizen. Enitharmon is suppressed and stifled with protection in the text, but in the designs, as we shall see, she becomes a powerful figure.

3. *The Spaces of Hell*

If the title page exhibits the lineaments of contraction and the Preludium displays a moderated and mediated expansion (accompanied by graphic unity of text and design), the first plate of the text proper [49] presents an image of radical expansion which is kept graphically distinct from the text. We have now been released by the guiding woman and left to run or fly through the "flames of desire" by ourselves; the fact that the figure is running to the left, against the current of our progress into the book, in the opposite direction from Enitharmon's flight, may suggest that these flames are armed with destruction and plagues like those which surround the Avenging demon called "Pestilence" in the Bible paintings or the figure of Hand in *Jerusalem* (see [50, 97]). We must also keep open the possibility, however, that these are the "thought-creating fires of Orc" (*SL* 6:6) which consume "the five gates" of the senses (*A* 16:22), and prepare to see our naked runner as an image of inspiration like the figure of the Holy Spirit sketched at the top of Blake's title page for Genesis (see [107]). If we restrict ourselves to the immediate text of *Urizen*, the ambiguity remains unresolved. The figure in plate 3 [49] might be on either side in the cosmic war whose outbreak is described in the text. On the one hand it might represent one of the Eternals in the prelapsarian eternity which Urizen perceives as "unquenchable burnings" (4:13), reacting against Urizen's laws "in the flames of eternal fury" (5:2). On the other it might be Urizen himself, looking inwards, fighting "with the fire; consum'd/ Inwards, into a deep world within" (4:14-15), "in unseen conflictions . . . unseen in tormenting passions" (3:14, 19), or perhaps Urizen suffering the reaction of the Eternals: "In fierce anguish & quenchless flames/ . . . To the desarts and rocks He ran raging/ To hide" (5:19-21). If we allow ourselves free rein in the imagery of *Urizen* the picture is of Orc who "with fierce flames/ Issu'd from Enitharmon" (19:45-46; cf. [76]) or Fuzon who "Flam'd out!" at birth (23:18; cf. [80]). The fact that the figure's face is turned away from us is Blake's very literal way of insisting that we contemplate all these possibilities, or, at a minimum, that we meditate on the basic ambiguities of the composition regardless of who is in it.

There is something maddening about this sort of omnidirectional ambiguity. We may be tempted to think Blake provides too little and asks too much, and that the design is more like a Rorschach test than a pictorial statement. At the risk of sounding like a true believer I would suggest that this is precisely what Blake intends. We might prefer that he tell us exactly who the figure is, where he is going, and whether those flames can singe a sleeve, but that would remove us from the action and give us a Urizenic illusion of an objective, nonparticipatory standpoint. This does not mean that any random association may be imposed on the picture and it does not mean that every reading is equally compelling: Fuzon and Orc are significant parallels to the figure in the picture, but they are probably not what Blake had primarily in mind when he designed it. What he certainly did have in mind was the tension between contrary feelings and interpretations in his composition, and a search for ways of making the viewer participate in that tension.

The next plate resolves at least one aspect of this tension: plate 4 [51] is an unambiguous vision of torment experienced by a human form combining the dynamics of expansion (the extended right leg) with a contracted clutching of his head. The ambiguity now shifts to the cause or nature of the torment: we can see the figure as sitting in a shower of dark rain, a thicket of subterranean or submarine vegetation, or a curtain of fire. The implicit synaesthesia of the earlier plates (Urizen's beard as a flood of frozen fire, the flame-vegetation of the Preludium) now becomes explicit, combining all four elements into a single system of forms. One way of gauging this ambiguity is to compare plate 4 with a relatively unambiguous presentation of a similar theme, the figure of Water in the *Gates of Paradise* series [52]. The rain of tears which washes this figure becomes in *Urizen* (as the text of plate 4 suggests) "cataracts of fire blood & gall" (4:46) which may be palpable, vegetative obstructions or "enormous forms of energy" (4:48). Later in the book Blake will make pictorial discriminations among the elements of earth, air, fire, and water [80], giving each a personality and composing a substantial number of his plates in terms of the dominance of particular elements (earth: 8, 9, 10 [61-63]; water: 12 [66]; air: 13, 14, 15 [67, 69, 71]; fire: 16, 18, 20 [72, 74, 76]). An equally important consideration, however, is their absorption into a unified sensory field. For Blake, synaesthesia (the "enlarged & numerous senses" of prelapsarian man; *MHH* 11, E 37) is not just a special state of awareness, but the basic condition of a healthy body and spirit. When it is suppressed by being shut up in a "ratio of the five senses," usually with the emphasis on sight, a reaction occurs. The unified field of sensation becomes a torrent of ambiguous data, an oxymoronic realm of "petrific . . . chaos (*U* 3:26), and synaesthesia reasserts itself as a world of confusion and disorientation. The figure crouching in the hellish rain of plate 4 clutches his head rather than his body (which is equally afflicted by the rain) because his affliction is more mental than corporeal. His problem is not that he is burning, drowning, or freezing but that, like the spectator, he cannot decide *what* he is feeling.

The next plate of *Urizen* [53] provides a relief from this sort of ambiguity: we now know that we are seeing Urizen unfolding his "book of brass" to display "the secrets of dark contemplation" (4:26) to us and to the Eternals. In four copies of *Urizen* (F,D,E,G), however, the absence of plate 4, which is the only plate that explains how Urizen writes his books, would make even this plate, and the title page, rather ambiguous. Another problem raised by the design (aside from the touch of putting mysterious hieroglyphics in the book in some copies, chaotic pigments in others) is the possible irony of the positioning of Urizen's book: Blake aligns its spine with the dividing line between his own columns of text. The effect of this placement is to identify Blake's own book with Urizen's book-within-the-book. Perhaps the "of" in *The Book of Urizen* is to be read like the "of" in Shelley's "Hymn of Apollo," and we are to see the Eternals who dictate Blake's verse as *including*, not just opposing, Urizen. Our analysis of textual structures would seem to confirm this: Blake's satire on Urizenic form includes the incorpation of it into the structure of his own work. Urizen greets us on the title page not only because this book is about him, but because it is by him. The fact that it was customary in illuminated literary manuscripts since antiquity to begin with a portrait of the author[28] must have amused Blake as he designed these portraits to satirize not just others but himself.

The ambiguity of the relations between Urizen and the other Eternals was, as we saw in the analysis of the text, a central way in which Blake undermined the moral distinctions of his Miltonic source. This ambiguity receives its most complex pictorial rendering in plate 6 [54], one of Blake's most extraordinary fusions of multiple iconographic themes into a new unity. The central paradox disclosed by the picture is obvious even before we deal with its more recondite aspects: this is clearly a fall into an inferno, either of the rebellious angels before creation or of the damned at the Last Judgment. But

[28] P. D'Ancona and E. Aeschlimann, *The Art of Illumination* (London, 1969), p. 8.

the central figure does not seem to know that he is part of a vision of torment. His calm dignity contrasts with the struggling contortions of the figures falling beside him, and his fall appears more like a graceful swan dive which, if viewed upside down, would look like a flight. The presence of numerous images of perdition and punishment—the constricting serpents, the threatening spears at the upper right, the flayed skins with their bestial faces amid the flames (all traditional images in renderings of the Last Judgment)[29]—does not neutralize the feeling of triumph conveyed by the pose of the central figure, and challenges us to find a perspective from which these contradictory impressions may be reconciled.

The immediate context in the poem is the war in heaven which Urizen is in the process of losing: "Fires pour thro' the void on all sides/ On Urizen's self-begotten armies" (5:15-16). Thus we can view this design from the perspective of the unfallen Eternals as the fate of the "primeval Priest" who, like that other mythical priest, Laocoön, defies the gods and is killed along with his sons by divine serpents. When Blake later engraved the Laocoön group he identified the central figure with "King Jehovah" (recalling Urizen's role as lawgiver) and his two sons with Satan and Adam. But this perspective cannot be very comforting for the Eternals: if Urizen is a priest like Laocoön, the void he has discovered is like the one in the belly of the Trojan horse—we ignore it and celebrate the fall of Urizen/ Laocoön/Jehovah at our peril. The design is too evocative of an upside-down crucifixion (the crime committed, Blake thought, by "the modern church"; see *VLJ*, E 554), with Christ's repose contrasted to the struggling of the two thieves, for us to be happy with this as an image of the defeat of our foe. Blake saw as early as *The Marriage of Heaven and Hell* that Jehovah was not simply the author of the laws on Urizen's stony tablets, but also a spirit of inspiration who "dwells in flaming fire" and is ultimately identified with the resurrected Jesus: "Know that after Christ's death, he became Jehovah" (*MHH* 5, E 35).

Suppose, then, that we try looking at this design from Urizen's perspective. From his point of view the life of the Eternals was a hell, and he begins his address to them with a rhetorical question:

[29] Michelangelo's Last Judgment includes a portrait of the artist himself as a flayed human carcass in the devilish hands of a hated rival. For further information on Blake's treatment of this theme, see my booklet "Blake's Visions of the Last Judgment," a special number published by the *Blake Newsletter* (Fall, 1975) for the 1975 MLA Blake Seminar.

"Why will you die O Eternals?/ Why live in unquenchable burnings?" (4:12-13, E 70). But this view of the design is subject to the same ironic undercutting we saw in the "eternal" view: "the fires of hell" are to the devils in *The Marriage of Heaven and Hell* "the enjoyments of Genius; which to Angels [and to Urizenic rationalists] look like torment and insanity" (*MHH* 5, E 35). Urizen's perspective distorts the blissful anarchy of eternity, making the "spiral ascent to the heavens of heavens" bend downward in the form of a constricting serpent ("thought chang'd the infinite to a serpent"; *E* 10:16, E 62). Urizen's perspective, like that of the Eternals, cannot be kept in focus. As Erdman suggests, "both parties can see this as the lot of their adversaries,"[30] but if both parties look hard enough they will begin to feel less secure about their respective positions.

One suspects, however, that the disquieting repose of the central figure in plate 6 is not just designed to make us "give the devil his due," whoever he may be. The design suggests an implicit parallel between the fall into hell, the Crucifixion, and the Resurrection, a metaphor which Blake did not develop explicitly in his poetry until the later prophecies, where he envisioned Albion imitating Jesus' sacrifice by throwing himself into the "Furnaces of Affliction" (see *J* 96:35, E 253). This act of "Self-annihilation" becomes the central focus in Blake's vision of personal and collective apocalypse, the imaginative act in which an old Selfhood dies and a new one is born. It is this image of regeneration which subverts the apparent context of war, defeat, fall, and perdition from any point of view, and which made Blake return to this design for the lineaments of Christ in his later painting of the Resurrection [55].

Given his absorption in cosmogony Blake may also have been acquainted with some form of the Orphic deity Phanes (also called Eros), who plays a large role in Neoplatonic creation myths and who is depicted with his body wrapped in a spiraling serpent and surrounded by the heads of animals [56].[31] Blake certainly knew of this deity in another form, as the winged cupid breaking out of the shell, an image he used in *The Gates of Paradise* [57], and which he would have seen combined with the spiraling serpent in Jacob Bryant's *Mythology* [58]. In this context the spiral serpent becomes an image of rebirth (a meaning which Blake could, of course, have

30 *TIB*, p. 188.

31 I am indebted to Judith L. Ott for calling this depiction of Phanes to my attention. For further discussion of Blake's use of the Phanes myth, see Kathleen Raine, *Blake and Tradition*, II, 149, 182-83.

derived independently from popular images such as the caduceus) and the animal faces amid the flames symbolize the new forms of life which spring up as Phanes is born from the cosmic egg. All of this must be regarded as highly tentative, however, until some firmer connection is established between the Orphic imagery and any engravings or descriptions which Blake could have seen.[32] Blake's use of the serpent-wrapped human body in his color print of *Elohim Creating Adam* [59] strongly suggests, however, that he saw the iconography of *Urizen* 6 as a complex metaphorical fusion of the Creation, the Fall, the Crucifixion, the Resurrection, and the Last Judgment into a single glowing form, a vortex which leads us to a new plane of perception.

In the context of the first section of *Urizen*, however, these images of hope remain ironic and unrealized, for the pictures which surround *Urizen* 6 stress its location in infernal regions. In plate 7 [60] we encounter someone to whom the fires of hell are clearly not the "delights of genius" but the "torments of insanity." It scarcely matters by now whether this is an Eternal, Urizen, Los, or a preview of Orc, since no character in the poem is left untouched by the "wrenching apart" of the eternal order. Still, the immediate context does suggest that this is primarily Los (described in the text on this plate), howling as "Urizen was rent from his side" (6:4). Los's gestures contrast significantly with those of the head-clutching figure in the dark rain of plate 4. The earlier figure seemed to be trying to hold a splitting skull together, or keep an insecure head on its shoulders; the torsion of Los's gesture suggests, on the other hand, that he is trying to pull himself apart, perhaps to ease the pains of delivering Urizen. The absence of foreshortening (Los's legs and hips seem directly attached to his shoulders) is a gruesomely literal way of saying that the wrenching of Urizen from Los's side has left him without a torso.

This and the next three plates in *Urizen* [60-63] constitute what might be called the "buried alive" phase of the pictorial narrative, centering on a theme which is not described explicitly in the text[33]

[32] There is a drawing (reproduced in Panofsky, *Hercules am Schweidege* [Berlin, 1930], pl. 9) attributed to Pierino del Vaga which is evidently based upon the Modena relief reproduced above, but I have found no evidence that Blake knew of it. Not surprisingly, Blake's treatment of the serpent-wrapped figure is closer stylistically to the original Mithraic bas-relief (which he could not have seen) than it is to the more sophisticated version provided by the seventeenth-century engraving.

[33] Burial alive is implied in the images of stony sleep, suffocation, and the

but which occupies a strong place in the illustrations. Although this series of plates lacks the obviously hopeful imagery that we found in plate 6, it does not present simple visions of defeated, buried life. The most ghastly vision, death itself (plate 8 [61]), is clearly an embryonic form, a suggestion that even the most contracted and dead form is like a fetus, a potentially new creature. Similarly, the literal depictions of burial alive (plates 9 and 10 [62 and 63]) are notable for their images of resistance and Sisyphus-like endurance, which provide a powerful counterthrust to the crushing stones around them. In plate 9 Urizen has come about as close to turning into stone as possible, and yet Blake had him say, in his caption for the separate print of this plate, "Eternally I labour on" (E 662). This counterthrust begins to have some effect in plate 10 as Los (or Urizen) pushes the rocks far enough apart to stretch his limbs.

We are reminded in plate 11 [64], however, that the masses of rock which confine these figures are really a mental state of "stony sleep" (6:7). Urizen and Los appear together, distinct now for the first time because their "wrenching apart" is completed, but clearly not yet healed. Their postures look more passive and defeated than those they assumed when buried alive, as if their struggle to rise and expand and "labor on" depended on the presence of an external counterforce of gravity and contraction. Given a surrounding space of expansive flames, as in plate 11, their reaction is passivity and contraction, a kind of perverse contrariety that Blake employs in a different way in plate 16 [72], his portrait of the element of fire as a crouching nude whose body is like a contracted stone or coal at the center of an expansive, radiant aura of flames. The stony enclosures which confined Los and Urizen now seem figuratively "within" them and literally "behind" them, a brick dome behind Los and a stone arch behind Urizen.[34] The scene is one of the most definite and literal in the whole book in terms of relation to the verbal narrative. Los's recoiling posture suggests that he is "shrinking from his task" (see 13:20) of giving Urizen a body, and his hammer is at rest, perhaps ready to slip from his hand. Urizen's minimal human form (skeleton, sinews, nerves, and blood vessels) has been completed and chained to the earth, although the absence of a chain in copy G makes the point that the real chain is the body itself or the

---

enclosure of various characters in globes, but the dominant sense of space in the text of the opening chapters is that of a vast, empty abyss.

[34] Erdman sees this arch as a leaning or falling tower (*TIB*, p. 193).

"bound mind" which inhabits it. The fires of Los's forge still surround Urizen, but they seem to be producing the cloud of smoke on which the text is printed, a suggestion that they are participating in Los's reaction to his creation: "His fires beheld, and sickening,/ Hid their strong limbs in smoke" (13:22-23, E 76). But the most obvious compositional statement is the parallel positioning of the legs of the two figures, a posture which demanded considerable distortion in Los's figure in order to show him recoiling from as well as imitating the form of his creation. This parallelism is Blake's way of restating the theme of entrapment by one's own creation, the idea which governs the first and last plates of *Urizen.* Los is shown "becoming what he beholds," a process which is even more compelling when the object you behold is a part of yourself, your own artifact.

4. *The Spaces of Heaven*

The void in which Los and Urizen appear has up to this point been portrayed primarily as a subterranean realm of stony contraction and fiery expansion, in a style which embodies tremendous tension and thrust even in motionless, imprisoned figures. As Los shrinks from his task, however, we move into a section of text and design in which the pressure of antagonism and contrariety seems to relax. Urizen stops being a Sisyphus: he appears as a sky-god huddled fearfully among the Eternals [71], or as an airborne Tantalus seeking a drink [69], or as a man who loves water being drowned in it [66]. The void is now conveyed by imagery of water and air, stressing the boundless indefinite rather than fiery underworld. As the fires in Los's furnace are banked Urizen experiences a new nightmare: "All the myriads of Eternity:/ All the wisdom & joy of life:/ Roll like a sea around him" (14:28-30, E 76), a situation which is depicted in plate 12 [66]. Urizen now faces a worse torment than burial in a "solid without fluctuation"—a space devoid of qualities, in which the thrusts of expansion and contraction have nothing to push against. Urizen seems to be trying both sorts of thrusts at once in plate 12 (his posture suggests a breaststroke), but the composition clearly stresses the futility of his struggles. The horizontal lines remain almost completely undisturbed by his movements, and the position of his beard suggests that he is not moving either up or down, but hovering motionless in a shadowy fluid despite his struggle to gain momentum. In a literal sense, then, it is difficult to see the space around Urizen as water or any material fluid: if it were, his movements would have more effect on it, or on himself. One way of explaining the effect of the picture would be to posit an "ethereal" fluid which fills Urizen's void, the substance of an absolute Newtonian space which is unmoved and unbounded, and which is free of the laws of gravitation (a phenomenon experienced by astronauts who have discovered how difficult it is to swim in the air at zero gravity). Another and perhaps simpler explanation is to see Urizen not just "in," but "as" the sea which rolls around him. Blake suggests this in most copies by rendering Urizen's beard in a series of rippling horizontals which parallel the flickering wave forms around him, and in copy G he virtually dissolves Urizen's body into the surrounding space, hiding his lineaments in a watery gloom which is relieved only by the highlights on his knees, feet, hands, and head. We have seen a similar blending of the body with its setting in earlier plates, Urizen treated as a stone amid stones, Enitharmon as a stylized version of the wave forms over which she floats.

The next plate (13 [67]) provides a very literal declaration of the idea that a human form can *be* the space around it, not merely reside in it. At the center of the page a starry night is unveiled by a woman whose hands dissolve into crescent moons or cloud boundaries and whose body looks like the clouds she pushes apart. Her pose is almost a reverse of Enitharmon's in the Preludium, a suggestion that Blake is giving us another guide, or invoking another muse. If the first muse was depicted as a prophetic scroll of drapery synthesizing the forms of fire and vegetation, the second is a cloudy sky-goddess composed of water and air. Her proper name is less certain. If we confine ourselves to the text of *Urizen* it can only be Enitharmon, "the first female form now separate" that we have seen since the beginning, beheld "Pale as a cloud of snow/ Waving before the face of Los" (18:10-12, E 77). If we allow ourselves slightly more latitude, this is Ahania, the female counterpart to Urizen, who upon the completion of Urizen's body and world can be seen "circling dark Urizen,/ As the moon anguishd circles the earth" (*Ah* 2:39-40, E 84; cf. illustration, *Ah* 1).

It is not hard to understand why Blake would want to reinvoke his muse pictorially at this stage in his progress through the book. Both the textual and pictorial narratives have reached an emotional nadir after moving through a series of increasingly bleak "visions of torment." Blake seems to have come to the point reached by Urizen in *The Four Zoas* in which the fall reaches its extreme limit, and every direction begins to seem up: "For when he came to where a Vortex ceasd to operate/ Nor down nor up remaind then if he turnd & lookd back/ From whence he came twas upward all" (*FZ* 72:16-18, E 342). Enitharmon appears at this point in the pictorial narrative because the process of claustrophobic contraction and disorientation can go no further. In the text, Los has finished his work of creating a body for Urizen and recoiled in despair from his own creation. But that is not the only emotion he feels. This is also the moment in which he begins to feel pity for Urizen, and in which that emotion takes on a life of its own, revealing itself as a cloud-woman who provides the first unambiguous image of hope since the Preludium.

The cloud-woman also symbolizes our release from the subterranean realm of the previous section, and the transformation of the obscure, shadowy void into a night sky:

> For in changeable clouds and darkness
> In a winterly night beneath,
> The Abyss of Los stretch'd immense:
> And now seen now obscur'd, to the eyes
> Of Eternals the visions remote
> Of the dark seperation appear'd.
> As glasses discover Worlds
> In the endless Abyss of space.
>
> (*U* 15:3-10, E 77)

Our vision of Enitharmon/ Ahania is similarly a "dark seperation" in the firmament of plate 13, still enveloped in Urizenic darkness, but it now has a seasonal, temporal definition: a "winterly night" implies a spring morning, a terminus in the abyss. The prophetic woman is, I would suggest, a personification of this new definition of night, a figure rather like the one who inspires Edward Young in his *Night Thoughts*: "whose modest, maiden beams/ Give us a new creation . . . whose mild dominion's silver key/ Unlocks our hemisphere, and sets to view/ Worlds beyond number" (Night IX: 1675-76, 1680-81). The fact that Blake's friend Stothard illustrated this passage of Young's work with a sky-goddess parting the clouds much like Blake's Enitharmon [68][35] suggests that Urizen's nightmare is being transformed into a night-vision of inspiration, and that the void is being redefined as a field for exploration and creativity, not rejected

[35] My thanks to Thomas L. Minnick for pointing out the parallel in Stothard's illustrations to Young's *Night Thoughts*. Stothard's figure cannot, of course, be a source for Blake's, since it did not appear until 1798.

as a purely negative "space undivided by existence" which strikes "horror into the soul" (14:46-47).

The next creative act we observe in the sequence of textual plates (plate 15 [71]) occurs, as we might expect, in the sky which Enitharmon unveils for us. Three human figures (four in copy G) and an eagle in folds of cloud-drapery hover over a dark hemisphere (presumably the "dark globe of Urizen," which now contains Los in his divided form), the youthful figure in the center reaching down to spread a wash of ambiguous colors over the globe. The text suggests that this is a vision of the Eternals who, appalled at Los's division into sexual forms, decide to abandon the world and enclose it in a "Tent of Science": "Spread a Tent, with strong curtains around them/ Let cords & stakes bind in the Void/ That Eternals may no longer behold them' " (19:2-4)—an act which seems the direct reverse of the unveiling Enitharmon has just performed. This may also be seen as a flashback to that earlier moment in the poem when "Los round the dark globe of Urizen,/ Kept watch for Eternals to confine,/ The obscure separation alone" (5:38-40). The vision also parallels, but does not directly illustrate, two other events: Urizen's enclosure of the world in a Web or Net of Religion, and the flight of Urizen's son Fuzon from "the pendulous earth" and the flood which follows ("And the salt ocean rolled englob'd"; 28:23). These parallels go beyond mere resemblances in action and verbal imagery. The wash of colors spreading over the globe resembles a flood more than a tent, and the beard of the Eternal at the right seems to be turning into a rain which contributes to the flood. The storm-cloud atmosphere, the aged faces of the Eternals who flank the central figure, and the pictorial echo of Urizen with his compasses (see [24]) in the downward-reaching gesture of the central figure all help to support what we saw implied in the text, that the Eternals' reaction to Urizen makes them become what they behold. In copy A Blake stresses their imitation of Urizenic paranoia by giving them wide, suspicious eyes, emphasizing their "Wonder, awe, fear, astonishment" (18:13) as they hover, "petrify'd" at creation. In copies B, D, and G they look rather gloomy and drowsy, an imitation of Urizen's melancholy and stony sleep.

The first creative act which occurs in Enitharmon's newly revealed sky, then, is at best ambiguous, perhaps only an imitation of Urizen's initial withdrawal from eternity. We can see the design as a pictorial allusion to God's disapproval of the world and his decision to destroy it with a flood. We can also see, on the other hand, a suggestion of a providential act of creativity, a pictorial echo of treatments of God dividing the waters from the dry land, an act which, like the creation of the "Tent of Science," will establish a basic order in Urizen's chaos.

In most copies of *Urizen*[36] Blake followed this vision of the Eternals' reaction almost immediately with a vision of the specific event to which they are reacting, Los giving birth to his "Pity" for Urizen in the form of a globe of blood which is the embryonic form of Enitharmon (plate 17 [73]). In a strict narrative sense this plate belongs just before plate 13, but Blake's freedom from this sort of concern should be evident by now: the plate always follows the one it logically precedes. Although this plate can be readily described with much of the language in the episode it illustrates, it is one of Blake's most radiantly independent visions, bringing the ambiguous Rorschach quality we have noted in other designs to a rare pitch of intensity and allusive breadth. Less well known than the portrait of Urizen with his compasses in *Europe*, it has the same archetypal inevitability, as if Blake had discovered the design rather than invented it.

At a sensuous level, plate 17 fuses the imagery of birth and creation, and their associated feelings of pleasure and pain. One view of the design will enlarge the globe to a diameter of eight thousand miles, placing it in outer space with a giant deity hovering over it. A blink of the eye reduces it to a human being alone in darkness, dreadfully wounded and pouring out his life in cataracts of blood. The setting of the picture is the most absolute void in the whole book—a dead blackness which offers no sign of element, horizon, or boundary. The synaesthetic networks of hair, veins, nerves, tears, and milk which flow from the figure produce a related ambiguity, forcing us to see the figure as weeping, bleeding, and suffering extreme pain (indicated by the rigid extension of the fingers), and yet simultaneously involved in a life-giving, nourishing, protective act, as if the process of impregnation, formation of womb and placenta, gestation, and birth were being undertaken as a single act of conscious, external creation. The maternal overtones are so strong, in fact, that it has

36 Plate 17 immediately follows 15 in copies D and G; there are two intervening plates in B and C, and one (presumably) in E. Copy A evidently puts 17 in the first section, after plate 7 (or after 11 in Erdman's hypothetical reconstruction; see *TIB*, p. 182).

been difficult for some viewers to see this as the male figure of Los; Keynes identifies it as Enitharmon.[37]

But the iconography is relatively unambiguous. It parallels, but does not illustrate, the description of Urizen's refuge from the angry Eternals as a womb, a black globe, and a heart in Chapter III, and the account of Urizen's heart in his rib cage in Chapter IVb. What it does illustrate is Los at the moment he feels pity for Urizen, giving birth to a literal embodiment of that pity as both a world and a fetus. We discussed earlier the common assumption that "Los's pity for the chained Urizen is totally misplaced."[38] This design, and the view of Enitharmon as cloud-woman on plate 13, does a good deal to undermine that assumption, suggesting that the birth of Enitharmon and the creation of a world of divided sexuality, while it may horrify the Eternals, is a rather good thing from the point of view of earth-bound mortals. One need only compare an earlier vision of labor pains (Los howling as Urizen is rent from his side, plate 7 [60]) to see that Los's offspring and his manner of bringing them into the world are improving. Another instructive comparison is to place the birth of Enitharmon [73] next to the picture of the Eternals covering the earth with the Tent of Science [71]. Both pictures depict the relationship between a world and a deity or deities: for Los, this relation is composed of "living fibres" which nourish the world at the expense of considerable pain; for the Eternals the relation is one of withdrawal, aversion, and wrath. The fibers and fluids they rain upon the earth will not nourish it, but close it off from eternity; at best their tent is "Stretch'd for a work of eternity" (20:1) which may take place under its protection.

5. *The Spaces of Earth*

This middle or "heavenly" section of Urizen's picture gallery is admittedly shorter and more subject to displacement than the first and last sections (it contains only two fixed text plates, 13 and 15), and serves more as a bridge or transition between the two halves of the book than a major phase in itself. The change in mood which occurs very clearly around the middle of copy D is there also in other copies, but is less explicit. A precise way of gauging this change of key is to compare plates which usually appear before plate 13 with ones that appear after it, especially ones that have in common

[37] *Census*, p. 71.

[38] Tannenbaum, "Blake's Art of Crypsis," p. 154n.

such themes as birth, creation, and exploration. The theme of birth, for instance, is treated exclusively in terms of its anguish in the first section (plate 7 [60]), but receives a more balanced and positive treatment in the births of Enitharmon (plate 17 [73]) and Orc (plate 20 [76]). The flames which burst out around the infant Orc seem more like a burst of purely positive energy than the ambiguous inferno which surrounds the naked runner of plate 3 or the falling Eternals of plate 6. Similarly, the portrait of Los with his hammer in his furnaces (plate 18 [74]) contrasts sharply with his appearances in the first half, burning in torment (plate 7 [60]), buried alive (plate 10 [63]), or in despair over his creation (plate 11 [64]). The flames are now seen as Los's element, his medium rather than his affliction. He now has room to work among the stones, and his posture implies "rest before labour" rather than dismay at the products of labor. Blake seems, in fact, to be playing with figural ambiguity in his eighteenth plate: if Los's grip on the hammer were changed ever so slightly we would see him not as resting but as poised in the backswing of a hammer blow. His cruciform posture, moreover, reminds us of the falling—but implicitly resurrected—Eternal of plate 6.

The theme of the creator beholding his creation is also treated in a way that discloses significant changes in the ethos of *Urizen.* The picture of Los crouching before Enitharmon after she has evolved into a female form [75] echoes the vision of Los crouching next to his first offspring, the chained body of Urizen in plate 11 [64]. The important difference between the two compositions (and the hint of "progress" in the pictorial narrative) is that Los's creation of Enitharmon provides an alternative or contrary to his state of contracted despair, not just a mirror image of it. When he finishes Urizen he "becomes what he beholds," but Enitharmon's flame-enveloped emergence from the word "Pity" in the text is like the flight of Oothoon in *Visions of the Daughters of Albion* [29], a vision of liberating possibilities (cf. p. 67 above).

A theme which emerges only in the second half of *Urizen* is that of exploration and wandering. When Urizen awakes from his stony sleep in Chapters VII and VIII he sets out to "explore his dens," a journey which gives him no joy, "For he saw that life liv'd upon death" (23:27). He is constantly "annoy'd/ By cruel enormities" (20:49-50) which spring up in his forsaken world, and he finds that "no flesh nor spirit could keep/ His iron laws one moment" (23:25-26). A satirical picture of this journey is provided on plate 23 [79], which shows Urizen as a mock Diogenes whose lamp has become a heavy iron ball emanating dull red rays which look more like spikes of "darkness visible." If Diogenes with his lantern was looking for an honest man, Urizen will settle for one who will merely obey his laws. He ignores or evades the lion at the side of his path, failing to recognize that "the just man rages in the wilds/ Where lions roam" (*MHH* 2, E 33), and may in fact appear as a wild, lawless beast in the light of his iron laws. Urizen's disgust with his own world, and his own implicit lawlessness, is suggested by a rather comic detail: he pushes against the frame of the picture as if trying to break the laws of pictorial illusion and escape from the universe in which Blake has placed him.

The climax of Urizen's journey occurs when he, like Los before him, feels pity for his creation and finds that emotion taking on a life of its own. As he wanders over the heavens his tears flow "down on the winds," producing "a cold shadow . . . behind him/ Like a spiders web" (25:4, 9-10) which covers the heavens and promises to evolve, like Los's globe of blood, into a woman, for "the Web is a Female in embrio" (25:18). This moment is depicted on plate 27 [84] as an inward flight, perhaps into that opening he was trying to find in the picture frame on plate 23. But the escape is clearly not what Urizen had hoped for. His gestures suggest alarm and dismay (compare the upraised hands of the fleeing hypocrites in *The Woman Taken in Adultery* [85], either fending off the enormities he is fleeing from or reacting to a worse horror on the other side of the vortex he is entering. In two copies (C and G) this enormity will be the birth of his sons, the four elements, a sequence which reverses the textual narrative; in all the other copies the final horror will be himself, caught in the Web which he is draping over the world. Urizen has finally seen himself in the mirror provided by the final plate.

The most comprehensive pictorial treatment of Urizen's role as explorer is provided by the full-page design of plate 14 [69], in which he appears as a muscular nude diving or doing a handstand amid swirling vapors and ambiguous stone-clouds. Its location as the fourteenth plate in the gallery of *Urizen* emphasizes its function as a parallel and parody of Enitharmon parting the clouds on plate 13, and as a contribution to the air-water imagery of the middle transition section. The sheer magnificence of the composition and the fact that it has no clear textual reference point, however, allowed Blake more flexibility in placing it, so we find it interpolated in the "buried alive" section in four copies (B,E?,F,G). We can see it as an illustration of Urizen "wandering on high" before his tears start to flow into a Web of Religion in the final section, or as a vision of him "self-balanc'd stretch'd o'er the void" (4:18) among the "merciless winds" which he discovers as he withdraws from eternity into himself.

The most striking feature of the composition is its fusion of contrary dynamics, the long curving line of the leg suggesting flight and fall while the contracted shoulders and arms imply arrested motion, recalling the "buried alive" posture. (Blake used this same arrangement of arms and hands in *Jerusalem* to depict a giant buried alive; see [70] and compare the hands of Grodna or Earth on plate 24 [80].) This encounter of opposites is restated in the contrast between the swirling wisps of vapor in the upper half of the picture and the stone-shaped clouds which Urizen encounters at the bottom. These parallels between the lineaments of figure and background provide another instance of the identity of the human form with its setting, an implication which Blake emphasized in his final version of this plate (in copy G) by coloring Urizen's body in the same tones as the clouds around him. As a total form, the picture provides a literal emblem of the paradoxical nature of Urizen's world, a cosmos which is both an "airy nothing" or void of insubstantial abstractions, and yet also a "wide world of solid obstruction" (4:23). The verbal equivalent of this sort of pictorial form can only be expressed in Blakean oxymorons like "petrific . . . chaos" (3:26).

The most rewarding view of the iconography of plate 14 is Hagstrum's suggestion that Blake is alluding to the myth of Tantalus,[39] a role which is hinted at in the text when Urizen is described as "craving with hunger" (20:30) as he explores his dens. Since Tantalus, like Urizen, cannot be killed for his crime by the gods, he is condemned to the kind of eternal torment which is associated with his name—the torment of being "tantalized" endlessly by the threat of annihilation (Pindar and Euripides place Tantalus in the air with a great stone hung over his head which continually threatens to fall) or with the ever-vanishing promise of gratification: he stands up to his neck in a river which disappears whenever he tries to drink from it, or reaches for food placed before him just as it is swept away by the wind.[40] Blake, in typical fashion, seems to have consoli-

[39] *Poet and Painter*, p. 46. See plates XXVIIIA and XXVIIIB.

[40] *Oxford Classical Dictionary*, 2nd ed. (Oxford, 1970), s.v. "Tantalus."

dated many of these elements into a single radiant form. He places Urizen in the air (perhaps following Goltzius' treatment of Tantalus floating upside down),[41] but he eliminates the threatening stone and stresses Urizen's searching, hungry aspect in the lower portion of the design. If Urizen is seen here as bending down to drink from a vanishing river, the irony of our earlier vision of him (plate 12 [66] drowning in a boundless sea ("Dip him in the river who loves water," *MHH* 5:7) is heightened.

But Urizen's thirst is more basic. He is looking for an "end," a stable center such as the one Blake describes in *The Four Zoas*:

> Where self sustaining I may view all things beneath my feet
> Or sinking through these elemental wonders swift to fall
> I thought perhaps to find an End a world beneath of voidness
> Whence I might travel round the outside of this Dark confusion
> (*FZ* 72:24-27, E 342)

Blake characterizes Urizen's goal in rather plain spatial metaphors: he wants to "get on top of things," find a position "on high" from which everything may be grasped in a single perspective, or "get to the bottom of things," and find a way of getting "outside of this Dark confusion." The composition of plate 14 suggests both of these hungers simultaneously. Urizen can be seen as a sky-god trying to part the clouds like Enitharmon on the preceding plate so he can see the world from above, or he can be seen trying to "touch bottom" and find the stony foundations of his world. But once again Urizen is afflicted with the synaesthesia he has tried to abolish: the substance he encounters refuses to declare itself unambiguously as either solid or vapor, stone or cloud. If we try to see him doing a handstand on a "solid without fluctuation" which will provide a firm basis for his abstractions, the solid melts into insubstantial vapors. If we see him trying to part the clouds and open a window or vortex through which the entire universe may be viewed, the stony, obstructive quality of the clouds reasserts itself. The ambiguity of the design is finally a strategy for inviting the reader to participate in the tantalizing search for an unequivocal point of view which torments Urizen.

Blake's satire of Urizen here differs from that in his portrait of him as a truly cynical Diogenes in plate 23 [79]. Urizen's search for a supreme fiction, the fiction of an absolute, is treated as heroic in plate 14, and tends to invite our participation rather than our

[41] See Hagstrum, *Poet and Painter*, plate XXVIIIA.

judgment. The search for a final resting place, a last perfect vortex, involves "creating many a Vortex . . . many a Science" (*FZ* 72:13, E 342) in the deep, each one involving a tantalizing hope for the absolute. But Blake does not see this search as utterly futile. Urizen is like the fool who persists in his folly till he becomes wise. When he passes through the next vortex, breaking out of the picture frame on plate 23 [79], or fleeing into the vortex on plate 27 [84] with "a Web . . . Shivring across from Vortex to Vortex . . . A living Mantle adjoined to his life & growing from his Soul" (*FZ* 73:32-34, E 343), he will at last see himself, if only to recognize his entrapment in his own nets. Urizen's self-deceptions are treated as the materials for self-knowledge, just as the "Human Illusion" created by Los is the prelude to a "Human Form Divine."

It might be well, then, to conclude our journey through these "visions of torment" with a meditation on Blake's final portraits of the artist and his family in the world of Urizen. It is not a happy picture. In plate 21 [77] we see Los, Enitharmon, and Orc in jealous, anxious intimacy. The bleeding wound in Los's side which gave birth to Urizen and nourished the embryonic globe of Enitharmon has now coagulated into a "Chain of Jealousy" which Los will use to bind down his son to the mountaintop. Los's flourishing beard suggests that his sacrifice of Orc is turning him into a Urizen very much like the one we find in chains on the next plate [78]. But Blake did not include a vision of Orc chained to earth in *Urizen* (a picture which does appear in the Preludium to *America*). Instead the pictorial and textual narratives are both broken off, and we are swept forward six thousand years to the London of 1794 and a vision of Orc as a begging or praying orphan (plate 26 [81]) with his howling "Dog at the wintry door" (25:2). The child abandoned on the primeval mountaintop has become the waif in the streets of London.

This picture is obviously a stylistic orphan among the titanic nudes and visionary, synaesthetic spaces of *Urizen*, confronting us with a deliberately stark naïveté and refusing to give our eye anything to feast on aesthetically. The horizontal and vertical structure of the door and the figures of boy and dog reassert the principle of identity between figure and background in a nonvisionary context, the rigid perpendiculars broken (but really reaffirmed) by the diagonal of "wand'ring light" (cf. "The Little Boy Found," *Inn*, E 11), which literally wavers and curves in copy B. The light varies from copy to copy, sometimes suggesting by its slanted angle the edge of a guillotine, sometimes—as in copy D [82]—disappearing altogether. If we view *Urizen* as a historical poem this is clearly the final plate, the one which literally brings us up to date. It is not a vision we can contemplate with any sort of pleasure, but it does compel attention, preventing us from turning away like the hypocrite on the following page (plate 27 [84]) who leaves the child to stay warm in a mantle of religion. The picture is most disquieting, however, because we cannot blame the child's condition solely on the rational "Urizenic carpentry"[42] which structures his world. The imagination (Los) has helped to build this world, and has in this poem abandoned the child to it. The picture is designed, in other words, to address us with embarrassing directness and to make us feel guilty. The child's appeal is not directed, like that of the lost boy in *Innocence*, to the elusive "wand'ring light" in his world, nor to those who victimize him in the poem (whose counterparts are, at any rate, found in every reader, in Blake's view), but directly outward to the nonplussed viewer.

Blake's refusal to make any concession to the rules of aesthetic distance or disinterestedness in the final vision of his pictorial narrative is only logical in view of the strenuous participation he has demanded from his audience throughout the book, and it is his way of suggesting that he wants something more than the intelligent contemplation of his artifacts. This does not mean that because Urizen fell we should take a chimney sweeper to lunch. What it does suggest is that the prophetic tradition refuses to allow the energies of art to be contained in a magic circle of mythic, archetypal irrelevance, and that to put them in this magic circle is to reenact the crime of Los and abandon Orc on the streets of London. The abandoned children of the imagination do not need our help so much as we need theirs, a point that Blake makes explicitly when he shows this same orphan [83] leading the aged, crippled wanderer of "London" (1794) and *Jerusalem* 84 (1818). If *Urizen* begins by showing us in the Preludium the child being led into the fallen world by a protective adult, it concludes with a vision of that child alone, now ready to show the adult a way out of that world. In copy D [82] Blake stresses the child's role as a guide by eliminating the knife-edged slant of "wand'ring light" and making the child a kind of forlorn beacon or candle that glows in the darkness around him.

The picture is a kind of final emblem, then, of the contrary energies in Urizen's world: the light of innocence is still to be found there, but accompanied by a howling dog who undoubtedly senses the evil spirits around him. The howl is a portent of disaster and

[42] Erdman, *TIB*, p. 208.

apocalypse ("A dog starved at his Masters Gate/ Predicts the ruin of the State"; "Auguries of Innocence," E 484); the child is the hope for revelation. We noted earlier that in the textual narrative Blake casts Los in the role of mediator between conflicting claims of the imagination. What should now be clear is that Los is also a symbol of the role demanded of the audience, a dual role of reader and viewer which requires us to mediate the often conflicting, problematic relationships of text and design, and to endure the paradoxes of a world in which "Fear & Hope are—Vision."

Chapter Five

LIVING FORM

Poetic and Pictorial Design in *Jerusalem*

BLAKE said that "if the fool would persist in his folly, he would become wise," which is perhaps why critics persist in attempting to discover a structure in his last great poem, *Jerusalem.* Interpretations of Blake's final prophecy (excluding those which dismiss it as inspired nonsense) have ranged from Swinburne's perplexed admiration at a safe distance to the modern tendency to deduce a structure based upon a judicious selection of quotations from the poem.[1] The clearest generalizations about the form of *Jerusalem* have come from critics who have kept their distance; the most useful readings, however, have come from those who, like Harold Bloom, persist in the folly of attending to the "Minute Particulars" at the risk of overturning their own theories.[2] Faced with the choice of being either a generalizing knave or an empirical fool about the structural question, one is tempted to take refuge in a paradox and propose that the form of the poem is some species of "antiform," that its structure is a denial of our usual ideas of structure. This paradox affords no refuge, however, if one engages in the folly of trying to prove it valid, which is what I propose to do in the following pages.

[1] Swinburne, in *William Blake: A Critical Essay* (London, 1868), admires Blake's ideas but not his poetic forms. Recent attempts to deal with *Jerusalem*'s structure are listed by Roger Easson in "Blake and His Reader in *Jerusalem*," *BSA*, p. 316 n., and will be cited as we proceed. For a thorough listing of commentary prior to 1956, see Karl Kiralis, "The Theme and Structure of Blake's *Jerusalem*," *English Literary History* XXIII (1956), 127-28.

[2] See Bloom's commentary in the Erdman edition, his chapter on *Jerusalem* in *Blake's Apocalypse* (New York, 1963), and his essay "Blake's *Jerusalem*: The Bard of Sensibility and the Form of Prophecy," *Eighteenth-Century Studies* IV (1970), 6-20.

I. STRUCTURE AND THE PROBLEM OF TIME: A FOURFOLD MODEL FOR NARRATIVE

Like Sterne, Blake was fascinated with the consequences for literary form of the subjective notions of time which emerged in eighteenth-century thought. We saw these concerns manifested in *Urizen* in Blake's descriptions of Los and Urizen as creators and measurers of time, and in the very form of that work as a complex texture of interwoven time schemes. By the time Blake began writing *Jerusalem* he had come to define the literary artist as one who reshapes the temporal forms of language in order to restructure consciousness, especially the consciousness of time. Los is Time, he creates Time, and he keeps "the Divine Vision *in time* of trouble" (*J* 44:15, E 191; italics mine). Our understanding of *Jerusalem* properly begins, therefore, with a reconstruction of Blake's idea of the relation of time to psychological states, and to the linguistic forms which describe and embody those states.

If poetry is primarily a temporal phenomenon, a linear sequence of lines, words, and episodes which must be apprehended in and through time, Blake would define four basic ways in which the fictive time of the poem can engage with the linear time demanded by the medium. At the simplest level of comprehension we assume that the medium is itself the message and that those events which are further along in the linear continuum are proportionately further along in time: the order of the telling corresponds directly to the temporal order of events narrated. Blake would call this the psychological state of Ulro, "Single vision & Newtons sleep" (E 693), the atomistic view of reality which sees time as a series of homogenous points on a line. Most language and literature, of course, frees itself from this lockstep and selects and arranges its moments from the temporal order in some imaginative order—*in medias res*, *ab ovum*, or *recherche du temps perdu*. All of these selective principles assume, however, that there is an order of nonhuman time which flows onward independent of any particular reorganization of its sequence. We say that this nonhuman time is "real" or "objective," and that human time is "subjective" or "imaginary." This bifurcated view of time produces narrative which employs devices like foreshadowing and the "flashback," and its creation and understanding depend to a large extent on the exercise of memory. The imaginative organization of time is perceived as a subjective artifice which distorts the real nature of time, for *in medias res* only has meaning if we assume that there is some objective, continuous *res* from which we select our middle. Blake calls this level of perception "double vision" or the world of "Generation," the normal condition of man in a dualistic world of "Division" between mind and nature, imagination and reality.

But Generation can become an "Image of regeneration" (*J* 7:65, E 149). The cycle of natural and human time can be orchestrated in a harmonious vision, what we call myth. The cycle of seasons, the ages of man, the times of the day can be perceived as metaphors for one another. Blake calls this state of reconciliation between human and nonhuman time Beulah, the land of lover and beloved, and the condition of the child or innocent who sees everything in sympathy with himself. Most pastoral poetry begins with this view of time, an interpenetration of man and nature such as we find in *Songs of Innocence*. The world of regeneration always threatens, of course, to slip back into Generation with the growth of individual self-consciousness and the perception of a discrepancy between man and nature. Hence most pastoral poetry adopts an ironic, satirical vision at some point: Colin Clout finds himself out of sympathy with nature, Innocence gives way to Experience, and the garden of *Thel* is replaced by a grave.

The garden, therefore, does not serve as Blake's final image for reconciling natural and human time. His highest vision employs the metaphor of the city, Jerusalem, an "artifice of eternity" like Yeats's Byzantium which detaches itself from the cycle of nonhuman nature and finds its structure in the widest reach of man's imaginative desires. The temporal and narrative order of a poem based in this view of reality need not be rationalized to accord with clock time nor harmonized with natural time; its contours are determined and limited only by the limits of the imagination: "if we raise ourselves/ Upon the chariots of the morning. Contracting or Expanding Time!/ Every one knows, we are One Family: One Man blessed for ever" (*J* 55:44-46, E 203). Time becomes a malleable substance, capable of being reshaped by the will into an artificial human environment: "the Sons of Los build Moments & Minutes & Hours/ And Days & Months & Years & Ages & Periods; wondrous buildings;/ And every Moment has a Couch of gold for soft repose" (*M* 28:44-46, E 125).

Blake places this art city of the imagination at the center of his ontology. The visions of the imagination are not illusions or distortions of reality but precisely the reverse: "The Visions of Eternity, by reason of narrowed perceptions,/ Are become weak Visions of

Time & Space" (*J* 49:21, E 196). In order for a poem to embody this view of reality, it must overcome the built-in limitations of the temporal medium of language, and therefore Blake calls English "the rough basement" and sees Los as building "the stubborn structure of the Language, acting against/ Albions melancholy" (*J* 36:58-60, E 181). A poetry of this order must satisfy two conditions: (1) it must dramatize the speciousness of nonhuman ideas of time; and (2) it must affirm the actuality of an alternative order in the present moment, rather than locating it in the memory of a lost Golden Age or relegating it to a wished-for future. We saw Blake experimenting with a poetry which satisfies the first condition in *The Book of Urizen*, where he continually undercut the apparently linear flow of poetic time with a system of recurrent archetypal patterns. The second condition was the governing principle of many of the lyric poems, which are quite conscious attempts to see " a World in a Grain of Sand"—or in a Sunflower. The Blake of the lyrics and the prophecies is sometimes treated as if he were two different persons. But his particular view of reality actually necessitates both forms, the lyric to affirm the efficacy of the human moment, the prophecy to redeem history, or all moments: "Los in Six Thousand Years walks up & down continually/ That not one Moment of Time be lost" (*J* 75:7-8, E 228). Los is not a prophet of the millenium awaiting the end of that "Six Thousand Years" (in fact, in an early draft of *The Four Zoas* he was content to range over a mere twenty years).[3] Rather he is concerned with redeeming all the "nows" of human time.

The real achievement of Blake's major prophecies, then, is his successful combination of the large form which invalidates nonhuman time with the affirmative vision of the moment; or, to define this achievement in terms of the actor rather than the form of action, the development of an epic hero (Los) who could function in a world of apparent temporal chaos, who could, quite literally, keep "the Divine Vision *in time* of trouble" (italics mine). The fact that Los never fully develops into the figure of "time-redeemer" in *The Four Zoas* may be one reason why Blake never engraved his manuscript epic. The redemptive force in *The Four Zoas* is the Council of Eternals, a group whose position outside of time and space was too close to the transcendent location of Milton's God to satisfy Blake's yearning for a deity who is "not a God afar off" but "a brother and

[3] See *FZ* 9:10, E 300; cf. textual note E 744.

friend" (*J* 4:18, E 145). Thus the prelude to *Jerusalem* is a poem (*Milton*) which stresses the descent from heaven, the repudiation of transcendence, and the entry into time and space as the critical acts in the renovation of the world. Those Eternals who close off the earth in a Tent of Science in *Urizen* are drawn down to earth by Milton's "unexampled deed," his rejection of the very heavens he had imagined in his own *Paradise Lost*.[4]

For Blake, the prophet had to serve as a bridge from a demonic world to a divine order which could only exist as a result of his own persistence in imagining and creating it. Without the Miltonic assumption of an untouched, perfect divinity in the heavens, the prophet cannot simply serve as the mouthpiece of God; if he is to be a seer, he must create what he sees. Hence the difficulty with Los in *The Four Zoas*. Blake could not make Los perfect, or he would have fallen into the same "error" Milton did in attempting to depict God directly, the error of postulating an absolute, Urizenic point of view. On the other hand, Los must not fall so far into time that he needs an external, transcendent redeemer to rescue him. He must simultaneously be far enough above time to see past, present, and future as a single pattern and far enough into time to find that visionary moment of human time, the "pulsation of the artery" in which "the Poets Work is Done." Between these extremes is located the "time of trouble," the nightmare of history dominated by Satan's "Watch-fiends" (*M* 23:40, E 118). Blake solved this apparently impossible problem by making Los not only the spirit of prophecy, but a direct personification of time itself (*M* 24:68). The struggle of the artist with time could in this way be recast as a struggle with the self. The drama of the poet's combat with his own doubts and fears becomes a metaphor for the prophet's quarrel with history, and the lyric moment of individual human time can be identified with the epic of collective, historical time: "Every Time less than a pulsation of the artery/ Is equal in its period & value to Six Thousand Years./ For in this Period the Poets Work is Done" (*M* 28:62-63, 29:1; E 126).

When we say, then, that *Jerusalem* has a structure of antiform, we mean that it treats as an illusion or fiction the temporal continuum which normally stands behind narrative, and that it is designed to subvert our assumption that the logical is equivalent to the chrono-

[4] For a fuller discussion of the theme of repudiated transcendence, see my essay "Blake's Radical Comedy: Dramatic Structure as Meaning in *Milton*," *BSA*, pp. 281-307.

logical. This does not mean a complex or obscure reordering of events, because that would imply some objective or ideal temporal order which the narrative rearranges. Antiform means that the poem's structure undercuts the whole notion of predictable linear chronology by embodying it as chaos.[5] The reader of *Jerusalem* is supposed to feel lost in time; he is supposed to be mystified by the inexplicable transitions, the repetitions, and the absence of cause and effect relationships. The narrative "goes nowhere" because time, as a causal chain, does not go anywhere. That is why it is so difficult to perceive any order of cause and effect or linear progression leading up to the apocalyptic conclusion of the poem. Although the theme is at least in part a quest or journey ("the passage through/ Eternal Death"; *J* 4:1-2, E 145), it is neither an odyssey nor a series of labors that lays all before us as we enter the poem with Los on the frontispiece.[6] What confronts us is a labyrinth, an encyclopedic vision of a nightmare world illuminated by and contrasted with an exploring imagination. Between the first and last plates of the poem Albion does not go anywhere or learn anything which can be said to "cause" his awakening. If anything, he knows less of himself in his death-sleep on plate 94 than he does in his conscious repudiation of the Saviour at the opening of Chapter I.[7] Los begins his task of reopening Albion's eyes on plate 5 and finds himself instantly threatened by his own Spectre and Emanation, who divide from him in a reenactment of Albion's division. On plates 87 and 88, just before Albion's awakening, Los is depicted in exactly the same situation. He has not in-

[5] The perception of non- or anti-linear elements has played an increasingly large part in recent interpretations of the poem. In the three essays on *Jerusalem* in *Blake's Sublime Allegory* the point appears in a variety of contexts. Roger Easson suggests that "the obscuring veil of narrative" is designed intentionally as a "tormenting and eternal labor of frustration" (p. 312); Stuart Curran argues that the form of *Jerusalem* is designed "to free man from that very sense of history, from the logical succession of events that constitutes narrative" (p. 345); and Karl Kroeber suggests that "Blake's poetry is uniquely graphic," and that the terms "applicable to the sequentiality of literary art . . . are not intended to elucidate graphic modes" (pp. 349-50).

[6] The scarcity of travel imagery in a poem introduced as a "passage through Eternal Death" is in itself notable. An instructive contrast is the pervasiveness of the journey motif in *The Four Zoas* and *Milton*.

[7] Frye notes in passing (while trying to show that "the structure of *Jerusalem* does not greatly differ from that of *The Four Zoas*") that there is "almost no working-up of climax" in *Jerusalem*: "We look back to see where the reversal of perspective occurred, but find nothing very tangible, and after so much churning, the mere silent appearance of the expected butter may seem almost an anticlimax" (*Fearful Symmetry*, pp. 357-58).

creased his mastery over the rebellious tendencies in his own soul; the struggle for the perfection of the self, like the building of the city of art, is a process of "Continually Building. Continually Decaying because of Love & Jealousy" (*J* 72, E 225). The capitulation of Los's rebellious "Female Will," Enitharmon, occurs not because of any motivated change in her behavior but because she recognizes that "The Poets Song draws to its period & Enitharmon is no more" (92:8, E 250). By all the measures of cause and effect, *Jerusalem* could have ended with the opening confrontation of Christ and Albion as Antichrist in the opening dialogue of the poem. On the other hand, it could have gone on indefinitely like *Tristram Shandy*. If the prophet's task is to insure that "not one Moment of Time be lost" (*J* 75:8, E 228), the work can never end.

II. GENERIC STRUCTURE: *JERUSALEM* AS COMIC ENCYCLOPEDIC ANATOMY

But *Jerusalem* does end at the suspiciously round number of one hundred plates, and it seems clear that the perception of antiform in the sequence of the work is only a prelude to the apprehension of some other form. The experience of *Jerusalem* as a complex, labyrinthine structure which intentionally subverts our expectations of temporal order and of narrative or dramatic development is based primarily upon a reading of the words. From a visual and spatial standpoint, however, the book discloses a contrary impression. We see a highly regular, symmetrical structure of four chapters of equal length, each prefaced by a full-page illustration and an address to a special audience, and each framed by half-page designs at the top and bottom of the first and last pages. The clarity of this structure is such a relief from the convoluted difficulty of the text that it has understandably served as a primary point of departure for structural generalizations. But none of the fourfold models proposed to explain the structure of *Jerusalem* has been compellingly successful in clarifying the progressive unfolding and ordering of parts in the text. The Zoas, the seasons, the times of the day, the four phases of history or of human life, the four Evangelists and their gospels, the four gates of Golgonooza[8]—all these provide suggestive analogies for the

[8] E. J. Rose suggests a structure based on the Zoas ("The Structure of Blake's *Jerusalem*," *Bucknell Review* XI [1963], 35-54); Frye sees "a drama in four acts" covering fall, struggle in the fallen world, redemption, and apocalypse (*Fearful Symmetry*, p. 357); and Joan Witke suggests that the four

four-chapter structure, but all of them seem to run aground on the Minute Particulars. One critic has argued that "the external structure of four chapters has little to do with" the "real nature" of *Jerusalem*,[9] and the most sophisticated reading of the poem to date finds it to be a system of seven interlocking structures, many of which cut across the boundaries of the four chapters.[10] One suspects that more structures will be discovered, and that they will continue to fall into three general categories: (1) linear, sequential models governed by the temporal patterns of sacred or natural history, including forms such as the epic journey, the quest, and the pilgrimage ("the passage through/ Eternal Death"); (2) dialectical, undulating, dramatic models governed by the contrast between a nightmare world ("the Sleep of Ulro") and the ever-present alternative of "awaking to Eternal Life"; (3) "vorticular," spiraling models constructed from the union of linear and dialectical organizations.

But the investigation into the structure of *Jerusalem* inevitably raises a prior question. What is the purpose of understanding structure? What do we gain by seeing seven or twenty "intertranspicous spheres" governing the organization of the text?[11] One answer is that we gain confidence, faith, reassurance that Blake is not just boasting when he claims that "every word & every letter is studied and put into its fit place" (*J* 3, E 144). And we seem to need more of this reassurance with *Jerusalem* because it is Blake's most formally exasperating work, the most demanding and least rewarding at an immediate sensuous level of all his illuminated books.[12] The pictures are the most erudite and iconographically complex of all of Blake's illuminations, exhibiting a kind of limit to which he would go in the use of literary, emblematic, allegorical designs. Our earlier generalizations about Blake's genius for iconographic simplification must be qualified for *Jerusalem*: he is still more economical than the emblematists or Dürer, but compared to his other illuminated books *Jerusalem* displays a great deal more allegorical machinery, more use

---

gospels control the structure ("*Jerusalem*: A Synoptic Poem," *Comparative Literature XXXII* [1970], 265-78).

9 Easson, "Blake and His Reader in *Jerusalem*," *BSA*, p. 316.

10 Stuart Curran, "The Structures of *Jerusalem*," *BSA*, pp. 329-46.

11 Curran, *ibid*., p. 340, adapts this phrase from Shelley.

12 Frye records "the initial impression of a harsh, crabbed and strident poem," a "dehydrated epic" in which Blake's symbols "had become a kind of ideographic alphabet and had thereby lost much of their immediacy" (*Fearful Symmetry*, p. 359).

of grotesques, more arcane literary allusions—the kind of thing we find in what is possibly a self-parody, the fantastic serpent chariot of plate 41 [111]. The austere simplicity of the *Milton* illustrations and the glowing single-mindedness of the *Urizen* designs has given way to a world in which the sensuous organization of pictures is governed more than ever before by complex ideas and hieroglyphic configurations.

This heightened intellectualism also governs the text and is one of the reasons for its lack of narrative, mimetic structure. *Jerusalem* is a "philosophic song" like the one Wordsworth hoped would come to him when "mellower years" would bring "a riper mind/ And clearer insight" (*Prelude*, I, 229, 236-37). It is in a very loose verse form which permits the frequent descent into prosaic "inferior" passages of definition and authorial commentary. It is an anatomy of the world with digressions, dialogues, drama, narration, vision, and "humours" of every description. The organization of these elements is governed, however, not by mimetic, narrative, dramatic concerns, but by ideas and relatively abstract images or ideograms. The initial inspiration for the poem comes not from Eternals, fairies, Daughters of Beulah or aged mothers, but from an *idea*: "This *theme* calls me in sleep night after night, & ev'ry morn/ Awakes me at sun-rise" (*J* 4:3-4, E 145; italics mine). The structure of the poem is not governed by a sequence of nine nights with an implicit historical progression as in *The Four Zoas*, nor does it move by a dramatic unfolding of action and reaction like *Milton*.[13] The overt structure is rather a rhetorical and oratorical one: we are reading four addresses, proclamations, prophecies (followed by chapters filled with fictive "exemplars of Memory and of Intellect"; *J* 98:30, E 255) directed at four audiences. Anyone who has spoken to different audiences on the same subject can grasp an essential feature of the structure of *Jerusalem*: it repeats itself constantly, but it is never quite the same. The good orator[14] will stress different themes to suit

[13] The formal and thematic distinctness of Blake's major poems is becoming more evident as more readers attend to the Minute Particulars. It is no longer enough to take the archetypalist view of these poems as stories of fall and redemption. That may provide a general basis, but it is hardly adequate for the practical problems of reading the major prophecies.

[14] Note that Blake defines the verse form of *Jerusalem* as adapted to the needs "of a true Orator" (plate 3). This suggests that the chapters of *Jerusalem* are seen as fictive illustrations or "exemplars" that are continuous with the overtly oratorical addresses that preface each chapter; the narrative is subordi-

his audience and address their condition, but the basic message will remain the same. We will return to this rhetorical and thematic notion of the four-chapter structure presently.

The intellectual character of *Jerusalem* is also revealed in the asceticism of imagery and values that pervades the poem. We find few of the lavish visionary spectacles that adorn the earlier prophecies: there are no celebrations of nature and love like those in *Milton*, and the apocalyptic conclusion of *Jerusalem* is rather restrained in comparison with the ninth night of *The Four Zoas*. Blake stresses "Mental Studies," "Intellectual Warfare," and "Art & Science" (see *J* 77, "To the Christians") as the keys to the gates of Heaven, an emphasis which becomes so pronounced that it threatens to lead him back into the mind-body dualism he had repudiated so consistently throughout his work. The address "To the Christians" that introduces the final chapter comes perilously close to adopting the conventional oppositions of spirit and body, duty and pleasure: "We are told to abstain from fleshly desires that we may lose no time from the Work of the Lord. . . . What is Mortality but the things relating to the Body, which Dies? What is Immortality but the things relating to the Spirit, which lives Eternally!" (*J* 77, E 229). Blake reminds us of his equal commitment to bodily energy by defining his radical Christianity as "the liberty *both* of body & mind to exercise the Divine Arts of Imagination" (*J* 77, italics mine), but his chief interest has clearly shifted to imagination as an "Intellectual Fountain," with the "lineaments of Gratified desire" and the "improvement of sensual enjoyment" placed in a subordinate position (but not abandoned).[15] The horses of instruction are evidently gaining on the tygers of wrath in the race to the palace of wisdom.

Jerusalem is best understood, then, not as an imitation of an action but as an encyclopedic anatomy of the world in which the exemplary actions, descriptions, and personae are drawn from the realms of myth, epic, and romance rather than (as is generally the case with anatomies) from the low mimetic world. If Northrop Frye had written his *Anatomy of Criticism* before *Fearful Symmetry*, one suspects that he would not have assumed that the four-chapter struc-

nate to the rhetorical and thematic concerns of the speaker as he relates to his audience.

[15] The "improvement of sensual enjoyment" never did mean simply to eat, drink, and be merry, in any case. Blake's emphasis was always on the "improvement" of the senses—the cleansing and expansion of the ones we have, and the discovery of new ones.

ture of *Jerusalem* corresponds to "a drama in four acts: a fall, the struggle of men in a fallen world which is what we usually think of as history, the world's redemption by a divine man in which eternal life and death achieve a simultaneous triumph, and an apocalypse."[16] He might have noticed that *Jerusalem* is far more adequately described by his own concept of encyclopedic anatomy,[17] a generic notion which links such diverse creations as *Finnegans Wake*, *Moby Dick*, *Tristram Shandy*, *Tale of a Tub*, and *The Anatomy of Melancholy*. Like most anatomies, *Jerusalem* has the reputation of being a farrago, a pastiche, the work of a slapdash eccentric. It deals, in Frye's words, "less with people as such than with mental attitudes"; it "resembles the confession in its ability to handle abstract ideas and theories," and it "presents people as the mouthpieces of the ideas they represent." It concentrates on evil and folly not as "social diseases," but as "diseases of the intellect," and presents the world "in terms of a single intellectual pattern," a pattern which "makes for violent dislocations in the customary logic of narrative." The short form of the anatomy, like many episodes in *Jerusalem* is "a dialogue or colloquy in which the dramatic interest is in conflict of ideas rather than character." Its exuberance is manifested "by piling up an enormous mass of erudition" in compilations and catalogues of places, names, and events.[18] It cannot afford to leave anything out: everything acted on earth must be recorded in the bright sculptures of Los's halls, so the artist must frequently resort to lists, summaries, and compilations which evoke matters (such as the history of Western religion) which he cannot treat in detail.

16 *Fearful Symmetry*, p. 357.

17 This genre is a compound of what Frye calls "anatomy," a form based in satire, and his concept of encyclopedic forms, "normally a scripture or sacred book in the mythical mode" (*Anatomy of Criticism*, p. 315). There is a risk, of course, of sounding like Polonius with his garbled mixture of "tragical-historical-pastoral" drama, but it is a risk we need to take if we are to attain any precision in defining the form of *Jerusalem*. Some critics will prefer to treat the poem as an epic, allowing, as Joseph Wittreich does (*BSA*, p. 23-58), wide latitude in what may appear in this form. The important thing, in my view, is to construct a definition that accounts for what is actually in the poem and that allows it to be related to and differentiated from other forms. Thus, although "epic" may ultimately be the best word for *Jerusalem*, it must be qualified sufficiently to distinguish it from a brief dramatic epic like *Milton* and a narrative epic like *The Four Zoas*. The concept of anatomy is very useful in making this kind of distinction, and it accounts for the extraordinary philosophical emphasis of the poem.

18 *Anatomy of Criticism*, pp. 309-10.

Many of these elements are things which critics might prefer to banish from *Jerusalem*, but they will not go away and they constitute an essential part of the poem, for better or worse. It may be objected that "anatomy" is simply a name we give to any massive literary masterpiece that demands a great deal of study and which resists structural analysis and generic classification. But the genre of anatomy shares characteristics other than an apparent formlessness with *Jerusalem*—the intellectual, philosophical emphasis, the deliberate disregard for mimetic form, the exhaustive scope, the dialectical procedure, and the insistence on an insomniac for its ideal reader. It is clearly unlike some anatomies in its lack of overt humor and in its tendency to refer to a presiding comic or apocalyptic resolution rather than a state of ironic irresolution. The typical anatomy is a losing race against death and corruption: Donne worries that the world will decay too rapidly for him to finish his analysis and Sterne knows that his humor cannot outrace death forever. For Blake, the only important death is the "Eternal Death" of a stifled, unproductive life, immersed in the nightmare of history. The race with this kind of death can be won at any moment, for "whenever any Individual Rejects Error & Embraces Truth a Last Judgment passes upon that Individual" (*VLJ*, E 551).

III. SPATIAL STRUCTURE: CENTER, CIRCUMFERENCE, AND THE SERPENT TEMPLE

Identifying *Jerusalem* as an encyclopedic anatomy does not release us from the task of discovering whether every word and every letter is in its fit place, but it may allow us to stop worrying about its failure to disclose a narrative or dramatic structure. We still want to know, however, how to find our place in the encyclopedia. The simplest place to begin is with the spatial structure of the world it describes:

> The Vegetative Universe, opens like a flower from the Earths center:
> In which is Eternity. It expands in Stars to the Mundane Shell
> And there it meets Eternity again, both within and without. . . .
> (*J* 13:34-36, E 155-56)

This passage is itself a microcosm or "opened center" in which the entire structure of *Jerusalem* may be seen: the poem is an account of the "Vegetative Universe" of Generation (Harold Bloom calls it a "long song of Experience")[19] which finds its contrary vision of eternity at both the center and the circumference. That is, the "total image" of the poem (its circumference) is a total picture of the fallen world contained within eternity. The "opened center," on the other hand, is located in the "Minute Particulars" of the poem and is therefore everywhere.

What this means for the reader is that he must approach the form of *Jerusalem* in two ways: (1) through a broad comprehension which sees all of the "Visionary Forms Dramatic" simultaneously; (2) with a focused attention which sees the total form of the poem crystallized in the individual moment. The first approach asks the reader to identify himself with Los in his spatialization of time so that he too may "walk up & down in Six Thousand Years" and see that "their Events are present" (*J* 74:19, E 227) before him. The second approach demands that the reader "Enter *into* these Images in his Imagination" (*VLJ*, E 550; italics mine); that is, he must enter the action of the poem with Los and continually focus the events before him in the light of Los's awakening perspectives. By a continuous exertion of the imagination the reader is expected to keep "the Divine Vision in time of trouble" and juxtapose it with the present moment of the poem so that he continually perceives the "Sleep of Ulro! and . . . the passage through/ Eternal Death" as containing an imminent "awakening to Eternal Life." This first kind of reading identifies us with the perfected Los, the prophetic bard who sees "Past, Present, & Future" at a single glance, like T. S. Eliot in "Tradition and the Individual Talent," spreading out the tapestry of Western culture. The second view casts the reader into the action of the poem to share in the doubts, hesitations, and momentary victories of the artist in a world which resists all imaginative organization. The first mode is essentially comic and cosmic; the second is primarily ironic and particularized.

Clearly, the "total image" or spatial form of *Jerusalem* is not available to us on the first reading, and perhaps not on the tenth, because the circumference of the poem, the total body of its verbal and pictorial content, steadily resists schematic structures or abstract models, including those based on the ostensible structure of four chapters. Blake acknowledges this difficulty when he assigns the idea of totality and circumference to the "Western Gate" of his fourfold system, which is "clos'd up till the last day" (*J* 13:11, E 155). In addition to the Day of Judgment, this "last day" refers to the literal end

[19] *Blake's Apocalypse*, p. 403.

of the poem (which obviously must be reached to discern the spatial form of the poem) as well as to the final assimilation of the total form or circumference of the poem in the mind of the reader. The center or "Minute Particular," on the other hand, is associated with the "Eastern Gate," the loins of Beulah or "sensual enjoyment," and the world of Generation as an "Image of regeneration." Even if the reader's imagination is incapable of comprehending the poem in a single spatial form, the particulars have been designed as centers for opening out his thought. In a certain sense, the narrative nonsequentiality of the poem is a rhetorical device to draw the reader's attention to the "Minute Particulars." Since events cannot be reconstructed in accord with any causal or temporal scheme which would give them relational meanings, the reader is forced to consider each moment of the poem in itself and in the light of the perspectives which Los as actor and Blake as narrator are focusing on these moments.

Blake employs these centrifugal and centripetal organizations of his poetic structure in an analogous fashion in his treatment of pictorial space. The points of the compass operate as a reference for orientation with respect to the picture-plane of the engraved surface: "the North is Breadth, the South is Heighth & Depth:/ The East is Inwards: & the West is Outwards every way" (*J* 14:29-30, E 157; see fig. 3). Many of the illustrations in *Jerusalem* seem to be constructed in terms of this inward-outward conception. In the frontispiece [86], Blake-Los enters the poem, and the fallen world, carrying the illuminated globe of his imagination in his right hand. This entry corresponds to the centripetal descent into the particulars of the poem, as Blake indicates by two glosses which he etched into the plate to introduce the theme of the "opened center": "Los . . . enterd the Door of Death for Albions sake Inspird"; "There is a Void, outside of Existence, which if enterd into/ Englobes itself & becomes a Womb" (*J* 1:8-9, 1-2; E 143). Los is entering a fallen world of death, an outside which can be "entered into," a boundless "Void" which is an enclosing globe, a tomb which is a womb. Like Milton "going to Eternal Death" on the frontispiece to his poem (cf. [18]), Los enters the fallen world of *Jerusalem* to make, with the reader, his "passage through/ Eternal Death." The journey to the center continues until plate 97 [87], where we find Los, his globe now a sun in his left hand, completing his journey through the fallen world with his "Naked Beauty displayd" (*J* 32:49, E 177). The reversal of the globe's position reflects Blake's consistent use of inversion to symbolize completion of a cycle, journey, or initiation

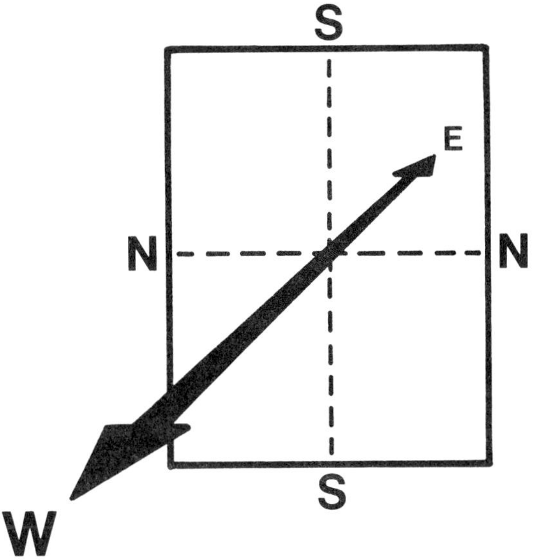

FIGURE 3.

and here represents the transformation of Los's perspective in the process of the poem. He begins at the "center" as a timid explorer in an unknown realm, only a step beyond the Diogenes of *Urizen* (see [79]), and emerges at the "circumference" as a triumphant explorer surmounting the last obstacle. The clothing of the two figures presents a similar contrast: the contemporary dress of the figure on the frontispiece (Blake himself is supposed to have worn a broad-brimmed hat like the one depicted) represents the immersion of the artist-reader in the space and time of the poem. The nude figure on plate 97 has shed these garments as he enters eternity. As he did through a similar pattern of reversals in the first and last plates of *Urizen*, Blake suggests that Los's end may be seen by holding up a mirror to his beginning: the triumphant artist-reader at the circumference is implicit in the tentative explorer entering the center. In the design called *Death's Door* in the illustrations to Blair's *Grave* [88] Blake made this identity explicit by placing both the entering and emerging figures in a single composition, transposing the theme into the context of death and rebirth.

If plates 1 and 97 depict the figure of Los at two critical points in his passage through the demonic world of *Jerusalem*, the hundredth and final plate [89] reveals him at the circumference of creation, facing outward toward the "Western Gate" which is opened on the "last day." A more accurate label for the central figure of plate 100 would be Urthona, the "eternal form" of Los, standing at rest with the whole range of the space-time world spread out behind him. Los himself is really "the Vehicular form of Strong Urthona" (*J* 53:1, E 200), who carries prophecy into the fallen world and gives that world a shape. The temporal, vehicular Los is shown at the left, setting out to the east (inward) with the sun of imagination on his shoulder. On the right is Enitharmon with her shuttle and distaff, weaving the space of the fallen world into a definite form so it can be redeemed. The two figures flanking the androgynous Urthona[20] represent, then, his own division into sexes, and the separation of eternity into space and time in the act of creation. The hammer and tongs suggest, in like manner, the active and passive aspects of the work of the artist as a Vulcan-blacksmith. In effect, the last plate tells us what we have already deduced from the poem, that the termination of *Jerusalem* is only the passing of *a* Last Judgment, and that the work of redeeming time and space does not end with the artist's (or the reader's) attainment of personal enlightenment. Los must set out on yet another journey into the "Void, outside of Existence" and Enitharmon continues to weave a protective space for the sleepers who remain in the fallen world:

> She Creates at her will a little moony night & silence
> With Spaces of sweet gardens & a tent of elegant beauty:
> Closd in by a sandy desart & a night of stars shining.
> And a little tender moon & hovering angels on the wing.
> And the Male gives a Time & Revolution to her Space
> (*J* 69:19-23, E 221)

Urthona in his stable, achieved form faces out at the "Western Gate" which is the circumference, balanced by his sexual, vehicular forms who continue the journey into the moment, the Minute Particular, which lies inward at the "Eastern Gate."

The "Rocky Circle & Snake" (*J* 92:25, E 250) of the Druid temple in the background connects the three parts of the composition and transposes the human theme into an emblematic earth-poem. Blake

[20] Urthona is given genitals in copy E, but his androgyny is still implied emblematically by his tools and by the cooperative labor of his male and female emanations.

undoubtedly based this form on an engraving of Avebury—*A Scenographic View of the Druid Temple at Abury*—which appeared in William Stukely's treatise on the subject in 1743 (see [90]). Stukely's explanation of this "serpentine temple" or Dracontium has particular relevance to Blake's idea of structure in *Jerusalem.* Druid temples, Stukely explains, were designed to imitate the various forms which God could assume. The circle represents God the Father in his timeless, pre-creative perfection, and the serpent represents the Son, the Logos or creative principle, which is also identified as "the nous, the other, or second mind of Plato, whom they affirmed to be the creator of the world."[21] The Dracontium, then, the temple which combined the forms of the circle and the serpent, was understood as an emblem of both God's perfect immutability and his descent into time and space.[22] Blake's human figures, of course, stand in just such a relationship, the perfected Urthona flanked by his temporal and spatial emissaries. Both aspects of the composition convey the central theme of the ongoing interpenetration of eternity and time which is promised in the last lines of the poem:

All Human Forms identified even Tree Metal Earth & Stone. all
Human Forms identified, living going forth & returning wearied
Into the Planetary lives of Years Months Days & Hours reposing
And then Awaking into his bosom in the Life of Immortality.
(*J* 99:1-4, E 256)

The serpent temple, as Blake noted in *Europe*, is an "image of infinite/ Shut up in finite revolutions" (10:21-22, E 62); but this is also the total image of the poem and the work of the poet which we find in *Jerusalem.* The stones of the temple are the one hundred plates of *Jerusalem* perceived as a total spatial form which unites closure and openness, eternal perfection and ongoing imperfection. Viewed as a translation of themes within the poem, the serpent temple is Golgonooza, the city of art-in-progress, the "new Golgotha" which is both the new place of sacrifice (Self-annihilation) that replaces the old doctrine of atonement, and the new "place of the skull," the new consciousness of eternity in time rather than beyond it.[23]

21 Stukely, *Abury, A Temple of the British Druids* (London, 1743), pp. 54, 61.

22 Stukely identifies the serpent as "the symbol of the fecundity of the deity, first exerted in producing the second person thereby, who with them was the creator of all things" (*ibid.*, p. 49). When wings are added to the image (see [91]) it becomes a symbol of the entire Trinity.

23 The image of the circle and the outstretched serpentine line is repeated

IV. STRUCTURE AND CAUSALITY: READING *JERUSALEM* BACKWARDS

But if all time can be said to be present in a single image before the orator-narrator of *Jerusalem* as it is for Urthona in the final plate, what principle governs his selection of particular moments to exhibit in his poem? We have already examined the negative principle which governs the *order* of his selections: they are arranged so as to invalidate any linear model which would suggest that time "goes somewhere," and to draw the reader's attention to the individual moment, pulling him inward rather than onward.[24] On the other hand, the particular actions which Blake chooses to present cannot be gratuitous; they must be accurate and typical examples of the events which

---

(and transformed) in at least two other illustrations, the halo and serpentine flames which surround the head and shoulders of "Hand" in plate 26 [97] and the winged globe which supports the figures of Jesus and Albion in plate 33 [92]. These two images reiterate the theme of eternity interpenetrating time in what might be called the emergence of "Eternal Wrath" and "Eternal Pity." Hand is the fiery warrior, a collective image of Blake's own Selfhood and of the fiery materials of his craft (the "Hand" which "seizes the fire" to create the Tyger is an early anticipation of this figure). He provides the means, the "Hand" by which eternal energy is incarnated in temporal form. The winged globe is linked to a portrayal of eternal forgiveness in the person of Jesus supporting the fainting Albion, who is still caught in the nightmare of time. The significance of circle and outstretched form is thus reversed in this latter emblem, the wings (which occupy the place of the serpent form in the Druid temple) now symbolizing the eternal support of Pity, which prevents the world (as Jesus prevents Albion) from falling indefinitely. It may strike some readers that this sort of hieroglyphical imagery is Blake at his worst—arcane, mysterious, and full of arbitrary symbolic portentousness. Before we dismiss this imagery too quickly, however, it might be interesting to compare its implications with the findings of a recent structuralist analysis of geometrical patterning in lyric poetry, James Bunn's highly stimulating "Circle and Sequence in the Conjectural Lyric," *New Literary History* III (Spring 1972), 511-26. Bunn suggests that "the combined circle and sequence" operates as a kind of deep structure for a great deal of nineteenth-century poetry.

24 Karl Kroeber's essay "Delivering *Jerusalem*" (*BSA*, pp. 347-67) develops a similar insight from a linguistic point of view. Kroeber contrasts *Jerusalem* with *Finnegans Wake*, distinguishing Blake's language by the way it "thrusts through the verbal surfaces in which Joyce delights," producing meaning which "depends upon the history of each word *in itself*, verbal wheels *within* wheels" (p. 349). Kroeber elaborates this intuition to argue that "inward expansion is perhaps the key to Jerusalem" (p. 354). The best treatment of Blake's poetics of inwardness is E. J. Rose's "The Symbolism of the Opened Center and Poetic Theory in Blake's *Jerusalem*," *Studies in English Literature* V (1965), 587-606.

constitute "the sleep of Ulro! and . . . the passage through/Eternal Death." Most of the principles of selection proposed by critics have included some implied teleology which necessitated the demonstration of temporal development in the themes they chose to consider. Thus Karl Kiralis finds his proposed structure of "Childhood, Manhood, and Old Age" frustrated by the Minute Particulars: "not all of the individual chapters have any apparent plan of growth. . . . But even though some planning is evident in these chapters, the time and space shifts, the once mentioned but not explained characters or symbols, the "reflections" and flashbacks . . . do not make for a clear and definite design of growth."[25] There are "designs of growth" in *Jerusalem*, but the one which governs the fallen world is the Polypus, the indefinite vegetative animal which sprouts in all directions simultaneously and serves as a parody of the fourfold vision which perceives all directions simultaneously.[26]

A more promising way of investigating *Jerusalem*'s structure is offered by Blake's distinction between "Natural Causes" (which operate in the fallen world of space and time) and "Spiritual Causes":

> And every Natural Effect has a Spiritual Cause, and Not
> A Natural: for a Natural Cause only seems, it is a Delusion
> Of Ulro: & a ratio of the perishing Vegetable Memory
> (*M* 26:44-46, E 123)

If we read *Jerusalem* looking for an order of "Natural" or secondary causes,[27] treating each episode as the cause of a later one and the effect of an earlier one, we quite literally experience (as Kiralis discovered) "the perishing Vegetable Memory" in the difficulty of remembering and isolating the prior cause of any event. This is particularly evident with the consummate action in the poem, the awakening of Albion. At the beginning of this episode, "Albion cold lays on his Rock. . . . The weeds of Death inwrap his hands & feet blown incessant. . . . England a Female Shadow . . . lays upon his bosom heavy":

25 Kiralis, "The Theme and Structure of Blake's *Jerusalem*," p. 142.

26 See the discussion of the Polypus in Chapter Four.

27 Blake's distinction between these two notions of causation is one of his firmest principles. We find it in his annotations on Lavater's *Aphorisms* in 1788 ("The Philosophy of Causes & Consequences misled Lavater as it has all his Cotemporaries. Each thing is its own cause & its own effect"; K 88) and in his annotations to Bacon's *Essays* in 1798 ("There is no Such Thing as a Second Cause nor as a Natural Cause for any Thing in any Way. He who says there are Second Causes has already denied a First"; K 403).

Over them the famished Eagle screams on boney Wings and around
Them howls the Wolf of famine deep heaves the Ocean black thundering!
Around the wormy Garments of Albion: then pausing in deathlike silence
Time was Finished! The Breath Divine Breathed over Albion

(94:1, 5, 7, 8, 15-18; *E* 251-52)

The apocalyptic moment steals in during a pause in the account of Albion's deepest death-sleep; it is not presented as the direct consequence of any particular creative or revolutionary action.[28] If we read back into the preceding episodes to find the event that has made the difference, we find only ambiguous signals, not efficient causes. One explanation is that the historical process has touched bottom: things cannot get any worse, and therefore the end is at hand ("if Bacon, Newton, Locke/ Deny a Conscience in Man . . ./ Contemning the Divine Vision & Fruition, Worshiping the Deus/ Of the Heathen, The God of This World, & the Goddess Nature/ . . . Is it not that Signal of the Morning which was told us in the beginning"; 93:21-26, E 251). Another signal is provided two plates earlier by Enitharmon's remark that "The Poets Song draws to its period & Enitharmon is no more" (92:8), but it is not clear whether the poem is reaching its climax because Enitharmon's separation from Los is about to end, or Enitharmon's separation must end because the poem is about to conclude. If we continue to read backward through the poem, a whole series of "turning points" are suggested: we can see the decisive moment as occurring when the total body of Error is revealed in the image of the Covering Cherub (89:9ff.); when Los finally sees the form of Jerusalem in "the opacous bosom of the Sleeper" (86:1ff.); when Gwendolyn repents her reduction of the male form to a "winding Worm" and tries to reverse the process "To form the Worm into a form of love by tears & pain" and encourages the other Daughters of Albion "to give their souls away in the Furnaces of Affliction" (82:72-79); or when Gwendolyn utters her false doctrine of female domination, "Forgetting that Falsehood is prophetic" (82:20).

But if every falsehood is prophetic, then every episode in the poem, including the opening vision of Albion rejecting Jesus, has

[28] Cf. Frye's sense of the ending, quoted above, note 7.

to be seen as instrumental in causing his awakening, serving as a "Signal of the Morning which was told us *in the Beginning*" (93:26, E 251; italics mine). The act of defining and clarifying and preserving the Minute Particulars of Albion's sleep is the means of waking him up; truth is established by the exploration of falsehood:

> Labour well the Minute Particulars, attend to the Little-ones:
> And those who are in misery cannot remain so long
>
> . . . .
>
> The Infinite alone resides in Definite & Determinate Identity
> Establishment of Truth depends upon destruction of Falshood
> continually
>
> (55:52-53, 64-65, E 203)

This does not mean, however, that the poem is merely a random aggregate of episodes, visions, and statements united only by their common concern with clarifying error. Blake's notion of "Spiritual Causes" suggests that there are identifiable *classes* of error, and that his poem may be organized thematically, in terms of these classes, rather than in temporal-spatial terms. Let us return, then, to the overt structure of the book as a series of orations or prophecies directed at particular audiences, examining the four chapters not as a temporal progression but as clarifications of particular kinds of error.

V. THEMATIC STRUCTURE: THE SEXUAL POLITICS OF ORATORY

Blake begins with the most universal audience, a public which includes both "Sheep" and "Goats" (plate 3), preaching a doctrine of universal forgiveness and reconciliation: "Heaven, Earth & Hell, henceforth shall live in harmony" (3:10). The error which is emphasized at the beginning of this chapter is the most universal one, the repudiation of faith, imagination, love, and forgiveness as mere illusions or "phantoms of the over heated brain" (see 4:24). Albion, who is the English-reading Public or Universal Man, is the dominant figure, opening the chapter with a repudiation of Jesus and concluding it with a long oration of despair (plates 21-25). The main body of the chapter gives an account of the divisions which particularize Albion's fall, his splitting into sons and daughters, the analogous division of Los from his Spectre and Emanation, Los's conflicts with Albion's children, and the absorption of Albion's

Emanation Jerusalem into Vala, the nature goddess. We also see the beginning of contrary movements: Los subdues (but does not defeat) his Spectre (plates 10-11), builds Golgonooza (plates 12-13), the city of art which is Jerusalem-in-progress, and perfects the "Spaces of Erin" (9:34) to serve as a refuge from Albion's melancholy, "Giving a body to Falshood that it may be cast off for ever" (12:13, E 153). Blake seems, in other words, to have designed his first chapter around his hypothetical audience, dramatizing its role as a universal public in the image of a universal man and surveying the entire range of themes that his poem will develop. It is difficult, in fact, to think of any character, theme, or action in the entire poem that is not in some way prefigured in this opening chapter.

As we move into the second chapter (addressed "To the Jews") the atemporal nature of the poem becomes obvious. Albion has just died in despair at the end of the first chapter, and yet we find him alive, if not well, at the beginning of the second (plate 28), doing the same sort of thing we saw him doing at the beginning of Chapter I—rejecting love as "unnatural consanguinities and friendships" (28:7; cf. "deceitful friendships," 4:26), rejecting faith in favor of "certainty and demonstrative truth" (28:11; cf. "By demonstration man alone can live," 4:28), and rejecting forgiveness in favor of a code of Sin and Moral Virtue (28:9, 15; cf. 4:31). But Blake is not merely repeating himself. The story of Albion's error is being retold to a new audience, a subset of the general public addressed in the first chapter. What we need to watch for, then, are shifts in emphasis which reflect Blake's understanding of the errors and visionary possibilities that reside in this special audience. Who are "the Jews," and how should the story of Albion's fall be recounted to them?

Blake's prefatory address to the Jews treats them not primarily as an audience whose errors must be corrected, but as a culture which has kept alive the tradition of prophecy and the possibility of a unified, humane society. The notion of Albion as a "Universal Man" is traced to the mystical Jewish tradition that "Man anciently containd in his mighty limbs all things in Heaven & Earth" (*J* 27, E 170). The appearance of a Saviour "as the Prophets had foretold" is linked to "The return of Israel" and "a Return to Mental Sacrifice & War" (*J* 27, E 172). What, then, are the errors Blake associates with Judaism? If we had to answer in one word, that word would be *patriarchy*. Blake thinks of Judaism not as a separate people or culture, but as a state of mind which is woven into the whole fabric of Western culture, "for all nations believe the jews code and worship the jews god" (*MHH* 13, E 38). The common denominator of Judaism is, for Blake, the "Patriarchal Religion" (E 169) which is absorbed by the revealed religion of Christianity and by the Natural Religion of Druidism ("the Druid Temples . . . are the Patriarchal Pillars"; *J* 27, E 169), and which survives in society as the "cruel Patriarchal pride/ Planting thy Family alone,/ Destroying all the World beside" (27:78-90, E 172). Behind these social and religious manifestations of patriarchy, however, Blake traces a psychological obsession with the "Masculine Portion" of human nature, the Spectre or Selfhood (see *J* 27:69-76), which is described as the author of "Moral & Self-Righteous Law" (especially the law of chastity), vengeance for sin, and codes of war.[29]

The second chapter retells the story of Albion's fall, then, in the context of a prefatory address which emphasizes the masculine half of that divided self described in the first chapter. This emphasis is sustained in the dialogues and exemplary actions which follow. Albion's opening dialogue is not with Jesus, but with his Spectre or "Rational Power" (29:5), his own masculine portion. The chapter is subsequently dominated by the male half of the Universal Man, the Sons of Albion, consolidated in the figures of Reuben and Hand, and the countermovements are chiefly directed at their activities: Bath preaches pacifism and forgiveness, and Los builds a lower world of Ulro, giving a form to Reuben and setting limits to the fall called "Satan" and "Adam," the lowest boundaries of the fall into "male will." There is little doubt that this chapter emphasizes (although it does not focus exclusively on) the errors Blake associates with masculinity—including the error of trying to redeem Albion by force, "to bear him back/ Against his will thro Los's gate to Eden" (39:2-3, E 184).

The ultimate error of the masculine "Spectrous" power is the transformation of the self into an atomistic ego, "a white Dot calld a Center from which branches out/ A Circle in continual gyrations" (29:19-20, E 173). This ego tries alternately to possess and to worship this external world, transforming it into a mysterious void animated by "the Female Will" (30:31-40, E 175). It is only logical, then, that the third chapter should anatomize this contrary error of "Female Will," associated with those who call "themselves Deists, Worshipping the Maternal Humanity; calling it Nature and Natural Religion" (90:65-66, E 248). The focus is now on the Daughters of Albion,

29 On Blake's use of Jewish mysticism see Asloob Ahmad Ansari, "Blake and the Kabbalah," in *Essays for Damon*, ed. Rosenfeld, pp. 199-220.

consolidated in Rahab (Natural Philosophy) and Tirzah (Natural Religion), who seek "To have power over Man from Cradle to corruptible Grave" (56:4, E 203). Much of the chapter reads like an apocalyptic satire on radical feminism, presenting the Daughters of Albion as a tribe of sadistic Amazons who are even more dangerous than their male counterparts, and expressing Blake's bitterest (and most easily misunderstood) antifeminist remarks. The Daughters are seen "dancing to the timbrel/ Of War," passing the "Knife of flint . . . over the howling victim" (58:2-3; 66:20), and reducing the males to slaves of women:

> . . . The Human is but a Worm, & thou O Male: Thou art
> Thyself Female, a Male: a breeder of Seed: a Son & Husband: & Lo
> The Human Divine is Womans Shadow, a Vapor in the summers heat
> Go assume Papal dignity thou Spectre, thou Male Harlot! Arthur
> Divide into the Kings of Europe in times remote O Woman-born
> And Woman-nourishd & Woman-educated & Woman-scorn'd!
>
> (64:12-17, E 213)

The "form of the Mighty Hand" (70:1) is exhibited once again, but this time "his feminine power" (70:18) is revealed: "Rahab/ Sat deep within him hid . . . Brooding Abstract Philosophy" (70:18-19, E 222). The countermovements in the third chapter also focus on the female side of the imagination: the Looms of Cathedron are tended by the Daughters of Los, laboring "for life & love" (59:37, E 207), and Jerusalem tells a story of Joseph forgiving Mary's adultery (61ff.), an exemplary tale of the abolition of female chastity.

It is clear, however, that Blake is not trying to place ultimate blame on the "feminine delusion," but to clarify the nature of "Feminine & Masculine when separated from Man" (67:14, E 218). Thus Los places intellectual and social contraries of all kinds on his anvil:

> He fixes them with strong blows placing the stones & timbers.
> To Create a World of Generation from the World of Death:
> Dividing the Masculine & Feminine: for the comingling
> Of Albions & Luvahs Spectres was Hermaphroditic
>
> (58:17-20, E 205)

The two middle chapters of *Jerusalem* are Blake's attempt to divide the sexes in order to reunite them at a new level. The first and fourth chapters, on the other hand, give roughly equal attention to both sexes, the first focusing on Albion's division into sons and daughters, the fourth anatomizing their consolidation in the apocalyptic form of error, the hermaphroditic Covering Cherub, a female hidden within a male (or vice versa), "Religion hid in War, a Dragon red & hidden Harlot/ Each within other" (89:53-54, E 246). This chapter is directed at the Christianity which unites the moral laws and patriarchy of Judaism with the natural laws ("Greek Philosophy") and matriarchy that finds its latest incarnation in the system of Deism. Blake's anatomy of the "feminine delusion" is not so much a prophecy of feminist political domination as it is an account of intellectual domination by naturalistic, rational, technological ideologies that reduce "Man" (read "mankind") to "a worm of sixty winters."

Jerusalem discloses, then, what E. D. Hirsch has called a "structure of emphases."[30] It is a thematically organized, encyclopedic anatomy of the human condition as a battle of the sexes. One question we still need to answer about this structure, however, is why Blake treats patriarchy before matriarchy in his scheme of spiritual causes. The answer to this question explains, I think, why temporal structure continues to be felt and investigated in *Jerusalem* in spite of the obvious resistance of the poem to being read in this way. The fact is that there are signs that the order of the two middle chapters reflects a vision of the historical development of consciousness as a movement from masculine to feminine dominance, a sequence which occurs quite explicitly in *Milton* (Milton and other male characters dominating the first half of the poem, Ololon and the Daughters of Beulah dominating the second half). These "signs of the times" are images of Albion's changing relation to the cosmos, the patriarchal era of Judaism referred to as the time "ere yet the Starry Heavens were fled away" from the limbs of Albion (30:20), and the matriarchal era of Deism referred to as the time when "now the Starry Heavens are fled from the mighty limbs of Albion" (75:27), presumably into the "Dragon wings coverd with stars" (54:30) of the universal female who begins to appear in this chapter. The change in sexual domination is defined historically, then, as the progressive alienation of mankind (Albion) from his world; man stops being a microcosm and becomes an atom, a tiny speck of intelligence adrift on a rock in a void or "Female Space."

The movement from patriarchy to matriarchy in the middle chapters of *Jerusalem* spills over into the final chapter as the Daughters

30 *Validity in Interpretation* (New Haven, 1967), p. 230.

of Albion, represented now by the warrior maidens Cambel and Gwendolyn, work out their "final solution" for dominating the Sons of Albion: "Unless we find a way to bind these awful Forms to our/ Embrace we shall perish annihilate, discoverd our Delusions" (82:3-4, E 237). Gwendolyn's answer is to surround the "cruel Warriors" with seductive luxury, the sweet delights of Babylon: "the fury of Man exhaust in War! Woman permanent remain/ See how the fires of our loins point eastward to Babylon" (82:35-36). Art will be enlisted to create decadent pleasure domes, degenerate parodies of the ideal civilization, Jerusalem:

> . . . let the Looms of Enitharmon & the Furnaces of Los
> Create Jerusalem, & Babylon & Egypt & Moab & Amalek
>
> . . . .
>
> See Sisters Canaan is pleasant, Egypt is as the Garden of Eden:
> Babylon is our chief desire, Moab our bath in summer
>
> (82:25-26, 30-31; E 237)

Gwendolyn believes this strategy will reduce the male to a helpless, dependent infant, insuring women's rule forever. But the process goes too far; the warrior does not merely degenerate into an infant, he regresses even further: "Hyle was become a winding Worm: & not a weeping Infant" (82:48). Her sister Cambel seems oblivious to this disappointment, envying Gwendolyn's power over her man, so Los allows her a similar power "To form the mighty form of Hand according to her will/ In the Furnaces of Los" (82:62-63). For the first time in the poem, however, the prophetic implications of error manifest themselves immediately to the one who commits the error. Gwendolyn has apparently persisted in folly long enough, for she

> . . . howld
> Over the forests with bitter tears, and over the winding Worm
> Repentant: and she also in the eddying wind of Los's Bellows
> Began her dolorous task of love in the Winepress of Luvah
> To form the Worm into a form of love by tears & pain.
> The Sisters saw! trembling ran thro their Looms! softening mild
> Towards London: then they saw the Furnaces opend, & in tears
> Began to give their souls away in the Furnaces of Affliction.
> Los saw & was comforted. . . .
>
> (82:72-80, E 238)

This reversal contrasts with the triumph of the Sons of Albion in Chapter II which serves only to create "A World where Man is by Nature the enemy of Man" (49:69), "A Creation that groans, living on Death./ Where Fish & Bird & Beast & Man & Tree & Metal & Stone/ Live by Devouring, going into Eternal Death continually" (50:5-7), and which causes Albion to utter "his last words Hope is banishd from me" (47:1).

Blake seems to be saying, as he does through Enitharmon in *Urizen*, Leutha and Ololon in *Milton*, and Oothoon in *Visions of the Daughters of Albion*, that the apocalyptic reversal of history is sparked by women, or by the feminine aspect of consciousness. At a psychological level, Blake is saying that the female imagination is the agency of inspiration that gives direction and meaning to the work of the male imagination; at a political level he is prophesying that, given the kind of power over men that men have over women, the women would have the sense to relent and abolish the whole game of domination, realizing that "Humanity is far above/ Sexual organization" (79:73-74, E 233). Needless to say, this prophecy is as much a hope and an exhortation as a prediction.

VI. THE PERFECT WHOLE AND THE MINUTE PARTICULARS

If we step back now and try to bring the total organization of *Jerusalem* into focus, we seem to have a contradiction. We began with a view of the poem as a structure of antiform, a labyrinth of atemporal, antinarrative moments or epiphanies, and ended with a picture of the poem as a historical progression with beginning, middle, and end. In between we suggested an intellectual, thematic structure based on the errors and visionary possibilities Blake associates with various audiences. It is this "in between" structure of ideas and "Spiritual Causes" that provides the center of gravity for the poem and that bridges its apparently contradictory uses of time. The thematic organization permits Blake wide latitude in the choice and sequence of actions, and it allows him to synchronize the necessarily lateral or linear movement of the poem with a centripetal, inward-moving sense of progression. We go from Chapter I to Chapter II not to find out what happens next, but to go deeper into what has already happened, and to come at it from a different perspective. The four chapters of *Jerusalem*, like the four gates of Golgonooza, are each fourfold, "Each within other toward the four points" (12:48); that is, each chapter contains a sense of the whole, implying and alluding to all the others but reviewing the whole in terms of a distinct emphasis.

But *Jerusalem* is not just a single, spatial form or "four-gated city"; it is also a woman, a living organism that discloses interfolded patterns of growth. Blake orders his thematic entries into the poem to suggest, in a very gentle and subtle way, that the ruling ideas and passions of consciousness have a history. By planting unobtrusive signs of progressive movement in the poem, Blake invites us to see the unfolding of his encyclopedia as a multidimensional narrative at the same time we see it as an omnidirectional kaleidoscope of intellectual patterns. The reader of *Jerusalem* can find, as numerous critics have, patterns of temporal progression and regression such as the ages of man, the cycle of seasons, the history of religion, and the poem is encyclopedic enough to provide "evidence" for all these models. We can feel, with Karl Kiralis, a pattern like that of a growing person,[31] or with Harold Bloom, a "gradually sharpening antithesis between two contrary forces" as in the Book of Ezekiel,[32] or with E. J. Rose, a journey "backwards in time" as in *Prometheus Unbound*.[33] More fundamentally, however, we must feel, as Karl Kroeber suggests, that "*Jerusalem* . . . moves inward to a point of transformation,"[34] a point which is located in every word and line, the centers which open into circumferences:

> He who would see the Divinity must see him in his Children
> One first, in friendship & love; then a Divine Family, & in the midst
> Jesus will appear; so he who wishes to see a Vision; a perfect Whole
> Must see it in its Minute Particulars. . . .
>
> (*J* 91:18-21, E 249)

VII. THE ILLUSTRATIONS: STYLE, SEQUENCE, AND ICONOGRAPHY

A full account of the illustrations to *Jerusalem* could occupy a book in itself. In the pages that follow, therefore, we will not be

[31] "The Theme and Structure of Blake's *Jerusalem*," p. 14.
[32] *Blake's Apocalypse*, p. 405.
[33] "The Structure of Blake's *Jerusalem*," p. 40.
[34] "Delivering Jerusalem," *BSA*, p. 352.

able to explore the *Jerusalem* designs with the same thoroughness that was possible with *Thel* and *Urizen*. What we can do, however, is to examine the basic characteristics of style and iconography and to survey the major "framing elements," the designs which are placed at the structural divisions of the text. If we cannot enter the city, we can at least study the symbolic ornaments carved on the gates. There is little question that the illustrations to *Jerusalem* are the most complex in Blake's illuminated books, both in their multiplicity of relations to the text and in their inherent iconographic difficulty. The technique of syncopation—placing designs at a physical and metaphoric distance from their best textual reference—is employed frequently, as is the device of reversing the meaning of symbols in different contexts. To cite a single instance: the image of the moon appears as a symbol of liberation on plate 4 [94], as an emblem of sexual enslavement on plate 8, as an ark of refuge on plate 24. None of these appearances is directly illustrative of a specific scene in the text; all must be seen as metaphorical transformations or displacements of verbal matters.[35]

[35] The moon with star on plate 4 coupled with the Greek motto "Jesus Only" suggests that this is a pictorial transposition of the liberating alternative offered by Jesus to Albion in the accompanying text. The moon on plate 8 is drastically removed from its textual reference, both physically and metaphorically. The closest verbal analogue occurs in 63:12, where "Fairies lead the Moon along the Valley of Cherubim." Since "Fairies of Albion" are "afterwards Gods of the Heathen," (*FZ* 4:3, E 297), this may be a lunar goddess like Diana, her role as a symbol of chastity indicated by the traces binding her breasts and loins. The "old moon with the new moon in its arms" which she pulls may be a folk emblem (see "The Ballad of Sir Patrick Spens") of the storms which this repression will produce. Erdman sees it as an emblem of female enslavement to natural cycles, a "menstrual chariot" (*TIB*, p. 287). The moon on plate 24 contains a different kind of fairy, one of those "Cherubims of Tender-mercy/ Stretching their Wings sublime over the Little-ones of Albion" described in the accompanying text (24:21-22), and it is part of the recurrent motif of "moony arks" which reappears on plates 18 and 39. Blake probably found this image in George Faber's *The Origin of Pagan Idolatry* (London, 1816), II, 90-91, where Faber suggests the following interpretation: "the Moon, which preserved his [Noah's] offspring while the waters covered the earth, and which subsequently became the parent both of the animal and vegetable creation, must inevitably be the Ark, which the old mythologists, in every part of the world, venerated under the astronomical symbol of the navicular crescent." In Blake's system it becomes a symbol of Beulah, the place of refuge and rest during the catastrophic floods of history. For more detail on this and other astronomical symbols in *Jerusalem*, see my Ph.D. dissertation. "Blake's Composite Art," Johns Hopkins, 1968, pp. 179-87.

We should also note, however, that Blake has abandoned some of the devices of the late Lambeth books which tended to separate the text from designs. *Jerusalem* returns to the visual interpenetration of text with graphic structures that we saw in the early Lambeth books, and it does not have a mobile gallery of free-floating full-page designs like *Urizen.* The few full-page pictures in *Jerusalem* are fixed solidly like pillars at the four gates of the poem. The only variations in the sequence of plates occur with some of the textual plates in Chapter II, a fact which tends to support the impression that nonnarrative principles of ordering are at work in the poem.

1. *Technical Discriminations: "A Variety in Every Line"*

We have already noted the increased use of nonhuman imagery, allegorical machinery, emblems, and hieroglyphics in the iconography of *Jerusalem* as a reflection of the heightened intellectuality of the poem. We should observe also that these iconographic riches are delivered to us in the most flexible and various graphic style Blake ever employed in his illuminated books. In his 1793 prospectus Blake described the graphic character of the Lambeth books as "a style more ornamental, uniform, and grand, than any before discovered" (E 670). On the elementary level of technique, the style of *Jerusalem* is certainly ornamental and grand, but it does not immediately strike us as "uniform." It discloses instead a wide range of degrees of pictorial finish and of graphic technique. Some forms are carefully articulated in fine lines, others are distinguished by only the barest suggestions of form, seemingly half-finished. Some plates are executed in white lines on a black background, others in black lines on a white background, and some even mix these two techniques in a single composition. Our first impression of the style of *Jerusalem,* then, is as a medley of extremes, combining sophisticated, highly accomplished graphic technique and formal invention with apparently naïve, rough sketches of simple forms that offer little pleasure to the connoisseur of engraving.

This apparently heterogeneous style is constructed, I would suggest, on two basically different conceptions of pictorial form, conceptions which may be illustrated by looking at the first and last plates of the book ([86] and [89]). The frontispiece to *Jerusalem* is essentially a line drawing on copper, the fineness of the lines suggesting (but not guaranteeing)[36] that they were engraved directly

[36] Erdman sees this, and the ten other *Jerusalem* plates in this style, as "intaglio etchings . . . or what Blake called woodcutting on copper" (*TIB,*

into the copper with a burin rather than etched with acid. The ink was then applied to the flat, uncut surface of the plate, and the incised "intaglio" lines were kept clean. Plate 100, on the other hand, is designed as a sculptured relief: the bodies are white masses which stand out from a black background that has been etched away with acid, the sinews of the bodies also etched in relatively thick, coarse lines that suggest an acid "bite" rather than the fine point of the burin. In this plate the "valleys" or cut-away portions of the plate were inked and the raised, relief masses were kept clean, precisely the reverse of the inking process in the first plate. While we cannot be absolutely certain that the first plate was not incised with acid, we can nevertheless discern a clear distinction between two notions of pictorial form, one conceived as a line drawing in which modeling and highlights are revealed by clustering lines together, the other as a sculptured relief in which shadows and masses are revealed by cutting away areas and lines. The first technique begins with darkness and introduces light; the second begins with light and introduces darkness.

A large number of combinations and modifications of these two techniques can be produced by a skilled printer with a wide repertoire of inking procedures. If a great many white lines are clustered together, the plate may begin to look like a black-line drawing, with white masses and backgrounds, as in plate 28 [98]. If, on the other hand, the sculptured relief process is carried far enough, so much black will be introduced that the print begins to look like a white-line drawing with thick lines, as in plate 6. It is also possible to combine the two techniques, as in plate 50 [99], where the human figures seem to be done in sculptured relief with some black engraved lines clustered at the edges of the etched shadows to produce a gray area (note especially the chest and stomach of the seated figure). The column of smoke surrounding the group of flying figures is modeled, on the other hand, in white lines drawn on a black background, as

---

p. 291). The fineness of the lines in these plates and their pointed extremities suggest, however, that they were cut directly into the plate with an engraving tool rather than bitten with acid. Arthur M. Hind points out that "the etched line nearly always has rectangular extremities, while the line cut with the graver tapers to a point" (*A History of Engraving and Etching*, p. 8). I will henceforth refer to these plates as engravings, not because I am certain that they were cut with a graver but as an economical way of reminding the viewer that there is a significant difference in the quality of line, aside from the distinction between relief and intaglio.

are the heavenly bodies and lightning in the seascape beyond. The stony island presents, however, another reversal, executed as it is in black-line cross-hatching on a white mass. I would not hazard a guess as to how every line in this plate was cut, but I would suggest that the sense of tension and turmoil that is represented in the forms of the picture is augmented and embodied in its restless, heterogeneous graphic style.

The designs of *Jerusalem* may be classified technically, then, in three general categories: (1) pure white-line engravings or "drawings on copper"; (2) pure relief etching or sculptured relief on copper; (3) plates using a mixed method. The white-line drawings (in copy D, plates 1, 2, 11, 26, 28, 31, 33, 41, 51, 53, 76) are the most prominent group in terms of size (all but the last full-page design are in this style) and placement (the frontispiece to each chapter is in this style). Their placement in the sequence—1, 11, 31, 41, 51—suggests that the idea of a series of ten-plate sections, each headed by a white-line drawing, may have been one of Blake's organizing principles, perhaps discarded as the work grew larger. Eight of the eleven plates in this style appear in the first half of the book, the three in the second half used as frontispieces (plates 51 [100] and 76 [103]) and as the heading to Chapter III (plate 53 [101]). The sculptured reliefs are far more numerous, then, especially in the second half of the book, and the mixed method is the scarcest, appearing only in plates 3, 23, and 50.

It would be foolish as this point to attempt to generalize about the significance of these stylistic groups: certainly we can rule out the notion that "good" subjects are reserved for one style and "bad" for another. Robert Essick's hypothesis that the line drawing technique is to be linked with the highly finished "Urizenic networks" of commercial engraving and the sculptured relief process with prophetic art is intriguing but inconclusive, and it threatens to become a disguised code for labeling the content of pictures as good or bad on the basis of style.[37] In *Milton*, as I have argued elsewhere,[38] this stylistic contrast is used to embody the difference between the world Blake/Milton/Los is leaving behind (the "finished" world of Milton's prophetic achievement) and the new world that is being (or about to be) created, and which is therefore seen as less highly finished.

[37] "Blake and the Traditions of Reproductive Engraving," *Blake Studies* V (1972), 59-103.

[38] "Style and Iconography in the Illustrations of Blake's *Milton*," *Blake Studies* VI (1973), 47-71.

The predominance of white-line drawing in the first half of *Jerusalem* and its relative scarcity in the second half may suggest a similar transformation, but we need much more evidence from particular designs before this can be substantiated.

What we can observe with some assurance are the basic effects created by Blake's repertoire of graphic styles, and their appropriateness to his theme. Perhaps the clearest point made by the style of *Jerusalem* is the relativity of black and white, a statement which is surely in keeping with a poem whose theme is the reconciliation of contraries like Sheep and Goats, Heaven and Hell, and male and female in a vision of Universial Forgiveness. Inseparable from this theme of forgiveness is the idea of universal liberation—including the liberation of the artist from popular notions of "uniformity" in engraving. Blake saw the conventional idea of "high finish" in the graphic arts as a hindrance to vision as debilitating as "the modern bondage of rhyming" was to verse. We should not be surprised, then, to find in his prophetic prints a rebellion against this "monotony," "a variety in every line" of the copper plate as of the poem: "I defy any Man to Cut Cleaner Strokes than I do or rougher when I please" (*PA*, E 571). The wide variety of "finishes" in the graphic style of *Jerusalem* is a sensuous means of eliciting visual flexibility from the viewer: connoisseurs are encouraged to "forgive what you do not approve," and "he who would see a Vision" is encouraged to exercise his senses, not resting in the contemplation of Blake's "finished" visions, but taking the tiniest, most tentative forms as the seedlings of new expanses to be opened in the imagination. The high finish of the line drawings and the rougher masses of the relief etchings interpenetrate like the perfect circle and outstretched serpent which symbolize the total form of the poem, embodying the interplay between the finished artifices of eternity and the ongoing processes of time and space.

2. *The Gates of the City*

Blake seems to have organized the major illustrations of *Jerusalem* in a rather straightforward fashion, to reflect the same thematic and rhetorical emphases that structure the poem.[39] The first three designs

[39] Henry Lesnick, "Narrative Structure and the Antithetical Vision of *Jerusalem*," *VFD*, pp. 391-412, investigates the same hypothesis that I propose here, that "the specific plates which introduce and conclude each of the four chapters help to define the material included in each chapter" (p. 391). His commentary differs from mine in that it posits a narrative pattern, "the succes-

(plates 1, 2, and 4) provide a pictorial summary of the epic theme, the frontispiece [86] showing Los commencing the "passage through/ Eternal Death," the title page [93] depicting Jerusalem as a cosmic butterfly-woman lying in the "Sleep of Ulro," and the headpiece to Chapter I [94] showing the possible liberation and "awaking to Eternal Life." As befits a series of plates introducing the entire poem "To the Public," these plates have a radiant, multipurpose iconography that can be read at many levels. At the literal level, Blake tells us in his marginal glosses that the frontispiece depicts Los "As he enterd the Door of Death for Albions sake" (*J* 1:9, E 143), the basic visionary act of Self-annihilation which is depicted similarly in the title page of *Milton* [18] as a journey into a vortex. Los reminds us of Diogenes/Urizen with his lantern in *The Book of Urizen* [79], but Diogenes/Los is not trying to break out of his world so much as he is trying to penetrate inward to its hidden heart in search of the indestructible honesty in mankind. At an archetypal level, Los is like Dürer's Apollo carrying his sun into the world of night, like Bunyan's Christian entering the Wicket Gate as he begins his journey to the heavenly city, or like Christ himself descending into death to begin the harrowing of hell. Perhaps most important is the rhetorical level, in which the traveler is the reader himself, a Theseus entering the labyrinth, the globe now seen as a golden ball of string already wound up to lead him in "at Heavens gate/ Built in Jerusalems wall" (*J* 77, E 229).

It is crucial to the understanding of Blake's allegorical technique to note that his picture resists being seen as a stratified, hierarchical system of meanings. The frontispiece provides a "publicly accessible" image in the most literal sense, in that it can symbolize with equal force the activities of the author, hero, or reader of the poem. To assert that the figure is "primarily" to be seen as Los is simply to restate this universality of reference, for Los symbolizes the imagination of *both* the author and the reader, personified as the hero of the poem.

If the opening plate is a comprehensive introduction to the theme of author, hero, and reader as pilgrim, the title page [93] is a vision of

sive stages of fallen existence" (p. 405), rather than a thematic structure. Our readings of particular pictures are not so much in conflict as different in emphasis. Lesnick tends to read many pictures ironically because he sees them as scenes in a journey which is incomplete; I regard this ironic level as a surface which Blake is asking us to penetrate in search of visionary openings, occasions for forgiveness.

the cosmos which he will explore, the "Void, outside of Existence" which lies on the other side of Death's Door, "A pleasant Shadow of Repose calld Albions lovely Land" (*J* 1:3). That gate was apparently a vortex, for the "traveller thro' Eternity" sees the world precisely as Blake describes it at the moment of passing a vortex, as a system of heavenly bodies, "a universe of starry majesty" contained in a human form (see *M* 15:21-35). This image of the cosmos as a sleeper surrounded by hovering, mourning attendants exerts far more influence on the subsequent iconography of the illustrations than the image of the traveler, perhaps because Blake knows his reader-viewer will play the role of traveler. The theme of the sleeping, supine victim attended by solicitous watchers (or, in many cases, fantastic demons and sadistic torturers like those in Fuseli's *Nightmare*) recurs throughout, the pose of the "melancholy observer" (the attendant just above the sleeper's head) an especially frequent motif, an adaptation, no doubt, of Dürer's *Melencolia I* [108], which hung above Blake's workbench.

If we had only these first two plates to define our opening theme we might expect a kind of Sleeping Beauty story, the passive heroine waiting for the traveler to awaken her. The headpiece to Chapter I [94], however, in a typical Blakean reversal, presents the female in an active role as the leader of an exodus to freedom, a flight from the bondage of the tyrannical woman who squats on the ground (this transformation is implicit, of course, in the butterfly-chrysalis imagery of the sleeper on the title page, and explicit in the intermediate marginal design of plate 3, where the sleeper seems to be rising). The basic movement of the poem from masculine to feminine dominance is thus summarized along with the dual themes of sleep and travel in the opening sequence of plates, and the headpiece to the first chapter focuses this movement as a choice between two images of the female: the naked, sexually liberated guide (cf. Oothoon, Ololon, and in *Urizen*, Enitharmon) who leads humanity to the realm of imagination and forgiveness ("Jesus Only") and the heavily clothed Vala-sibyl who keeps her subjects' minds (rather unsuccessfully) on mundane matters. This is a pictorial transposition of the choice Albion is making below in the opening episode of the text: the seated man with his head turned away from the liberating exodus parallels the Albion who (in the accompanying text) "away turns down the valleys dark," rejecting Jesus as a "Phantom of the over heated brain" (4:22, 24, E 145). Many of the plates which follow will present further transpositions of this choice in terms of other antitheses:

Los versus his Spectre in plate 6, the prophetic swan-woman versus the fashionable goldfish-woman of plate 11, the fleeing Abraham versus the "vegetated" Skofeld in plate 15, the interwoven wings of seraphim versus the meshing "Wheels of War" on plate 22, and the moon of liberation versus the moon of enslavement, which is prefigured by the presence of two moons (and two earths) in the wings of the sleeper on the title page. All the major thematic actions of text and design—the journey, the sleep, and the choice or judgment—are thus exhibited for us clearly in the opening sequence of plates.

After Albion makes his mistaken choice in the opening episode of the poem; the predominant motif of the pictures in Chapter I is, as Erdman suggests, "Albion's fall and entrapment."[40] Since Albion is "the Public" at one level of the allegory, this seems only fitting for the chapter addressed to this audience. Jerusalem's role as the sleeping victim surrounded by watchers (presented on the title page) is thus transferred to Albion in the body of the first chapter. He appears as a slain warrior on plate 9, as a melancholy sleeper in his tomb (or perhaps only the marble effigy) on plate 14, as a fallen Gulliver on plate 19, a netted bird on plate 22 (top), and a victim in a torture chamber on plate 25 [95].

This last plate, the tailpiece to the first chapter, provides a summary of Albion's fate in the opening phase of the poem. We see him "ere yet the Starry Heavens were fled away/ From his awful Members" (30:20, E 174), fainting with agony in the "Threefold" realm of female domination, his daughters turning into his mothers, a trio of Parcae or Fates. On the right is Tirzah, the physical mother of his mortal part whose apron strings are the "living fibres" of the umbilical cord. We can also see Tirzah as a torturer disemboweling her victim, an unappealing idea that Blake may have borrowed from Poussin's *Martyrdom of St. Erasmus* [96].[41] If Blake was working from this source, however, he clearly modified it in several important details. The cord emerges from Albion's navel, stressing its umbilical character, rather than (as in Poussin) from the upper abdomen of the victim, and Tirzah's action is more ambiguous than that of the

[40] *TIB*, p. 304.

[41] This source was suggested by Morton Paley and Deirdre Toomey, "Two Pictorial Sources for *Jerusalem* 25," *Blake Newsletter* V:3, no. 19 (Winter 1971-72), 185-90. The likelihood that Blake was working from the St. Erasmus theme is increased by the fact that it was adapted for satiric political prints in the eighteenth century. See the review of Herbert Atherton's *Political Prints in the Age of Hogarth* in *Times Literary Supplement*, 23 August 1974.

torturer of St. Erasmus. The saint's entrails are pulled taut by the full force of his torturer and wound up on a winch in the background; Albion's "cord" has considerable slack in it, and Tirzah can be seen as a midwife "milking" the umbilical cord downward to the navel to preserve the life fluids before cutting and tying off. The fact that the Fates or Parcae were associated with childbirth and midwifery (*parica* means "childbearing") suggests that we should see this as a picture of giving and sustaining life as well as taking it away.

If Tirzah is the physical mother or midwife who controls Albion's birth, the central female is Vala, Mother Nature spreading the tent of creation (or the fibrous womb and placenta) in which the newborn Albion will live. The woman at the left is Rahab, the "mother of sorrows" who receives her dead son's head in her lap like a melancholy *Pieta*. Her right hand is hidden behind her back and her legs are crossed, gestures which Blake associates not simply with deceit but also with the dramatic irony of "prophetic falsehood" in which error reveals a contrary truth (cf. Gwendolyn, plate 81). The irony in the picture cuts in two directions: we can behold a scene of man in the fallen world of birth, life in nature, and death, surrounded by solicitous mothers who are really torturers (Rahab a hypnotist who mentally enslaves her victim, Tirzah the physical torturer, Vala the one who keeps the whole atrocity secret and mysterious); or we can see the apparent torturers as giving life to their victim, commiserating and mourning over him like the melancholy watchers on the title page. Like the ambiguous vision in *Urizen* of Los giving birth to Enitharmon as a globe of blood [73], the design focuses its iconography in a symmetrical vision of hope and fear. The very image of Albion's fall into the "Void, outside of Existence" shows that void becoming a womb from which the new man may be born.

Blake continues to use the major "framing designs" (frontispiece, headpiece, and tailpiece) as pictorial summaries of the thematic emphases that govern each chapter. As we have noted, the second chapter is concerned primarily with "male will," the patriarchal institutions of moral law, vengeance for sin, and war as embodied in the actions of the Sons of Albion. The aggregate form of the Sons of Albion is the figure of Hand (see 8:43), whose major pictorial treatments appear in plates 26 and 50 [97 and 99], the plates which frame Chapter II. The other framing design, the headpiece of plate 28 [98], is a lovely ornamental vision of the liberated sexuality which must be condemned by the jealous male: "All these ornaments are crimes, they are made by the labours/ Of loves: of unnatural consanguinities and friendships" (28:6-7, E 172). We will return to this picture for closer examination presently.

The frontispiece to the second chapter presents a reversal of the sexual victimization we saw at the end of Chapter I. The dying Albion is reborn as his Promethean son Hand, an ambiguous Orc figure whose flames coil around his arms like the brazen serpent on the crucifix and whose wounded palms threaten to turn from their cruciform gesture to hurl down destruction and plagues, like the demon who showers revenge on Egypt [50]. Hand must be seen, in other words, as an ambivalent force in the work of the imagination, not simply as a symbol of evil.[42] Like Los's own demonic Spectre, he cannot be banished, but must be compelled to "labour obedient" in the furnaces of art. Blake suggests, in fact, that his adversaries are the very stuff of his art, identifying the Sons of Albion as the flames in his furnace, the Daughters as the metals which are forged:

> . . . I took the sighs & tears, & bitter groans:
> I lifted them into my Furnaces; to form the spiritual sword.
> That lays open the hidden heart: I drew forth the pang
> Of sorrow red hot: I worked it on my resolute anvil:
> I heated it in the flames of Hand, & Hyle, & Coban
> Nine times; Gwendolyn & Cambel & Gwiniverra
> Are melted into the gold, the silver, the liquid ruby
> . . . .
> . . . I behold the soft affections
> Condense beneath my hammer into forms of cruelty
> (9:17-23, 26-27; E 151)

This is Blake's way of saying that his art cannot lift itself by its bootstraps directly into some transcendent, ideal realm. The spiritual sword must be forged with the materials of this world, just as the vision of a unified eternity must be embodied in the dualistic, temporal meduim of language, the "stubborn structure" of English. In *Milton* Blake calls for his inspiration to descend from the subjective, ideal realm, "From out the Portals of my Brain . . . down the Nerves of my right arm . . . into my *hand*" (*M* 2:5-7, E 95; italics mine), where it may be incarnated in concrete, particular forms. The fact that these forms may be "condensed" into perversions of the visionary state by the corrupting influence of the "Hand" which forges them does not vitiate their prophetic value:

[42] See note 23, above.

> But still I labour in hope. tho' still my tears flow down.
> That he who will not defend Truth, may be compelled to defend
> A Lie: that he may be snared and caught and snared and taken
> That Enthusiasm and Life may not cease. . . .
>
> (9:28-31, E 151)

Vision is revealed not just by opposing or denying error, but by forcing it to manifest itself in clear and definite form. An art which tried to eliminate "Hand" and treat the material, historical world as an insubstantial vapor would, in Blake's view, be both impossible and irrelevant. He depicts Hand, therefore, as a figure of terrible beauty; the artist in this world, like the creator of the Tyger, must have a "hand" that dares to "seize the fire" and mold it into prophetic forms.

The tailpiece to Chapter II [99] presents Hand without this mitigating ambivalence of beauty and terror. His internal conflicts have now been externalized as a grotesque form with "Three strong sinewy Necks & Three awful & terrible Heads/ Three Brains in contradictory council brooding incessantly" (70:15, E 222). Hand's melancholy "brooding" causes a "Giant-brood" to issue from "a hideous orifice" in his chest and to rise "as the smoke of the furnace" (Hand's prophetic fire degenerating into obscurity?) in a funnel-shaped pillar of cloud or "vortex of the dead." The text tells us that this breeding will continue until Hand is divided into all Twelve Sons of Albion, and then they will reunite "into Three Forms, named Bacon, & Newton & Locke" (70:15, E 222). The background of the design suggests that this vortex is an apocalyptic manifestation of error: the heavens are filled with portents such as the giant meteorite or comet driving between the sun and moon on the right and the jagged river of lightning which issues from the mouth of a cormorant above the moon on the left.[43]

The general significance of "Threefold" figures and groups in Blake's art could occupy a study in itself. He reverses the traditional numerological preference for heavenly triads to earthly tetrads, associating the triad with the fallen psyche (the Individual, his Spectre and Emanation), the fallen society of "Three Classes of Men"

[43] Lesnick, *VFD*, p. 397, suggests that the bird is a cormorant, linking it with Milton's comparison of Satan to a cormorant in *Paradise Lost* IV:195. The fact that Hand is described with talons and a "rav'ning beak" (9:13) supports this identification. The fullest study of the figure of Hand is E. J. Rose's "Blake's Hand: Symbol and Design in *Jerusalem*," *Texas Studies in Language and Literature* VI (1964), 47-58.

(*M* 4:4), the corrupt justice represented by the three "Accusers of Theft Adultery Murder," and "Satans Holy Trinity. The Accuser, the Judge, and the Executioner" (inscriptions to "Our End is Come," E 660), the perceptual tyranny of three spatial and temporal dimensions, and the religious tyranny of the Christian trinity which consolidates all these other triads ("in Milton; the Father is Destiny, the Son, a Ratio of the Five Senses. & the Holy Ghost, Vacuum!"; *MHH* 5, E 35). In *Jerusalem* we have already seen the threefold group of females as symbols of the natural cycle of birth, life in nature, and death, and the second chapter seems especially rich in variations on this theme: the threefold psyche of Los reunites in plate 44, Albion writhes in a dance with his split Emanation in plate 47, Jesus hovers over the birth of the sexes in plate 31, a triple serpent provides yoke and wheels for the time chariot of plate 41, and Satan's Watch-fiend, the tyrant of clock-time, appears as three horsemen in one with his triple bow drawn in plate 35.

The occurrence of a figure with three heads, however, is sufficiently rare in Blake's iconography to suggest that he has something more particular in mind than merely another threefold demon. (The only other use of this motif in Blake's art is in a fairly literal illustration of Cerberus, the three-headed dog in Dante's *Inferno*). The fact that the three heads are described in the text as counselors who are involved in intellectual as well as physical "brooding" (70:15, E 222) suggests that Blake derived the figure from the tricephalous representations of Prudence, Good Counsel, and Time found in many emblem books.[44] Time was often depicted with three faces (usually animal) to represent past, present, and future, and a three-faced man signified the proper use of memory, intelligence, and foresight as the keys to good counsel and prudent action. Blake's remark that "Prudence is a rich ugly old maid courted by Incapacity" gives us an idea what kind of emblem he would have designed if this more grotesque tradition had not been available. But the motif of a three-headed figure gives him a way of connecting his critique of prudence and time with religious and psychological tyranny. The temporal reasonings on which prudence depends are, like Milton's trinity, composed of memory (which formulates the idea of destiny), intelligence (the ratio of the five senses), and foresight (which sees nothing, or vacuum). Hence the figure of Hand presents the three

[44] The following discussion is based primarily on Irwin Panofsky's "Titian's *Allegory of Prudence*: a Postscript," Chap. IV of *Meaning in the Visual Arts* (New York, 1955).

heads of Prudence as "Three Brains in contradictory council" and as a demonic trinity of accusers which is "The God of This World" (see the epilogue to *The Gates of Paradise*). Hand, who started out as an ambivalent energy figure, ends by appropriating godhead,[45] debasing himself in the process and becoming a parody of the prophetic bard who "Past, Present, & Future sees" at a single glance.

The third chapter of *Jerusalem* concentrates, as we have noted, on the triumph of female will or Deism. Plate 51 [100] introduces this theme in an imperial, courtly context, exhibiting the heavily robed Vala as queen, Hyle as her chief minister, and Skofeld as the warrior who is leaving to execute her commands. The design is pervaded, however, not with a sense of triumph but with an overwhelming feeling of oppression and infernal gloom, the figures bowed under the lineaments of contraction. The prophetic irony is that Vala's triumph is really a defeat, that it is not better to reign in hell than serve in heaven. Vala's twelve-pointed crown (an emblem of her rule over the Twelve Sons of Albion and of her role as the aggregate form of the Twelve Daughters) looks more like a spiky crown of thorns than a victor's spoils. Her sceptre, capped with a fleur-de-lis which signifies the demonic triad (and the rule of female chastity), leans useless against her side. Her posture shows that she has "become what she beheld"; her position, her head leaning on her left hand, relates her to the melancholy watcher and suggests the furthest development of this motif. Melancholy can plunge no deeper. Vala cannot bear to watch her court and subjects. Her minister has reached a "limit of contraction," turning into a self-enclosed stone like the matter which his name (Hyle) signifies. Her soldier still shows some signs of energy (he walks, and flames emanate from his back), which is perhaps why he has to be chained; Hyle is securely fettered with mind-forged manacles, but Skofeld (Blake's real-life accuser of treason) is a "hapless soldier" who might desert the whole scene if loosed from his chains. A gloomier reading would link Skofeld with the figure of Despair in Blake's color print of *The Lazar House* illustrating *Paradise Lost* (XI: 477-90). In that design a figure like Skofeld is depicted as the agent of a blind sky-god (Death), moving among the sick with his dart of death, perversely killing the hopeful and sparing those who wish to die. In *Jerusalem* we see him

[45] That is, insofar as he is seen as a figure of the Trinity. For background on this theme, see R. Pettazoni, "The Pagan Origins of the Three-Headed Representation of the Christian Trinity," *Journal of the Warburg and Courtauld Institutes* IX (1946), 135-51.

as the vehicular form of the despair which pervades his entire world, an embodiment of Albion's last words in the second chapter, "Hope is banishd from me."

If plate 51 shows the nadir of the relationship between the sexes as a mutual tyranny in which master and slave grow alike, the headpiece to Chapter III [101] portrays the fallen world itself as an imperial female, combining the vision of Jerusalem as a cosmic seraph (see the title page [93]) with the theme of the melancholy observer. The design is a deeply ambiguous fusion of the images and roles associated with Jerusalem and Vala, a fusion which is reflected in the widely different interpretations that have been suggested for this picture.[46] If we look at the corresponding headpieces to the first two chapters, however, the progression which leads to plate 53 becomes clear. The first chapter is introduced with a clear pictorial choice between Jerusalem and Vala [94]. The headpiece to the second chapter [98], which we saw earlier as a vision of liberated heterosexual activity, also illustrates the ambiguous lesbian union of Jerusalem and Vala described in the first chapter:[47]

> [Albion] . . . found Jerusalem upon the River of his City soft
>   repos'd
> In the arms of Vala, assimilating in one with Vala
> The Lilly of Havilah: and they sang soft thro' Lambeths vales,
> In a sweet moony night & silence that they had created
> With a blue sky spread over with wings and a mild moon
> (19:40-44, E 163)

[46] S. Foster Damon initially saw the figure as "Beulah, mercifully veiling the Sun of Eternity from our eyes" (*Philosophy and Symbols* [New York, 1947], p. 472), but changed this to "Vala, who wears the papal tiara" in *A Blake Dictionary* (Providence, 1965), s.v. "Sunflower." Anthony Blunt accepted the Beulah identification, pointing out that the figure was probably based on a picture of a Hindu deity in E. Moor's *Hindu Pantheon* (see *The Art of William Blake* [New York, 1959], p. 38). John Grant provides the fullest context for understanding this design, relating it to the whole range of Blake's floral symbolism in "Two Flowers in the Garden of Experience," *Essays for Damon*, ed. Rosenfeld, pp. 333-67. Grant seems in accord with the general opinion that this is a pernicious woman, probably Vala or Rahab (p. 357), but does not deal with her resemblance to textual accounts of Jerusalem or to the picture of Jerusalem as a cosmic seraph on the title page. Erdman (*TIB*, p. 332) suggests that she is a "parody of Jerusalem," a bit of irony which may, as we have seen, cut in more than one direction.

[47] Grant, "Two Flowers," pp. 355-62, should be consulted for the fullest account of alternative views of the design. The embracing couple seem to be male and female in some copies, both female in others. Either way, Albion sees them as incestuous.

It is Albion's view of this embrace as an instance of "unnatural consanguinities" that introduces the sinister overtones, however. Blake does not treat the lesbian union as evil or unnatural, but as an image of a prelapsarian harmony and freedom which looks evil from a fallen perspective, and which *is* evil insofar as it absorbs or disguises the visionary form of Jerusalem in the image of Vala or Nature.

The melancholy female of plate 53, then, is a composite form of Vala and Jerusalem which intertwines the fallen and eternal perspectives. We can see her as a cosmic form of the female tyrant on the previous page, the outline of her wings and pyramidal coiffure forming a fleur-de-lis like the cap of Vala's sceptre (a concrete example of the vegetative universe opening like a flower from a minute particular), a transformation of the free-flowing Lilly of Havilah into a symmetrical symbol of imperialism. The popish triple crown connects her with the tyrant of the Lambeth books (see *Europe* 11 [26]) and restates (along with the threefold form of the fleur-de-lis) the theme of the demonic triad. The twelve stars in her wings transpose the symbolism of Vala's twelve-pointed crown on plate 51, and her role as a "veil" which obscures eternity is implied in two images of solar eclipse, one produced by her wings, the other contained in her wings (note the way the moon on the left seems to stand between the earth and a sun which would be off the left side of the plate). The starry heavens have now fled from the limbs of Albion to the wings of the universal female, a nature goddess who has assimilated the hope of liberation (Jerusalem) into her realm of threefold illusions.

But this vision of Vala, no matter how many demonic images we may find in it, clearly does not express the kind of despair we saw in her lineaments on plate 51. Her union with Jerusalem is not just an ironic subversion of the liberating ideal by Natural Religion; it also permits that religion to have a hidden core of prophetic truth, a vision which will be perceived by Los in the final chapter:

> I see thy Form O lovely mild Jerusalem, Wingd with Six Wings
> In the opacous Bosom of the Sleeper, lovely Three-fold
> In Head & Heart & Reins three Universes of love & beauty
> Thy forehead bright: Holiness to the Lord, with Gates of pearl
> Reflects Eternity beneath thy azure wings of feathery down
> (86:1-5, E 242)

Even as her "opacous Bosom" blots out the sun, the cosmic nature goddess floats on her sunflower, like Brahma on his lotus, an emblem of the melancholy longing for "that sweet golden clime/ Where the travellers journey is done."[48]

Chapter III closes with a vision [102] of the female will in its most debased form, paralleling the exposure of the Sons of Albion at the nadir of their condition at the end of Chapter II. Two crowned females with scaly loins (probably Rahab Babylon, the double female described in the accompanying text) are wrapped in and apparently connected to an apocalyptic seven-headed coil of dragon-serpents (cf. the seven-headed dragon of Rev. 12:3). The design is very much like plate 25 of *Urizen*, which illustrates the birth of Urizen's daughters from "monsters, & worms of the pit," and it evokes the archetypal visions of the beautiful female with the serpentine lower body found in Spenser's Error and Milton's Sin.[49] Blake has grafted the male dragon of Revelation to the Great Whore, producing a "Mighty Hermaphroditic Form," the "Male within a Female hid" (75:15, E 228). The male is not hidden completely, however; if we look closely at the lower center of the melange of female serpent-dragons we find

[48] In "The Fate of Blake's Sunflower," *Blake Studies* V (1974), 7-49, John Grant amplifies the argument made earlier in "Two Flowers," suggesting that this image is totally sinister "because it has been magnified out of all proportion by an unimaginative and illiberal vision of ultimate reality. Instead of aspiring bravely or desperately toward the sun . . . Vala is sunk into a complacent distraction that turns its back on the divine sun and thus blocks the true source of all light" (p. 48). I would agree with some of these observations, adding that the rigid symmetry of Vala's pose, contrasted with the dynamic asymmetry of the Lilly on plate 28, is in itself a rather sinister gestalt. But I would also quarrel with some of Grant's assumptions. That Vala is "magnified out of all proportion" is a rather curious objection to make to Mother Nature, and it begs the question of what it is that serves as the basis or norm in determining proportion; Vala is seen sitting in the center of a flower, a position which could be said to *reduce* her out of all proportion. The claim that she is complacent seems even more tenuous. In the iconographic context of *Jerusalem* she is clearly melancholy, not complacent, and is thus connected with the pathos and time-weariness symbolized by the sunflower. The fact that she blots out the sun (rather unsuccessfully) is, of course, sinister, but it should not blind us to the presence of Jerusalem in her "opacous Bosom," nor to the differences between this Vala and the infernal tyrant of plate 51.

[49] Spenser's description of Error appears in *Faerie Queene* I: 14: "he saw the ugly monster plain,/ Half like a serpent horribly displayed;/ But th'other half did woman's shape retain,/ Most loathsome, filthy, foul, and full of vile disdain." This description probably derives primarily from Hesiod's account of the snake goddess in *Theogony* 301, which Blake would also have known. Like Keats with his Lamia, Blake transforms the archetype of the snake-woman into a much more ambiguous, complex figure than it was for Spenser or Milton.

the musculature of a male back, his neck in the grip of the female at the left, his dragon head nuzzling or perhaps whispering in her ear (recalling Satan as a toad whispering in the ear of Eve). Blake suggests, at one level, that the transformation of woman into Error or Sin is really a consequence of the male mind inventing a code of chastity and then condemning the female for failing to live up to it. Pictorially speaking, the reason the females in this design have serpent bodies is that the male in their grip has a reptilian head.

Within the constricting coils of the hermaphroditic dragon, however, we see another kind of coil composed of intersecting circles like the wheels of Eden which are shown filled with overlapping angels in the upper part of the page. These are coils "which/ Wheel within Wheel in freedom revolve in harmony & peace" (15:20, E 157), unlike the constrictive wheels of the serpent form which move "by compulsion each other" (15:19). As in his vision of Vala as cosmic nature goddess on plate 53, Blake intertwines fallen and visionary perspectives, inviting us to probe inward, entering into his images to discover first the male hidden within the females, then the form of Jerusalem within the hermaphroditic dragon. For the closed imagination the female form is a crushing, devouring serpent; to the visionary, as we learn at the end of the poem, it becomes the mediating presence between individuals, the collective emanation by which any entity becomes connected with any other: "And I heard the Name of their Emanations they are named Jerusalem" (99:5, E 256).

Blake's genius for designing pictures as vortices which draw the reader inward, into a dialectic of ironies, ambiguities, paradoxes, and concentric unfoldings, is never more fully revealed than in the magnificent frontispiece to Chapter IV [103], a crucifixion addressed to the Christian audience that has consolidated all the errors of Deism, Judaism, and the general public into Christendom, the basic fabric of Western civilization. The first thing we might note is that this could very well be a Blakean satire on the typical Christian error, the worship of the dead "vegetated" god rather than living humanity. The cross is replaced by an oak tree to update and naturalize the event, making it a crucifixion of the human form on the limbs of Natural Religion, the Deism whose ancestry Blake traces back to Druidism (superstitious nature worship) and the rational naturalism of the Greek philosophers, all consolidated in the "Atheistical Epicurean Philosophy of Albions Tree" (67:13, E 218).

And yet this satiric view of the picture, although it is easily supported with textual references to "Vegetated Christs" as "Satanic Selfhoods" which must be put off, does not quite satisfy.[50] In the first place, the humanity and pathos expressed in the crucified Christ make if difficult to behold him ironically. In the second place, Albion's stance at the foot of the tree does not suggest a rigid imitation or worship of Christ's death-image, but a living transformation of it into a dance, the famous "Dance of Albion" pose (seen from behind; cf. [25]) that Blake consistently associated with liberation: "Albion rose from where he labourd at the Mill with Slaves/ Giving himself for the Nations he danc'd the dance of Eternal Death" (E 660). This is, then, like the rising of Samson from the mill where he worked with slaves, a dance of death for life, the act of Self-annihilation. Albion is not worshiping the dead body of Jesus but perceiving and reenacting in his own body the prophetic crucifixion which is both an historical event and a timeless archetype. The Druidical oak tree (its fruits suggesting the tree of knowledge) is so faintly drawn, especially in the black and white copies, that it has become practically invisible, leaving us with a primarily human confrontation. The best textual analogies to this scene, then, are the apocalyptic conversations of Albion and Jesus at the end of the poem, when they meet face to face for the first time since the beginning and Albion questions the necessity of crucifixions: "Cannot Man exist without Mysterious/ Offering of Self for Another, is this Friendship & Brotherhood[?]" Jesus answers: "if God dieth not for Man & giveth not himself/ Eternally for Man Man could not exist! for Man is Love:/ As God is Love: every kindness to another is a little Death/ In the Divine Image" (96:20-21, 25-28, E 253).

Albion cannot use this sense of the crucifixion, as the modern church does, to crucify Christ upside down and excuse the execution of criminals, because he is not perceiving the act externally, as an atonement for his sins, but internally and empathically, as an act which must be reenacted in the annihilation of his own Selfhood. Albion's role has changed, in other words, from that of adversary (and, paradoxically, beneficiary) of Christ's act to that of disciple and evangelist. That Blake has this meaning very literally in mind is suggested by the fact that his composition is based on the traditional renderings of the Crucifixion with St. John the Evangelist (the only disciple who witnessed the Crucifixion) at the foot of the cross (see [104]). There are two sunrises in the picture, one on

[50] Lesnick, *VFD*, p. 399, gives the fullest argument for an ironic reading.

the left horizon, the other around Jesus' head. We might surmise that Blake is giving us another ambiguous choice (compare the two eclipses in plate 53 [101] and the two moons and two earths in the title page [93]). Perhaps one is the natural sun, the other the spiritual —but which one? The answer is both, or neither, because the important sunrise in the picture is Albion himself, rising like Samson (whose name was translated as "sun"),[51] shaking off his spiritual darkness and blindness. Small wonder the mistaken (but accurate) title "Glad Day" (based on Shakespeare's personification of the sun rising in *Romeo and Juliet*) remains attached to this figure despite the efforts of scholars to correct it.

If Albion is taking on the roles of sun-god and evangelistic prophet of apocalypse in Blake's crucifixion design, this suggests that he is beginning to be identified with Los, the creator and carrier of the sun throughout *Jerusalem* and the personification of prophecy. When we turn the page to the headpiece of Chapter IV [105], it is precisely these roles that we find consolidated in the figure with the eagle's head (which several commentators see as a cock)[52] sitting on Albion's shore. This eagle-man, as we noted earlier[53] unites the iconography of St. John [106 and 107] with the pose of Dürer's *Melencolia I* [108] to produce an emblem of the apocalyptic prophet as melancholy artist. These images would normally be associated with Los: he is the "Watchman of Eternity" who spends his nights watching for "Signals of the Morning". In *The Four Zoas* his visions are explicitly compared with St. John's ("John Saw these things Reveald in Heaven/ On Patmos Isle"; 111:4-5, E 371); and the melancholy pose of our eagle-man is a rather direct transposition of the description of Los in the accompanying text ("Los laments at his dire labours, viewing Jerusalem,/ Sitting before his Furnaces clothed in sackcloth of hair"; 78:10-11, E 231). Given the appearance of Albion as St. John in the preceding picture, however, it appears that the Universal Man and the Prophet are becoming one, a fulfillment of Moses' wish that all the Lord's people were prophets.

The reader who has passed over the crucifixion scene on plate 76 as a satire on the "Vegetated Christ" may see this bird-man as a grotesque gargoyle, a symbol of fleshly desire like the dog-headed

[51] McKenzie, *Dictionary of the Bible*, p. 767.

[52] Joseph Wicksteed, *William Blake's Jerusalem* (London, 1954), p. 226. Lesnick (*VFD*, p. 400) and Erdman (*TIB*, p. 357) prefer to see it as Hand with his "rav'ning beak," an emblem of ignorance.

[53] See the discussion of Dürer's *Melencolia* I in Chapter One.

figure of Egypt (Damon), "ignorance with a rav'ning beak" (Erdman), or "a symbol recalling Peter's denial of his Lord" (Wicksteed).[54] Beneath these appearances, however, we can see the eagle of genius who can gaze into the sun—or at us—without blinking, and the cock who signals the morning, Albion and Los united as one man, introducing us to the final, apocalyptic chapter of the Bible of Hell.

It is clear that there is a great deal more to be said on the matter of the presence of St. John in Blake's verbal and visual art. Although the explicit textual references are not numerous, the feeling of a pervading style and presence is quite strong. The emergence of the evangelist at the crucifixion on plate 76 [103] and the prophet of Patmos in plate 78 [105] is foreshadowed, for instance, by a clear pictorial allusion to St. John on plate 62 [109]. The giant figure whose body is covered by the text of this plate is the "mighty angel" whose feet are described as "pillars of fire" in Revelation 10:1, and the tiny figure between his feet is St. John. Any doubt that Blake had this allusion in mind is dispelled by his own painting of *The Angel of the Revelation* [110] in his series of Bible illustrations. Blake has altered the composition in significant ways, of course, stressing (as he does in the accompanying text of plate 62) the torments of visionary perception. The rainbow described around the angel's head (Rev. 10:1) is replaced in Blake's design by a coiled serpent plumed with eyed peacock feathers, another variation on the winged circle motif, and a symbol of seraphic wisdom, the many-eyed vision of angelic knowledge. It is interesting in this context to note that the figure of the "mighty angel" with his characteristic gesture (one hand stretched downward, holding the little book that St. John will consume, the other "lifted up . . . to heaven"; Rev. 10:5) also appears in the title page for Genesis [107] along with the figures of the four evangelists. Here the angel is present as what we may surmise to be one of the four figures of divine inspiration: the winged figure of the Holy Spirit at the top, the aged Jehovah at the right, Christ at the left, and our "mighty angel" of Revelation at the bottom.

All these allusions must be interpreted, of course, in terms of the transformations Blake imposes on them as he absorbs them into his own vision. The tiny St. John figure at the bottom of plate 62 is, in context, Los beholding "the Divine Vision among the flames of

[54] Damon, *Philosophy and Symbols*, p. 473; cf. "Egypt" in his *Blake Dictionary*. See also Erdman, *TIB*, p. 357; and Wicksteed, *William Blake's Jerusalem*, p. 226.

the furnace" (62:35, E 211) or Blake himself as a tiny homunculus confronting another of his "Giant forms," as he does in the design on plate 37. One suspects, in fact, that the most important aspect of St. John's presence in Blake's art, aside from his obvious function as a model of the prophetic and apocalyptic artist, would be his role as patron saint of engravers, printers, makers of books, and art dealers. St. John is not just a remote, visionary model but the tutelary spirit of the very crafts, techniques, methods of distribution—in a word, the "hands"—with which Blake manifests his vision in concrete forms. If the eagle-man of plate 78 is meant to recall the verbal descriptions of "Hand" with his "rav'ning" beak (see 8:43-9:13, 19:23-24, 78:2-3), then surely we are seeing him transformed here from predatory adversary to prophetic ally, using his eagle's head for vision, not violence.[55]

As Blake's cast of Visionary Forms Dramatic approach their "Resurrection to Unity" in both the text and designs of the final chapter, it naturally becomes more difficult to name the figures in the illustrations with complete certainty. The awakening, expansive, embracing human forms which appear in the final six plates resolve the conflicts and complex thematic strands in a crescendo of unification which is experienced not as the tantalizing ambiguity and irony we have seen in the problematic iconography of earlier plates, but as a kind of imagistic radiance. Erdman conveys this effect in his commentary on plate 96:

> . . . as the first lines of text on this page annouce, "England who is Brittannia" (and with whom all the female persons of the drama are now amalgamated) will enter "Albions bosom rejoicing" (2), as we are shown on plate 99. All the male persons now speak "in" this Jehovah-like Albion or "Universal Father," and in this "Vision of Albion" (97:5-6) we see male and female, age and youth . . . rising in the clouds. . . . Yet the interpolation, Plate 95, of Albion as naked youth, repeated on Plate 97 to show us youthful Albion as Los-Urthona-Jesus, prevents our settling down with the incongruity of the Universal Man as solely pater familias! In Plate 99, regardless of the apparent sexual garments, the young person will have to represent all youth, the elder all

[55] In the conclusion of the poem Hand's earlier role as the predatory terror who accuses and frightens Jerusalem will be transformed into the role of mediator between masculine and feminine principles: "the Hand of Man grasps firm between the Male & Female Loves" (97:15).

> age. With time ended, all these aspects vanish and come to life in one plenitude of Universal Brotherhood and Human Form Divine. This does not erase but validates all the Illuminations in these one hundred plates, just as it preserves the Druid temple in the one hundredth.[56]

In plate 99 [112], the final text plate, all the conflicts of *Jerusalem* (and, indeed, of Blake's entire corpus of illuminated prophecies) are brought to a consummate resolution: Thel has found her father-lover, Oothoon embraces Theotormon, Orc is reconciled with Urizen (especially in copy E, where the young woman becomes masculine), and all the battles of the sexes and the generations are resolved in a synaesthetic explosion of flames, gushing fountains, and living fibers. Anthony Blunt relates the picture to the pictorial tradition of the prodigal son's return,[57] a touchstone which reveals even more precisely the character of Blake's invention. The old man's embrace of the young woman (or man, an androgyne rather than a hermaphrodite) is not just paternal but sexual, and the overt moral of the prodigal son tale, the forgiveness of the erring soul by a perfect, merciful father, is transformed by the cruciform gesture of the young woman into a scene which says that "*Mutual* Forgiveness of each Vice/ Such are the Gates of Paradise" (italics mine). It is the patriarch who receives forgiveness and redemption as much if not more than the young woman.

Jerusalem does not end with this vision, however, but with the dominant seventh of plate 100 [89], a picture of resolution, completion, and rest complicated by the images of a new beginning and continued work. The perfect, closed form is also open and ongoing; the rest of the satisfied artist is balanced by the images of continuing labor and exploration, just as the serpentine Druid temple (its stones an emblem of the one hundred plates of *Jerusalem*) couples the closed perfection of the circle with outstretched serpent, an icon of the interpenetration of eternity and time,[58] "living going forth & returning wearied/ Into the Planetary lives of Years Months Days &

[56] *TIB*, p. 375.

[57] *Art of William Blake*, p. 81.

[58] A fuller study of this image is clearly needed. The circle with serpent is, as we have observed in note 23, a pictorial and metaphoric relative of the winged globe which supports the fainting Albion on plate 33, and of the halo-disc flanked by serpentine flames around the shoulders of Hand on plate 26 [97]. Kathleen Raine has found a probable source for these images, combining the winged disc with the outstretched serpent, in Bryant's *Mythology*, I (1774), pl. VIII. See *Blake and Tradition*, II, 261, and [91] in this text.

Hours reposing/ And then Awaking into this Bosom in the Life of Immortality."

VIII. A CONCLUSION IN WHICH NOTHING IS CONCLUDED

It is clear that a great deal more critical "going forth & returning wearied" is required before *Jerusalem* is fully understood, or even before we will know if it is accessible to full understanding in the same degree or kind as *Paradise Lost* or *Ulysses.* I am still not entirely convinced that "Every word and every letter" and every picture *is* in "its fit place," not because I can point to things which should have been elsewhere, but because in many cases I cannot explain why they should *not* be elsewhere. What this suggests is that our notion of "fit place" as a location in a linear or spatial matrix may have only a limited application to the structure of *Jerusalem.* Blake's concept of fit place seems, in other words, less relational than centripetal or concentric: the fit place is where you are, and the proper direction is both inward and onward. This can be very disturbing to the rational explicator who insists on knowing exactly where he is in relation to the whole. My theory is that Blake intentionally designed *Jerusalem* to allow only an approximate sense of structural orientation, and that this is in part a rhetorical strategy for drawing our attention inward, onto the Minute Particulars of text and design which lie before us.

This sense of approximate structure and centripetal focus is closely related to Blake's request that his reader "forgive what you do not approve, & love me for this energetic exertion of my talent." It may well be impossible to "approve" every word and image in *Jerusalem*, not just in the sense of commending its truth or beauty but in the more fundamental sense of "proving" or demonstrating the meaning of every particular in a practical way. Blake asks us, in other words, to read in a spirit of faith and forgiveness as well as demonstration, and not to repeat the error of Albion by making these two into antithetical habits of mind. "By demonstration, man alone can live, and not by faith" (4:28, E 145) is the rebuke with which Albion separates himself from Jesus. This clearly does not mean mindless acceptance or blind faith, but a modicum of trust in a poet whose ample demonstrations of genius should allow us to forgive his darker passages when we cannot illuminate them.

The leap of faith which Blake requests of his reader is nothing beside the one he demanded of himself. The remarkable thing about his commitment to "open the Eternal Worlds, to open the immortal Eyes/ Of Man inwards into the Worlds of Thought" (*J* 5:18-19, E 146), and the thing which makes this exertion of talent so worthy of love, is that it is conducted with a sane humor and self-awareness that overcomes the threat of a crippling self-consciousness. Blake knows there is something absurd about setting up as a prophet in an age which does not believe in prophecy and which hearkens after the false "modern prophets" who traffic in prediction. But instead of becoming obsessed or crippled by this absurdity, he cheerfully absorbs it into his system. Take, for instance, plate 41 of *Jerusalem* [111], an elaborate emblem of Blake's own art as a chariot of genius which carries a drowsy old couple (Albion and either Jerusalem or Vala—that is, Blake's audience) who are too sleepy to manage the reins. The chariot is an impossible rattletrap of old mythologies: a coiled three-headed serpent furnishes the wheels and traces, which are harnessed to a pair of bulls with old men's faces, lion's manes, and spiraling unicorn horns that end in hands pointing in opposite directions! Astride these beasts are two prophetic eagle-men (the nearest, Los or Blake himself with pen in hand) spurring them on—the whole thing incapable of actually moving in its present form, but full of a coiled energy which, if flexed, would tear the contraption apart. This monstrosity is a self-parody, a satiric vision of Blake's own epic machinery, the elements of his craft,[59] and of his total art form as a composite system of contrary, heterogeneous elements. Blake transforms the potentially crippling sense of the absurdity of his work into a vision which resides on the perilous border between the sublime and the ridiculous, absorbing both these realms, and the viewer, into a larger, divinely comic world.[60]

It will be objected that "absurdity" is a modern word that names a concept and emotion only discovered in the twentieth century. Even if that were true (which I doubt), the evidence seems overwhelming that Blake would have appreciated, if not used, this word in its modern sense. That is, Blake understands his work as a human affirmation of meaning in the face of a cosmos from which all transcendent, objective guarantees of meaning have vanished, whether those meanings are traced to the impersonal forces of nature (Deism)

[59] See Erdman, *TIB*, p. 112, on the printing house in hell.

[60] For a version of the chariot of genius which has a better chance of going somewhere, see Beatrice's chariot in the illustrations to *The Divine Comedy* (no. 88).

or to the agency of a personal patriarchal deity. The work of Los, like that of Sisyphus, is a process of "continually building & continually decaying . . ./ In eternal labours" (*J* 53:19-20, E 201), and his work does not end when he reaches the summit, as we see in the final plates of *Jerusalem.* Nor does it simply start over at the bottom again. As Camus declares in the *Myth of Sisyphus*, affirmation in the face of absurdity "silences all the idols. In the universe suddenly restored to its silence, the myriad wondering little voices of earth rise up," and "this universe henceforth without a master seems to him neither sterile nor futile. Each atom of that stone, each mineral flake of that night-filled mountain in itself forms a world. The struggle itself toward the heights is enough to fill a man's heart."

What Camus saw as the absurd, Blake envisioned as a void, the absence of a protecting father which sent Thel fleeing back to the Vales of Har, the vast abyss of subjectivity explored by Urizen, and the "Void, outside of Existence" which Los enters in *Jerusalem.* In these voids Blake confronts the forces for despair which he finds in himself and the world—the spectrous, egotistical doubter and accuser, the obdurate "Hand," the allurements of feminine repose—and he transforms these antagonists into dramatic forms in a comic epic anatomy of his own melancholy. At the darkest moment in *Milton* Los

> . . . gave up himself to tears.
> He sat down on his anvil stock; and leand upon the trough.
> Looking into the black water, mingling it with tears.
> At last when desperation almost tore his heart in twain
> He recollected an old Prophecy in Eden recorded . . .
> . . . .
> That Milton of the Land of Albion should up ascend
> Forwards from Ulro from the Vale of Felpham. . . .
> (*M* 20:53-57, 59-60, E 114)

The cheerful improbability of this turning point in the poem, like the similar improbability of the stalled chariot in *Jerusalem* 41, is, in a sense, the central meaning of Blake's art. The comic resolution of history is grounded in an absurdly joyous leap of faith in the present moment and the individual genius as the catalysts for collective awakening. The tradition of prophecy is independent of the silent idols men have worshiped; Milton is reborn in the Vale of Felpham. For Blake, the human race may yet be born in its full maturity: all art, science, liberated work or expression are the means of delivering us into the human family, and the individual is a participant in this task, the collective enterprise of our species to discover and create its own nature.

Jerusalem ends with the regenerated artist facing outward to the circumference of his creation, resting on his tools, and finding it good. But this repose is like the hour of rest Camus gives to Sisyphus, a rest before labor. The work is already beginning again, as we see from the activities of Los and Enitharmon in the background. Blake brought his final illuminated book to a conclusion around 1818, but his labors were not done either. At a similar point in his career William Butler Yeats looked back over his achievement:

> "The work is done," grown old he thought,
> "According to my boyish plan;
> Let the fools rage, I swerved in naught,
> Something to perfection brought."
> ("What Then?"—*Last Poems*)

But Yeats's sense of completion is immediately disturbed by the nagging voice of Plato's ghost asking, "What then?" Blake may also have heard this ghost, but his capacity for boyish plans was undiminished. He had before him the illustrations to Job, Dante, and Virgil, the zenith of his career as a graphic artist, and three more opportunities to link his prophetic genius with visionaries of the past. Behind him lay the canon of his illuminated poems, unread and unsold, but still glowing images of the Blake who did not die in 1827:

> Reengravd Time after Time
> Ever in their youthful prime
> My Designs unchangd remain
> Time may rage but rage in vain
> For above Times troubled Fountains
> On the Great Atlantic Mountains
> In my Golden House on high
> There they Shine Eternally

Index

Index

Bracketed numbers refer to illustrations in this text.

INDEX

ILLUSTRATIONS

1. *Songs of Experience*, copy I. Frontispiece
4, 144

2. *Songs of Innocence*, copy Z. Frontispiece
4, 144

3. Albrecht Dürer, *St. Christopher with Head Turned Back* (1529)–6

4. *Christian Reading in His Book*, from Blake's designs for Bunyan's *Pilgrim's Progress*–8

5. Drawing from the manuscript of *Vala*, or *The Four Zoas*, p. 66 –8, 44n

6. *America*, copy N. Plate 8 –9

7. *America*, copy N. Plate 10 –9

8. *The Marriage of Heaven and Hell*, copy C. Title page –10, 75

9. *Songs of Innocence*, copy I. Plate 10: "The Little Black Boy," second illustration–12

10. Otto van Veen, *Amoris Divini Emblemata* (Antwerp, 1660), emblem 13: Guardian Angel Presenting the Wayward Soul to God–12

11. *The Expulsion*, from Blake's illustrations to *Paradise Lost*–19

12. *The Expulsion*. Engraved by Rothwell after E. F. Burney, *Milton's Paradise Lost* (London, 1799)–19

13. William Hogarth, *A Harlot's Progress*, pl. 1: Arrival in London–25

14. George Wither, *The Choice of Hercules*, from *A Collection of Emblems* (London, 1635)–28

15. Paolo de Matteis, *The Choice of Hercules*, in Shaftesbury, *Second Characters, or The Language of Forms* (Birmingham, 1773)–28

16. *Jerusalem*, copy D. Plate 46(32)–28, 51

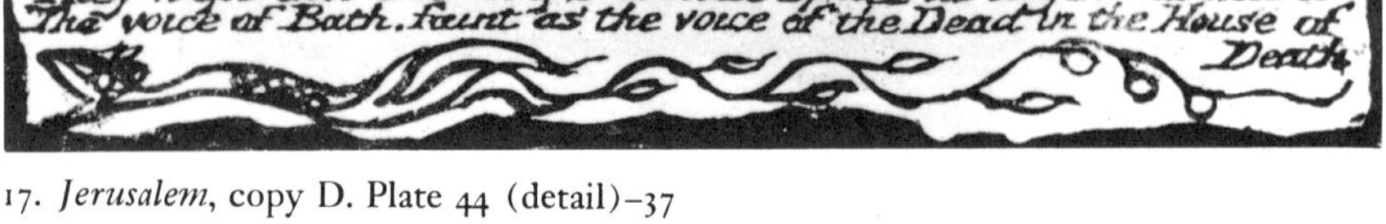

17. *Jerusalem*, copy D. Plate 44 (detail)–37

18. *Milton*, copy A. Title page –43, 178, 198

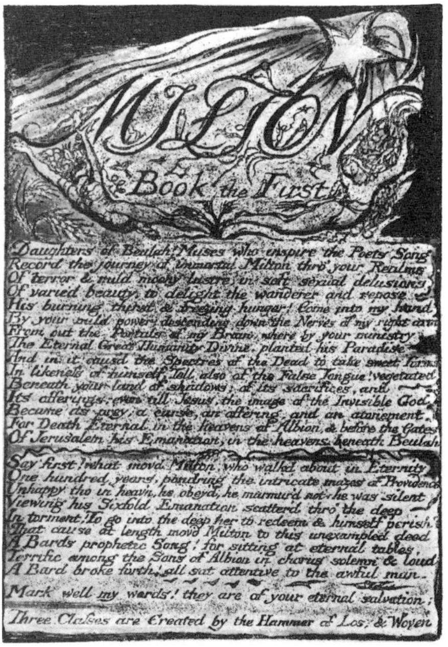

19. *Milton*, copy A. Plate 2–43

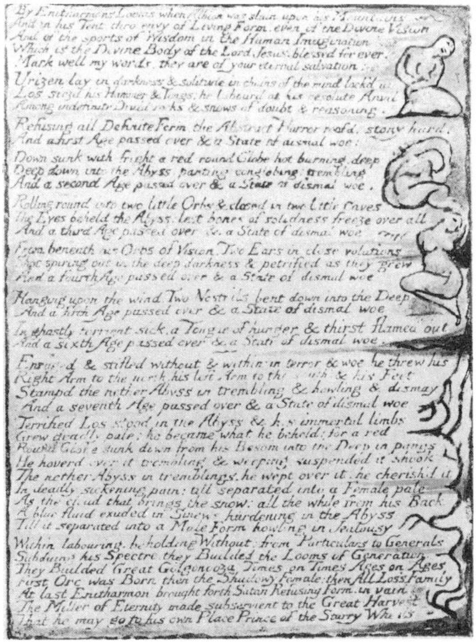

20. *Milton*, copy D. Plate 3–43

21. Blake, engraving after Hogarth, *The Beggar's Opera*, Act III: "When My Hero in Court Appears" (1790)–46

22. *Newton*–49, 51, 63, 73

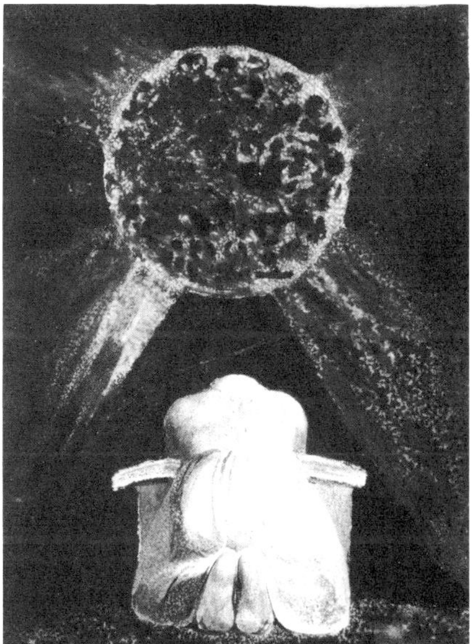

23. *Song of Los*, copy A. Frontispiece 51

24. *Europe*, copy I. Frontispiece–54, 155

25. *Albion rose*, color print–54, 210

26. *Europe*, copy K. Plate 11–56, 207

27. *The Marriage of Heaven and Hell*, copy B. Plate i: "Our End is come"–63

28. *America*, copy N. Plate 9 (detail)–64

29. *Visions of the Daughters of Albion*, copy J. Plate 4 (detail)–66, 158

30. Francis Quarles, *Emblemes* (London, 1635), Book V, emblem 9 –66

31. *Europe*, copy I. Plate 2 –68

32. *The Angel Michael Binding the Dragon*
69, 73

33. *The Epitome of James Hervey's Meditations among the Tombs*
66, 69, 73

34. *The Lord Answering Job from the Whilwind*–63, 69

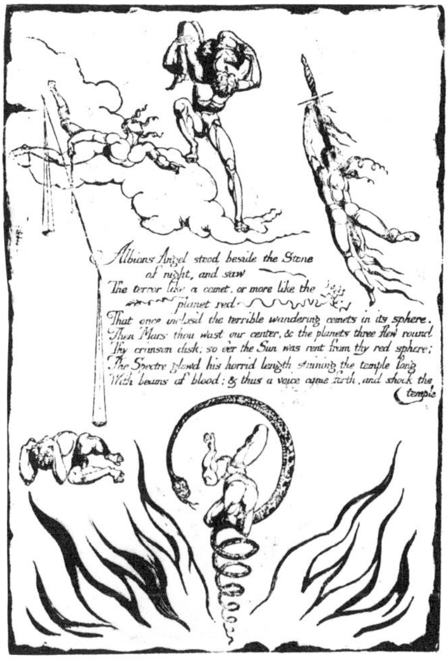

35. *America*, copy N. Plate 5 –73, 109

36. *The Punishment of Rusticucci and His Companions*, from Blake's designs for *The Divine Comedy*–63, 73, 105

37. *The Book of Thel*, copy O. Title page
69, 79, 97, 104

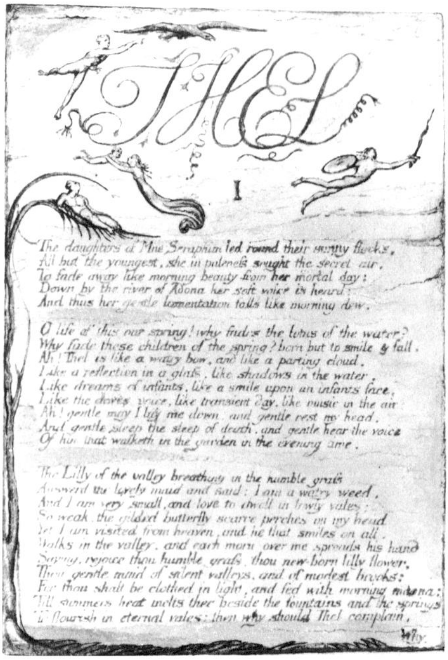

38. *The Book of Thel*, copy O. Plate 1
79, 99

39. *The Book of Thel*, copy O. Plate 2
100, 104

40. *The Book of Thel*, copy O. Plate 4
101, 104

41. *The Book of Thel*, copy O. Plate 5
101

42. Francesco Francia, *The Madonna Adoring the Infant Jesus*–102

43. Albrecht Dürer, *The Nativity* (detail)
102

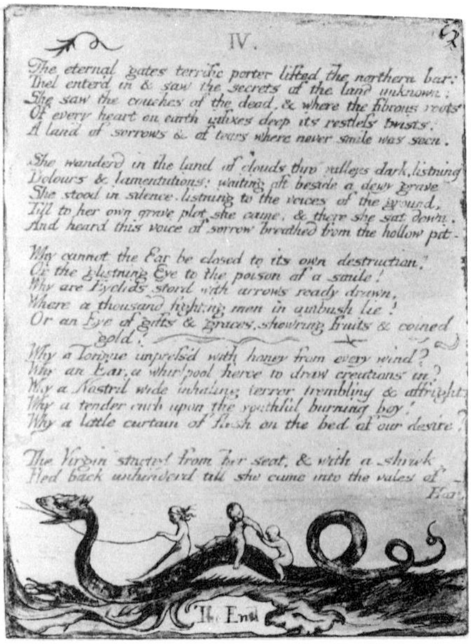

44. *The Book of Thel*, copy O. Plate 6
79, 84, 103, 144

45. *Song of Los*, copy B. Plate 6 –110

46. *The Book of Urizen*, copy B. Title page 13n, 64, 113, 140

47. *The Book of Urizen*, copy B. Plate 28 64, 140

48. *The Book of Urizen*, copy B. Plate 2 111, 142

49. *The Book of Urizen*, copy B. Plate 3 145

50. *Pestilence: The Death of the First Born*–145, 202

51. *The Book of Urizen*, copy B. Plate 4 146, 150

52. *Gates of Paradise*, copy F. Plate 2: *Water*–146

53. *The Book of Urizen*, copy B. Plate 5 143

54. *The Book of Urizen*, copy A. Plate 6 –57, 69n, 109, 147

55. *The Resurrection*–57, 149

56. Relief of the Orphic God Phanes, Modena–149

57. *Gates of Paradise*, copy F. Plate 2: "At length for hatching ripe he breaks the shell"–149

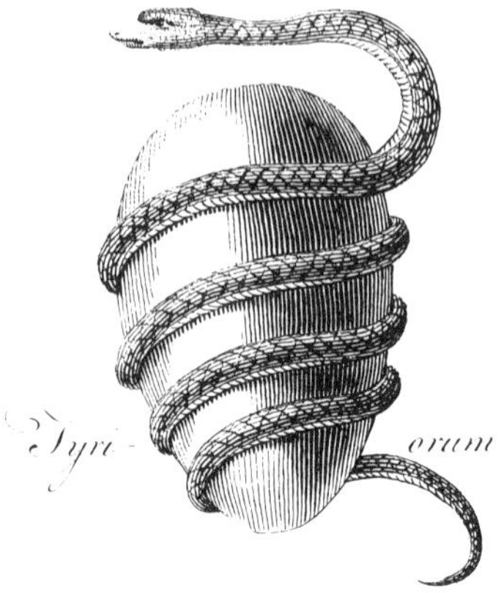

58. *The Mundane Egg*. From Jacob Bryant, *A New System, or an Analysis of Ancient Mythology* (London, 1774-76)–149

59. *Elohim Creating Adam*–150

60. *The Book of Urizen*, copy B. Plate 7
150, 158

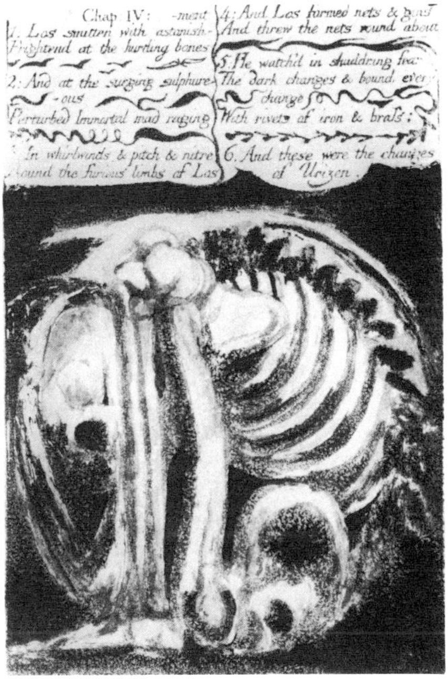

61. *The Book of Urizen*, copy B. Plate 8
63, 146, 150

62. *The Book of Urizen*, copy B. Plate 9
109, 146, 150

63. *The Book of Urizen*, copy B. Plate 10
109, 143, 146, 150

64. *The Book of Urizen*, copy G. Plate 11
109, 151, 158

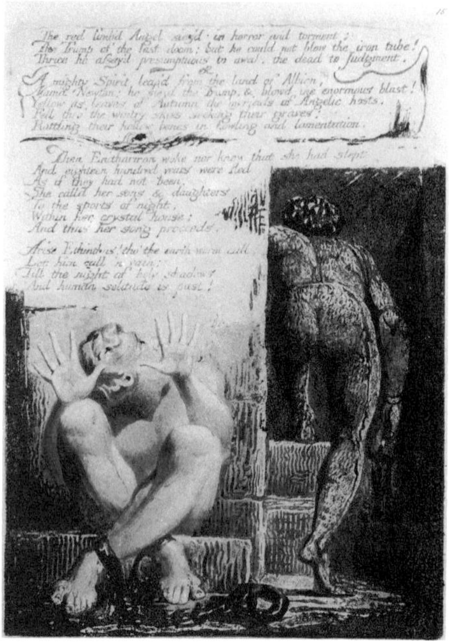

65. *Europe*, copy K. Plate 13 –58, 109

66. *The Book of Urizen*, copy B. Plate 12
146, 152, 161

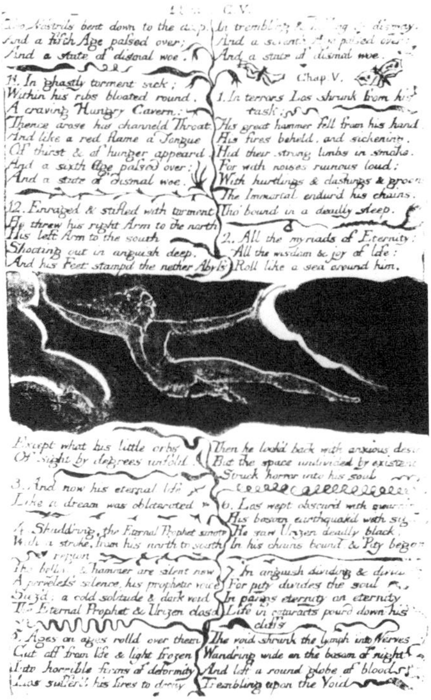

67. *The Book of Urizen*, copy B. Plate 13
128, 138, 146, 153

68. *Night*. Engraved by J. Neagle after Thomas Stothard, *Night Thoughts by Edward Young, D.D.* (London, 1798)
154

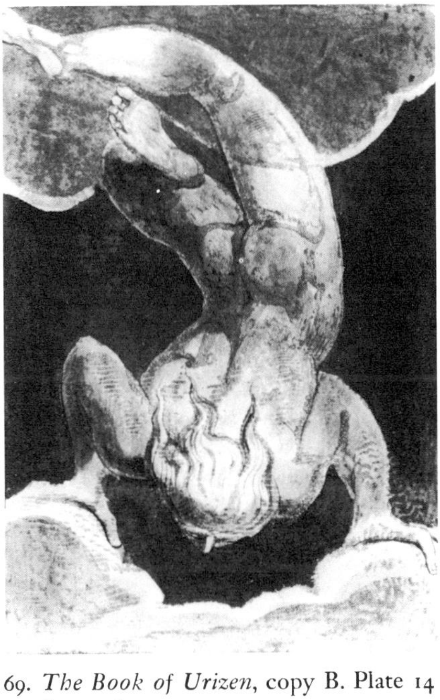

69. *The Book of Urizen*, copy B. Plate 14
69n, 146, 152, 159

70. *Jerusalem*, copy D. Plate 23 (detail)
160

71. *The Book of Urizen*, copy B. Plate 15
146, 152, 155

72. *The Book of Urizen*, copy B. Plate 16
146, 151

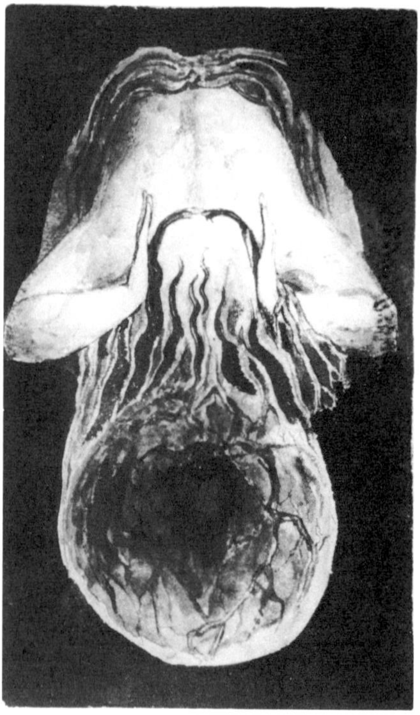

73. *The Book of Urizen*, copy B. Plate 17
60, 156, 201

74. *The Book of Urizen*, copy B. Plate 18
138, 146

75. *The Book of Urizen*, copy G. Plate 19
67, 158

76. *The Book of Urizen*, copy B. Plate 20
145, 158

77. *The Book of Urizen*, copy B. Plate 21
162

78. *The Book of Urizen*, copy G. Plate 22
109, 162

79. *The Book of Urizen*, copy B. Plate 23
158, 161, 179, 198

80. *The Book of Urizen*, copy G. Plate 24
138, 145, 160

81. *The Book of Urizen*, copy B. Plate 26
58, 63, 162

82. *The Book of Urizen*, copy D. Plate 26
162

83. *The Songs of Innocence and of Experience*, copy Z. Plate 46: "London"
163

84. *The Book of Urizen*, copy B. Plate 27
69n, 159, 162

85. *The Woman Taken in Adultery*–159

86. *Jerusalem*, copy D. Frontispiece–51, 178, 194, 198

87. *Jerusalem*, copy D. Plate 97 –51, 178

88. *Death's Door*. Etched by Schiavonetti after Blake, Robert Blair's *The Grave* (London, 1808)–51, 100, 179

89. *Jerusalem*, copy D. Plate 100 –180, 194, 214

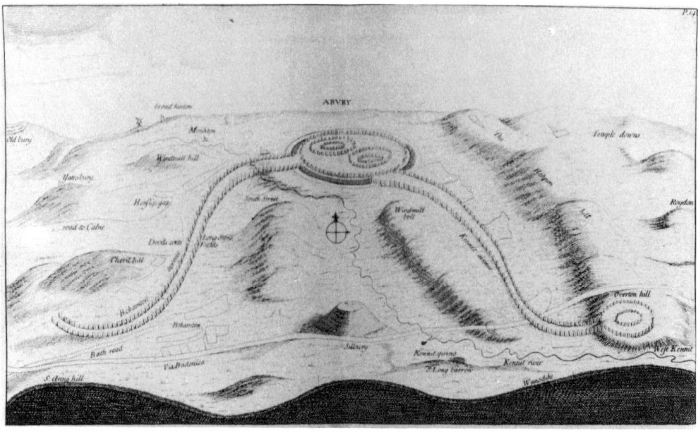

90. *A Scenographic View of the Druid Temple at Abury.*
From William Stukely, *Abury, A Temple of the British Druids* (London, 1743)–181

91. *Winged disc and serpent.* From Jacob Bryant, *A New System, or an Analysis of Ancient Mythology* (London 1774-76)–181n, 214n

92. *Jerusalem*, copy D. Plate 33(37)–47, 181

93. *Jerusalem*, copy D. Title page–49, 198, 206, 210

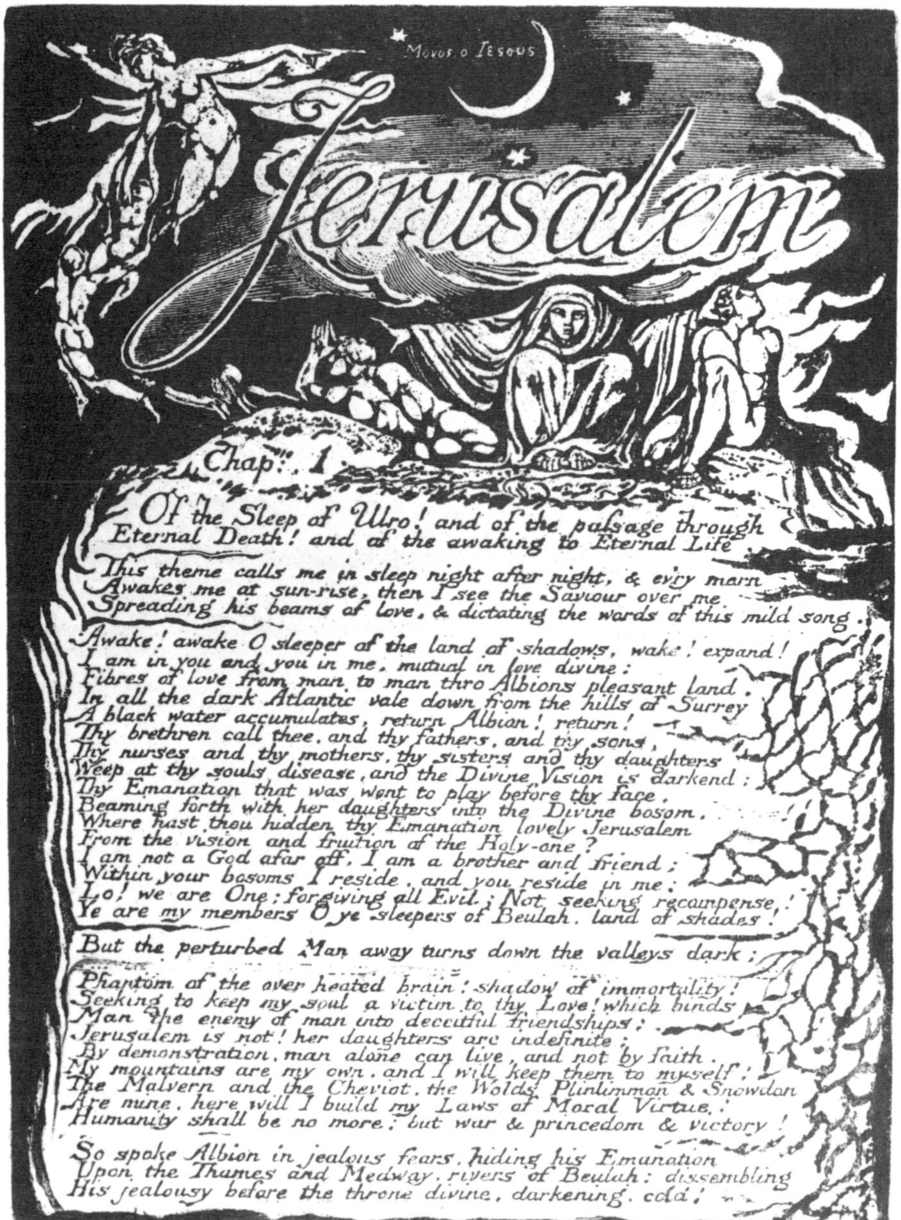

94. *Jerusalem*, copy D. Plate 4 –193, 198, 206

95. *Jerusalem*, copy D. Plate 25
200

96. Engraving after Poussin, *The Martyrdom of St. Erasmus*
200

97. *Jerusalem*, copy D. Plate 26 –56, 145, 201, 214n

98. *Jerusalem*, copy D. Plate 28 –195, 201

The Atlantic Mountains where Giants dwelt in Intellect;
Now given to stony Druids, and Allegoric Generation
To the Twelve Gods of Asia, the Spectres of those who Sleep:
Swayd by a Providence opposd to the Divine Lord Jesus:
A murderous Providence! A Creation that groans, living on Death.
Where Fish & Bird & Beast & Man & Tree & Metal & Stone
Live by Devouring, going into Eternal Death continually:
Albion is now possessd by the War of Blood! the Sacrifice
Of envy Albion is become, and his Emanation cast out:
Come Lord Jesus, Lamb of God descend! for if; O Lord!
If thou hadst been here, our brother Albion had not died.
Arise sisters! Go ye & meet the Lord, while I remain—
Behold the foggy mornings of the Dead on Albions cliffs!
Ye know that if the Emanation remains in them:
She will become an Eternal Death, an Avenger of Sin
A Self-righteousness: the proud Virgin-Harlot! Mother of War!
And we also & all Beulah, consume beneath Albions curse.

So Erin spoke to the Daughters of Beulah. Shuddering
With their wings they sat in the Furnace, in a night
Of stars, for all the Sons of Albion appeard distant stars.
Ascending and descending into Albions sea of death.
And Erins lovely Bow enclosd the Wheels of Albions Sons.

Expanding on wing, the Daughters of Beulah replied in sweet response

Come O thou Lamb of God and take away the remembrance of Sin
To Sin & to hide the Sin in sweet deceit, is lovely!!
To Sin in the open face of day is cruel & pitiless! But
To record the Sin for a reproach: to let the Sun go down
In a remembrance of the Sin: is a Woe & a Horror!
A brooder of an Evil Day, and a Sun rising in blood
Come then O Lamb of God and take away the remembrance of Sin

End of Chap. 2d.

99. *Jerusalem*, copy D. Plate 50 –195, 201, 203

100. *Jerusalem*, copy D. Plate 51 –205, 207

Jerusalem
Chap 3

But Los, who is the Vehicular Form of strong Urthona
Wept vehemently over Albion where Thames currents spring
From the rivers of Beulah; pleasant river! soft, mild, parent stream
And the roots of Albions Tree enterd the Soul of Los
As he sat before his Furnaces clothed in sackcloth of hair
In gnawing pain dividing him from his Emanation;
Inclosing all the Children of Los time after time.
Their Giant forms condensing into Nations & Peoples & Tongues
Translucent the Furnaces, of Beryll & Emerald immortal:
And Seven-fold each within other: incomprehensible
To the Vegetated Mortal Eye's perverted & single vision
The Bellows are the Animal Lungs. the Hammers, the Animal Heart
The Furnaces, the Stomach for Digestion; terrible their fury
Like seven burning heavens rangd from South to North

Here on the banks of the Thames, Los builded Golgonooza,
Outside of the Gates of the Human Heart, beneath Beulah
In the midst of the rocks of the Altars of Albion. In fears
He builded it, in rage & in fury. It is the Spiritual Fourfold
London: continually building & continually decaying desolate!
In eternal labours: loud the Furnaes & loud the Anvils
Of Death thunder incessant around the flaming Couches of
The Twentyfour Friends of Albion and round the awful Four
For the protection of the Twelve Emanations of Albions Sons
The Mystic Union of the Emanation in the Lord; Because
Man divided from his Emanation is a dark Spectre
His Emanation is an ever-weeping melancholy Shadow
But she is made receptive of Generation thro' mercy
In the Potters Furnace, among the Funeral Urns of Beulah
From Surrey hills, thro' Italy and Greece, to Hinnoms vale.

101. *Jerusalem*, copy D. Plate 53 –206, 210

102. *Jerusalem*, copy D. Plate 75 –208

103. *Jerusalem*, copy D. Plate 76 –68, 209, 212

104. Piero della Francesca, *Crucifixion*, with the Virgin and St. John–210

105. *Jerusalem*, copy D. Plate 78 –27, 211, 212

106. *St. John the Evangelist with an Eagle's Head.* From the Bible of St. Bénigne–27, 211

107. Sketch for a title page to Genesis (second version)–145, 211, 212

108. Albrecht Dürer, *Melencolia I* (1514) 27, 199, 211

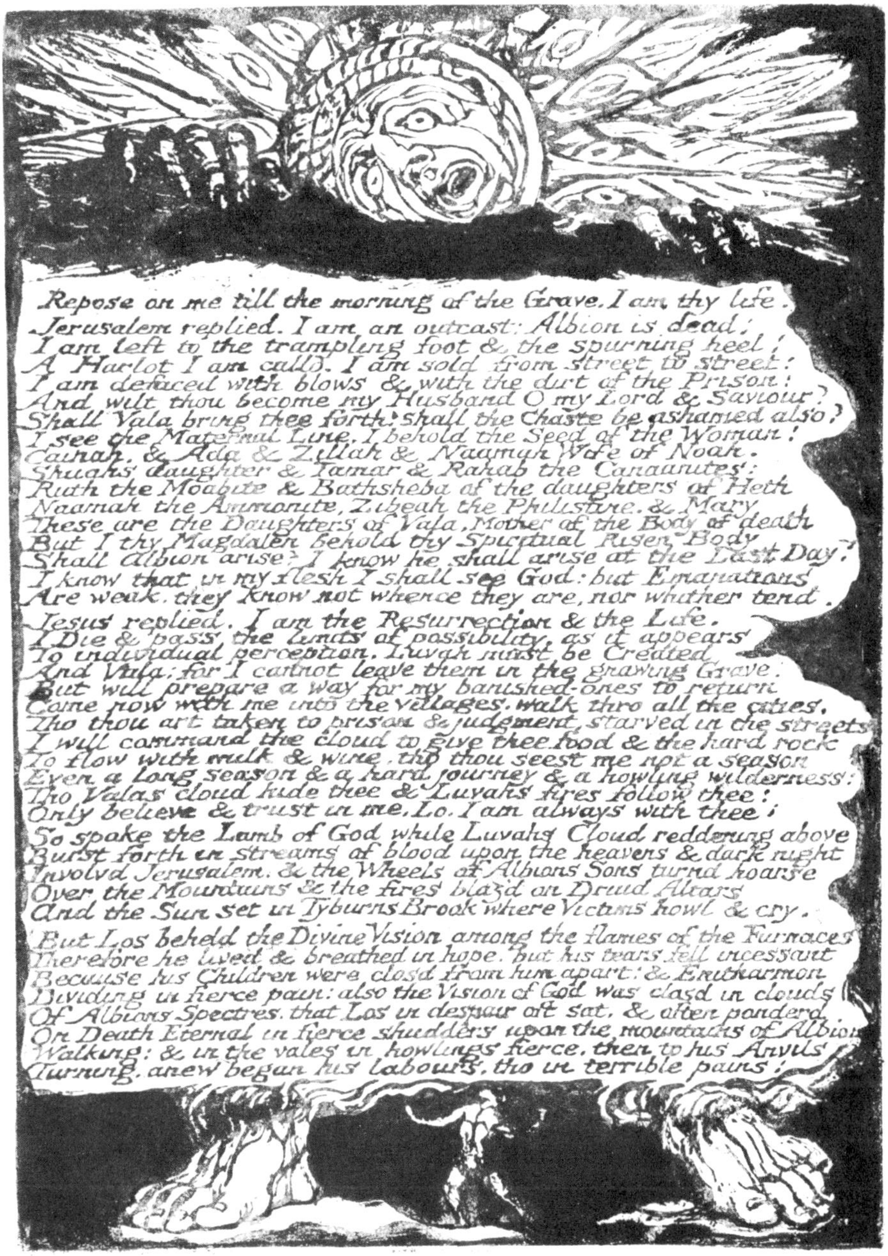

109. *Jerusalem*, copy D. Plate 62 –212

110. *The Angel of the Revelation*–212

111. *Jerusalem*, copy D. Plate 41(46)–173, 216

112. *Jerusalem*, copy D. Plate 99 -213

LIBRARY OF CONGRESS CATALOGING IN PUBLICATION DATA

Mitchell, W J Thomas, 1942-
Blake's composite art.

Includes bibliographical references and index.
1. Blake, William, 1757-1827—Criticism and interpretation.
2. Blake, William, 1757-1827—Aesthetics. 3. Illumination of books and manuscripts, English. I. Title.
PR4147.M5 821'.7 77-7116
ISBN 0-691-6348-6

JU